THE FUTURE OF METAPHYSICS

ROBERT E. WOOD was born in Racine, Wisconsin, and studied at Marquette University. He is the author of *Martin Buber's Ontology* and is at present Associate Professor of Philosophy at St. Joseph's College in Rensselaer, Indiana.

THE FUTURE OF METAPHYSICS

Edited by
ROBERT E. WOOD

CHICAGO
Quadrangle Books
1970

 For information, address the publisher at 12 East Delaware Place, Chicago 60611. Manufactured in the United States of America. Published simultaneously in Canada by Burns and MacEachern Ltd., Toronto.

Library of Congress Catalog Card Number: 70-116094

Preface

The contemporary attack upon metaphysics has been launched from many quarters: the positivists call for its elimination as nonsense; the linguistic analysts claim that it will disappear with a little verbal therapy; existentialists advocate the "overcoming" of traditional metaphysics; religiously committed people demand its dissociation from their faith; logicians speak of logic and ethicians of ethics without metaphysics; pragmatists consider it outmoded; Marxists and psychoanalysts term it a rationalization of economic or irrational desires. Indeed, the age is spoken of as the era of "the end of ontology."

All this in spite of claims in the early part of the century of a "resurrection of metaphysics" (Peter Wust), claims that metaphysics would soon have the status of a science (C. S. Pierce), and that historically it always buries its undertakers (E. Gilson). Today we hear new voices speaking of giving publicly recognizable legitimacy to metaphysical proof (J. Owens), of establishing metaphysics on such a basis that any attempt to refute it would end up convicting itself of contradiction (E. Coreth), of the necessity of moving beyond the clarity of analysis to certain "metaphysical affinities" (J. N. Findlay). Even those outside the field have spoken of the need for a "renaissance of metaphysics" (former Secretary of Defense Robert McNamara), or of the demand for an ontology on which to ground psychological practice (Rollo May).

The rising interest in metaphysics is as inevitable as the tide, for the inevitability of metaphysics as a pursuit is implicit in the structure of all propositions affirming or denying something to be the case. Of what can one affirm or deny that it is the case? Though it is disputed, it seems obvious that the field of affirmation or negation covers the whole range of actuality and possibility. Implicit in every affirmation or negation is a reference to the Whole of what is or can be. Openness to the Totality is characteristic of man, on account of which he transcends the present situation, can question its adequacy, evaluate it, and project alternative possibilities. Man is physical-metaphysical, immanent in immediate contexts while referred beyond them all to the Whole. Metaphysics as a reflective enterprise grows out of this reference as an explicit attempt to form a view which takes in the Whole.

As the reader will note throughout this volume, such an enterprise is variously termed "metaphysics" or "ontology." The terms are used differently by different thinkers—at times employed interchangeably, at times distinguished. Thus in Neo-Scholasticism a distinction is made between consideration of the most general principles of reality (ontology) and consideration of transphysical entities (metaphysics). And in the Husserlian tradition, the study of the most general features of types of objects is called ontology, while questions transcending object-questions in the direction of the subject of awareness and the subject of being are metaphysical questions. Given the latter two usages, one could conceivably have ontology without metaphysics: (1) if there are no trans-physical entities, or (2) if that which transcends the status of objects is unknowable. But, of course, one's usage of the term "metaphysics" depends upon one's view of what the "physical" is which metaphysics is "meta."

We are suggesting that transcendence of immediacy in the direction of the Whole is the "meta" of metaphysics in human experience. Heidegger attempts to move beyond or beneath traditional metaphysics to this reference in the light of which metaphysics itself is possible as a study of entities: this move Heidegger terms "fundamental ontology." Such reference is the basic mode of experiential presence, a fundamental orientation toward entities which establishes the sustaining "mood" or "feel" for things. It is articulated in different ways in different cultures, in different epochs and in differing individuals, though there are pervasive tendencies in a culture or an epoch.

Visual dominance, involving an experiential detachment of subject and object—and consequently a tendency socially toward isolated individuals, psychologically toward the splitting off of cognitive from affective components, linked up with the will-to-power expressed in technology—has created the sustaining mood of Western culture for the past few centuries. The anti-metaphysics of positivism grows out of this stance. In the emergent counter-culture, tactile and audile concerns offset visual dominance, linking individuals in relations of communal dependency and mutual involvement, establishing connection between various levels within the self. An attempt is thereby made to reintegrate the sub- and trans-rational features of experience, expressing itself in concern with the occult (the "metaphysical," as many popular accounts would have it) as well as in the serious practice of mediation and inward illumination. The latter recaptures the *Nunc stans* of qualitative depth from the *Nunc fluens* of a quantified system whose subjects are turned outwards toward the incessant flow of novelty production. The experiential base for the concept of spirit and of the eternal in man is being recovered. And, as Louis Lavelle remarked, the recovery of the spirit and the recovery of metaphysics go hand in hand.

Out of the "corruption of the youth" in fifth century B.C. Athens came the metaphysical speculations of Plato and Aristotle; on the crest of the wave of the nascent youth culture and concomitant rediscovery of nature in the twelfth century, the great metaphysical syntheses of the Middle Ages appeared; and out of the *Sturm und Drang* of German Romanticism grew the systems of speculative Idealism. Whether they be elements in the pathological syndrome of a culture in upheaval or symptomatic of a cure, metaphysical systems have a way of appearing at critical junctures in history. Today seems to present one of those critical junctures: the times seem ripe for a resurgence of metaphysics.

Paying heed to this situation, in the summer of 1969 a group of distinguished metaphysicians gathered at Catholic University, Washington, D.C., for a conference on "The Future of Metaphysics," in which this book had its origins. An attempt was made to draw upon the major competing and complementary approaches that constitute the contemporary spectrum of metaphysical orientations: Linguistic Analysis, Phenomenology and Existentialism, Process Philosophy, Scholasticism, and Oriental

Thought, along with a renewed Hegelianism. From every approach, the future of metaphysics appears favorable. Indeed, what is remarkable is the return of interest in the common enemy of contemporary anti-metaphysics: Hegel. Four of the papers in this volume give sustained and favorable attention to Hegel. Heidegger's claim that Hegel was the end point of Western metaphysics may have to be modified as Hegel appears to be giving birth to a new wave of metaphysical speculation. It is my fond hope that the essays in this volume may contribute to that new birth.

I wish to thank Professor Jude P. Dougherty, Dean of the School of Philosophy, and Rev. Robert Paul Mohan, Director of the Summer Session, both of Catholic University, for their cooperation in making possible the conference from which these papers have come. Thanks also to Mrs. Mary Homan, Mrs. Toni Tomlin, and Miss Marylyn Mahony for their help in preparing for the conference. Finally, my appreciation to Miss Ramona Paryse and Miss Terri Tracy for their aid in the preparation of the manuscript.

ROBERT E. WOOD

Rensselaer, Indiana
April 1970

Contents

Part II: METAPHYSICS AND THE DISCIPLINES

THE FUTURE OF METAPHYSICS

Part I

THE CONTEMPORARY SPECTRUM

The Problem for Metaphysics

Paul Weiss

Metaphysics is the persistent, self-critical pursuit of those finalities which are presupposed by all knowledge and by all contingent beings. The exposition of its methods, claims, and results is hard to separate from an account of other approaches to knowledge and reality, for its justification, in good part, lies in the fact that it finds a place for basic truths which the other approaches inevitably and regrettably neglect. This fact becomes a little more evident when the positions of common sense, analysis, science, existentialism, and mysticism are surveyed, and their limits indicated. It then becomes possible to make a little more plausible the answers that are to be made to current objections to the intelligibility, testability, or legitimacy of the metaphysical enterprise.

Most of what men claim to know has been gathered in the course of daily living. Each man learns almost untaught some of the crucial differences that separate the old from the young, the wise from the innocent, and the reasonable from the naive. Slowly, and often painfully, each human being learns the way in which men and women differ in outlook, rhythm, and aim; and each human being sooner or later takes account of telling differences in the needs, demands, and values of other humans. Gradually, each man learns to separate the plausible and the useful from the foolish and the futile. Before many years have passed, all men have come in some contact with birth and death, with fear, anxiety, and joy. Few men are without the confidence needed to tell day from night, or what a change in the seasons portends. We pay too high a price for a system of philosophy if its principles lead us to doubt or to deny the well-conned commonsense truths that other humans also exist, that men can think and will, that there is good and bad, the beautiful and the ugly, and right and wrong.

Little of our knowledge is pure, freed from all admixture of tendentious belief and inherited errors. Little is clear. All of it is filtered through language and custom. Indeed, men are deemed normal only so far as their speech and acts, and therefore what they really claim to be, know, and believe is in consonance with what is acceptable to the rest. This is true even when one man with considerable justification affirms a truth the rest never knew. Even in the most advanced societies his claims will be dismissed as at least irrelevant and at most mistaken until he wins support from those who are in power because of their authority or their mass. Although truth does not depend on consensus, still it must be widely consented to if it is to have the effectiveness it deserves, and be accepted without question.

Learning takes place more or less haphazardly. The contingencies of existence and the exigencies of life dictate in good part what it is that will be encountered. And what is encountered grounds most of what we know. No mind, though, is filled only with a miscellany of unrelated bits of information. Common language and practice provide categories which determine how items are to be classified. Unfortunately, those commonsense categories are neither well bounded nor unalloyed.

Commonsense men observe carelessly; usually they speak quite loosely. They testify under oath, with evident sincerity, about what they could not conceivably have seen. Few know how to use technical terms or complex instruments with precision. Too often they overlay what they confront with questionable conventions. What they experience is soon obscured by superstitions and arbitrary beliefs.

Were common sense more careful, we would not be so ready to analyze, except occasionally and then for a short time. Were it more precise and better organized, mankind would not so quickly turn to science for its answers. Were its vision steady and its values keyed to man as he stands by himself, there would be less need to vitalize common sense in existentialistic and other personalistic ways. Were its items final or self-explanatory, men might not be so tempted to look to mysticism, and try thereby to get to whatever might lie beyond the daily world.

And were all of common sense to form a single, self-critical, comprehensive system, there would be less reason to engage in speculation, trying somehow to understand what is at the root of all that is and can be known.

Common sense has a vulgar muscularity which has prevented it from being crushed by any other agency. Reid, Moore, Peirce, and Austin have made the English-speaking philosophic community see how vital and surefooted common sense is. But, the more they insisted on the validity of commonsense claims and the soundness of commonsense discourse, the more evident it became that they had difficulty in finding room for abstract mathematics, formal logic, theoretical science, universal ethics, and revelational religion. Each one of these challenges common sense at some crucial point. The necessities, the prescriptions, the formalities, the obligating good, and the final judge of which these disciplines speak are not altogether within the grasp of commonsense experience, methods, or discourse. To be sure, common sense is sometimes pliable enough to accommodate faint versions of them. But it never finds a place for them in their full rigor or shows adequate respect for their austere beauty.

Common sense too often replaces what is hoped for and believed by what is known, proved, or really encountered. It is too often dogmatic where it should be slow-moving and detailed. One would feel less desire to abandon it could one hold its impulses in check, refine its vocabulary, and give it a steady and sure direction. Analysis is a sharp instrument enabling us to achieve something like these ends.

Analysis looks for the joints in things. It seeks to break up phenomena or discourse into more manageable and, if possible, more reliable and manipulatable parts. Today it depends considerably on the wit of men to use the distinctions of grammar or logic to tell them where to cut into things so that they can find the units in terms of which all else is presumably to be understood. But this is only one of many ways it might proceed.

Analysis enables us to know exactly what it is that we are saying. It is a method which can be extended to embrace the assertions and objects of any discipline whatsoever. Wherever there is meaning and wherever there is something asserted, evidently analysis can be used there to lay bare the components, and therefore the import of what is said.

Analysis waits for other enterprises to give it material on which to work. Although it follows its own bent, it is still a dependent enterprise. Nor does it examine the presuppositions on which its data rest; it does not know whether or not those disciplines on which it operates have anything which answers to them in fact. And, of course, it knows no way of relating one discipline to another. The most it can do is to show that all are divisible into elements.

There are analysts who boldly affirm that the elements to which they finally come are the atoms of the world or of language. Hume, the early Russell, and the early Wittgenstein held this view. But their justification is hard to find. Perhaps that is why these three acute thinkers soon turned from this position to attend instead to other subjects or to take up other approaches.

Analysis should be guided by the structure of things. That structure, because it is embedded in the things, is most readily known by attending to what is encountered. An analysis which does this will, more likely than not, so divide entities that widely dispersed common factors will be found, enabling one to restate what had already been learned in a rough and uncritical way. But something more will be needed if what is sought is an explanation or a prediction, or if one wants to evaluate the claims of all disciplines without making an antecedent judgment regarding their respective merits.

Technology has transformed the shape of the West to give it a distinctive tone and drive. Behind that technology is science, a triple-pronged affair, more widely practiced and praised than understood. One occupation of science has to do with the production of experiments, deliberately set in ideal and controlled situations so as to enable one to get exact answers to exacting questions. Another occupation is with observations, usually achieved with the aid of tightly calibrated instruments. A third occupation is with the creation of theoretical formulations of the connections that hold between the law-abiding occurrences discovered in experiment and observation. When those theories are freed from their initial base and developed independently, they assume the shape of comprehensive explanations and predictions of what can be known in other ways.

In all its guises, science offers a challenge to the tacit claim of common sense to have reached foundational or inexpungeable truths. It does not, however, cast all common sense aside. In the end, every scientific claim must be checked by commonsense men confronting commonsense scales, numbers, signals, lights, and photographs. But science points to realities not within the capacity of common sense to acknowledge and sometimes even to understand; the two meet only on the surface.

We need not, and we should not, stand on either side of the barrier that separates some of the analysts from some of the positivists. We need not deny that what we know in commonsensical ways exists as surely as what we discover in controlled experiments, refined observations, and through the help of scientific theories. There are, however, other things to understand, not reachable by any of these methods. A strenuous effort should be made to try to attend to all avenues of knowledge, to reconcile their demands and claims, and to present the result in a single, well-organized, comprehensive account. Existentialism, mysticism, and metaphysics all claim to know what is beyond the competence of common sense, analysis, or science. But they do not accord well with the temper of the day. Still, the distinguished thinkers of the Western world who have pursued them, and the challenges these disciplines offer, require an honest inquirer today to try to find out what such disciplines can and cannot do.

Science seeks cold, impersonal truth. It deals with some items which occurred a long time ago, as well as with others scheduled to appear in the remote future. It interests itself as much in the composition of stars as it does in the appetites of men. This catholicity and objectivity some find pretentious and therefore offensive. Existentialists are among its most outspoken critics today. They object not so much to the results or methods of science as they do to its attitude. For them there is little of value, solace, or even truth in any view that does not express man as he authentically is. All else they think is desiccated, abstract, or too alien to man to be anything more than an exhibition of the folly of detachment and of the attempt to be objective.

Despite their conflict, existentialism and science share a common attitude toward common sense and analysis. Both find the first too crude and the second too naive. But all four positions, I think, have a place in the civilized pursuit of knowledge. What science knows is merely on a plane different from that which interests the existentialist; but both are concerned with aspects of the commonsense world, and the meanings of both can be made clearer by having recourse to analysis.

In their different ways these diverse approaches keep the mind focused on rather limited areas and tasks. None pays sufficient attention to the fact that men are constantly confronted with the wondrous and the perplexing. They do not seem to be sufficiently alert to the occasional moments of terror many experience when the familiar world falls away to leave one confronting a vast, dark awesomeness. They also seem to be insufficiently aware of a continuity beneath the separated items that are dealt with in daily life or are the objects of language, theory, or human concern. They are insensitive to the fact that every distinctive thing we know might be a fractionated, distorted form of one single, all-encompassing reality. That at least is the contention of some singular men who have dotted the course of history.

These men insist that there are realities which escape the mesh of other enterprises. They want to identify themselves with those realities, or simply to live with them. Methods which involve conceptualization, they think, inevitably distort what everyone can glimpse, if only for a moment and only occasionally. They refuse to remain within the orbit of thought or even of human concerns. What is real they assert is quite different from what is normally known.

These men are mystics, natural or supernatural. The natural mystic—such as Schopenhauer or Bergson—claims to be able to penetrate beneath phenomena to a quite different reality. He speaks of 'insight' or 'intuition' as means by which he can escape the thrall of daily discourse and understanding. His counterpart, the supernatural mystic, starts instead with a religiously grounded claim and tries to trace it back to its source, at the same time cutting himself free from all restraining dogmas.

There seems to be a large core of agreement amongst these men, so far as one can judge from their somewhat metaphorically expressed claims. But there is no sure way of knowing this. They offer no definite criteria, no clear tests, and no reliable evidence. That is, however, no adequate reason for dismissing them. They are evidently sincere and have something important to say; they make an unusual effort to arrive at that which is beyond all human contriving, distortion, or fragmentation. It would be wise to see if it is possible to come to know in another way that to which they seem to point. This is one of the things that a metaphysician tries to do. He thinks he sees at the heart of common sense, science, and existentialism indications of final realities which seem to be somewhat like what the mystics report is ultimate reality. But the metaphysician tries to reach his finalities through the use of a distinctive philosophic method, and tries to express what he knows through the agency of a fully integrated system, where item supports item, and all is made subject to the critically used criteria of clarity and completeness.

This is a world in which there are many things of many kinds. I call them all 'actualities.' Some are known in a partially obscured or distorted form by common sense. Other actualities, quite minute or startlingly gigantic, are the topic of the sciences. It is conceivable that some of them might be reached by analysis. Existentialists seem to get to the root of those actualities which have considerable bearing on man's destiny. Were all of these approaches together to exhaust the universe, there would be little left to do unless it were just the relating of all of them, an examining of their presuppositions, or a forging of a language in terms of which one could discourse on any of their objects. But they do not seem to exhaust all that can be intelligibly grasped. Some things remain inexplicable unless we take account of the presence of other realities which are distinct in location, nature, and function from any of the things we can encounter. It is these realities which interest the metaphysician.

All actualities seem to be subject to at least three compulsions, the source of which are the realities we now seek. One of these compulsions is brute, keeping actualities coordinate in time. Another is prescriptive, dictating what the actualities can be and do. A third is agglutinative, affiliating some with others from which they sometimes diverge quite radically in nature, value, and function. Each deserves a word.

1. Some things are sluggish and others swift, but all enter the

next moment together. What keeps them temporally abreast? An Aristotelian would say that they are all confined within a single area where they are temporally counted in a common way. Leibniz would say that they had been preordained to always be coordinate. The former makes them move as a collection, though they had been taken to be independent in being and function. The universe seems to be far more open, larger, and peopled with beings which are more interdependent than those that Aristotle acknowledged. On the other hand, Leibniz translates the temporal into the nontemporal, and therefore has difficulty with the question of the coming to be and passing away of things. It seems more correct to say that all things are swept along by the movement of a single, cosmic, dynamic, extended power, compelling all things to enter into the next moment together.

2. Nothing will be unless it can be. But what can be is the possible. Because the possible limits the degree of freedom that is open to present actualities, predictions can be made and expectations may be justified. Some of the possibilities are imperious and impose conditions to which all things must conform. It is these possibilities that concern mathematicians and logicians. Other possibilities promise enhancement to whatever will realize them; they are the possibilities which obligate. All are locatable in a single reality toward which actualities point and which in turn makes them intelligible.

3. Some things attract one another; others are mutually repellent. Some of these attractions and repulsions are understandable by reference to notions such as electric currents. Some perhaps are adequately explained by a theory of chemical attraction or valency. But there are other affiliations which occur without regard for the nature of the bodies of actualities. These affiliations are most conspicuous in the commerce of human beings. Suddenly, but with confidence and certainty, men sometimes make contact with other men, and sometimes with animals or things, with whom they have no evident common background or experience. Attenuated forms of that attraction can be discerned throughout the animal kingdom; electric and chemical attractions seem to be special forms of it. In any case, it offers testimony to the presence of a power of affiliation which is strong enough to bring disparate entities into close concordance, even when they are quite remote in space and differ considerably in nature. One does

not depart much from a long, deeply established tradition if one speaks of this affiliating power as God.

All three powers affect actualities. As not exhausted in any one operation on any particular set of actualities, they are powers which must be recognized to have a being distinct from those actualities and the way these are related to one another. Whatever encounter we have with them is never more than fleeting, and is never clear edged. To know them with some clarity one must supplement insight with reason. The agencies for accomplishing this are dialectic, the consideration of what would complete what one already knows, and system, the integrated articulation of realities as they stand apart from one another, as they condition one another, as they affect one another, and as they manifest themselves in limited forms within the confines of one another.

These are not, I think, the only finalities, but I believe enough has been said to show that their study involves a nest of issues, and yields results that appear to be rather distant from anything men usually know or are interested in. As a matter of fact, a study of them enables one to understand a little better and to interrelate a little more coherently a whole range of inquiries which would otherwise seem to be without connection and without a rootage in the nature of things. Art and history are private and public ways of relating us to an insistent extended Existence; ethics and politics are individual and common ways of relating us to a prescriptive Ideal; and personal and communal religion are ways of relating us to an affiliating God. Existence, Ideality, and God are thereby known, not as they operate over the cosmos of actualities, but from more limited perspectives. All three of them, in addition, have more absolute forms, where they stand away from their relation to actualities and help constitute another domain there. It is one of the objects of metaphysics to study them severally and together, in relation to actualities, and in relation to one another.

An account such as this raises two types of questions: substantive and methodological. Have the realities been properly characterized in themselves and in interrelationship? Can they be known, understood, and spoken about intelligibly? Adequate answers to the first question will lead one far into the internal workings of a rather elaborate system. Fortunately, they are adumbrated in the answers to the second question.

It is common today to say that metaphysical assertions are at best poetic and at worst nonsensical, and surely vague and unverifiable. Neither the language of common sense nor that of science can accommodate them. I think this criticism is just in the main. Although unkind to poetry and overimpressed with science, it is surely right in remarking that metaphysics cannot be expressed in ordinary terms or in conformity to the criteria appropriate to the contentions of common sense, analysis, science, or existentialism.

Metaphysics speaks in a 'metalanguage' which gives coherent and communicable sense to transcendental terms that are recalcitrant to our ordinary grammar. It forges a new language in which such terms as 'unity,' 'being,' 'possibility,' 'truth,' and 'the good' are intelligibly related by attending to the nuances of compelling powers and what these demand. Those terms, shorn of a reference to the compelling powers of Existence, Ideality, and God, take paradoxical turns, disruptive of conventional practice. Metaphysics starts with such terms as aberrational items—and in a sense always leaves them that way—as it moves on to understand how, in the light of what is ultimately real, they can be interrelated and significantly used.

Again and again, the metaphysician, like everyone else, finds himself confronted with incoherencies, paradoxes, and apparent contradictions. In the attempt to exhibit the rationale behind these, he alters his vocabulary and grammar. His discourse does not have a set of antecedently known and tried rules, but instead is a creative, freshly minted agent constantly altered to accommodate and quiet new perplexities. It looks to ultimate beings to find out what distinctions and stresses are to be made in accepted categories and claims.

There are some who hold that metaphysics, like all else, is economically, politically, or socially conditioned. What were problems once, they think, are problems no longer; what once was unknown is problematic now. Philosophy in all its branches is for them tentative, dependent, and a creature of the times. They note that the nature and rights of slaves is not a major issue for us today, and that megalopolis, international law, space travel, and the rights of minorities are now to the fore. But the fact that there are problems that come and go does not mean that there are none that remain with us always. Birth, death, joy, pain, love, hate, peace, war, and injustice, growth and decay, mind and body, male and female, and youth and age explode again and again into a multiplicity of issues and questions as soon as we refuse to accept without criticism the unexamined answers that common sense and science provide, or refuse to ignore some of the things that exist outside experience.

Metaphysics begins with the wondrous. Whatever awakens surmise as to its ground or bearing on whatever else is or is known can prompt the beginning of a long and hazardous dialectical journey. One knows that one has come to the end of that journey and finally touched on an ultimate Being when, upon returning to the world of things, one finds that everything has become wondrous—more wondrous even than the initial items had been before—but more clearly demarcated and understood. Wonder does not disappear as a result of philosophic inquiry; instead, it becomes manifest everywhere. Metaphysics does not dissolve or solve problems. It traces them back to their origin, and thereby discovers why the problems arise and are always with us.

Scholasticism and Metaphysics

Joseph Owens

I

The object of this paper is to inquire into the role of Scholasticism in contemporary metaphysics.

Of the two terms, "metaphysics," perhaps surprisingly, turns out to be by far the easier to pinpoint and bring into manageable focus for the purposes of the present discussion. In no small measure does it owe this relatively common acceptance as an understandable term in contemporary American philosophy to the initiative of Paul Weiss in founding a society to represent, as it were officially, American metaphysical endeavors, and in starting the *Review of Metaphysics* to provide a public forum for their expression. Twenty-five years ago the historical welter of views that passed under the caption of metaphysics, their apparently irreconcilable divergencies and radical opposition to one another, and their seeming inability to communicate among themselves or with the general philosophical mentality of the first half of the present century were enough to put the prospect of any fruitful cooperation in this area beyond the pale of respectable hope. Yet the Metaphysical Society of America in the first article of its constitution was able to define its purpose as "the study of reality," and bring the allegedly irreconcilable and despairingly centrifugal tendencies under a common viewpoint. And, strangely enough, it worked! Nor is there any reason to fear that this pragmatic test will not be met as the ongoing impulse for wider metaphysical discussion extends these efforts to the intercontinental scene in the new International Metaphysical Society.[1] The formula may or may not have to be modified, but the prospect of a *common* formula seems assured.

This agreement makes comparatively easy the task of giving a manageable signification to the term "metaphysics" in the present context. Metaphysics can be understood as the study of reality, in the way in which that study has been pursued over the last two decades at the meetings of the Metaphysical Society and in the pages of the *Review of Metaphysics*. The notion is distinctive enough. Other sciences may claim peripherally that they are dealing with reality, but they do not focus upon that aspect. A chemist or a physicist would maintain he was dealing with reality and not with fancy or fiction, but what operative role does the notion play in his formulae? He is just not interested in approaching his subject matter from that viewpoint, and as a chemist or physicist has no need to. It would, in fact, be a distraction for him. The experience of Western metaphysics from the time of Parmenides, however, shows conclusively enough that there is a distinct approach to things from the viewpoint of their reality. It is that approach, as followed out in practice during the last two decades of our metaphysical enterprise in America, that gives distinct and recognizable contours to the meaning of metaphysics in the present discussion.

II

Unfortunately, the notion of "Scholasticism" offers no such relatively facile criterion for probing its meaning. Over forty years ago a historian who was writing on the topic of Moslem and Christian Scholasticism was able to say that "It would be difficult to find in the history of the human spirit a notion more disputed than the concept of Scholasticism." [2] The situation does not seem to have changed notably during the intervening decades. The importance of a correct understanding of the notion and the prevailing lack of clarity in regard to it have in the meantime been stressed by Gilson: "Overwhelmed by more than five centuries of floods, the ignorance of itself is the most serious evil from which Scholasticism is suffering." [3] Yet no satisfactory notion of Scholasticism has emerged in current literature. Scholars working on the problem, at least those to whom I have listened, have not been able to present a notion that will cover all the facts.

What is the reason for the difficulty? The term itself is relatively late, and its history is yet to be written. It is used currently for a disconcertingly wide variety of ways of thinking. It is applied to the theology and logic of the Christian Middle Ages, to Moslem Scholasticism and Hebrew Scholasticism,[4] to what Carlo Giacon calls the "second Scholasticism" of the sixteenth and seventeenth centuries,[5] to Protestant Scholasticism,[6] to neo-Scholasticism, and to "contemporary Scholasticism." [7] The last is surprisingly different in spirit and tone even from the neo-Scholasticism of the late nineteenth and early twentieth centuries. But similarly profound differences will be found in all the varieties of Scholasticism just listed. The difficulties in reaching a common notion under which they may be subsumed become apparent. Certainly a merely historical characterization, such as "the theology and philosophy of the Middle Ages," will not do. The extent in time is much greater, and the designation would be about as meaningful as "ancient thought" or "modern thought." Nor will the rather widely accepted notion of the organization of all human knowledge under the domination of sacred theology meet the situation. This would exclude the Italian universities, where the studies were geared to medicine and not to theology,[8] and would require the unorthodox currents to be labeled "anti-Scholastic." [9] Still less can the aim of Scholasticism be looked upon as "the exposition of Christian dogma in its relations to reason." [10] The Moslem and Jewish versions would be left out, as well as long treatises on logic that cannot even in the most farfetched way be regarded as instances of "the exposition of Christian dogma." Conversely, we are familiar today with many rationalistic and modernistic explanations of Christian dogma that cannot by any flight of fancy be brought under the notion of Scholasticism, at least without fear of causing considerable umbrage in their proponents.

What, then, is the basic notion conveyed by "Scholasticism"? The earliest occurrence listed for the word in the *Oxford English Dictionary* (s.v.) is in the second half of the eighteenth century. No other instance is offered until the last half of the nineteenth century, when the term becomes common. From the beginning its basic meaning is "the doctrines of the Schoolmen" (*ibid.*). "Scholastics," in this sense of the medieval theologians, is regular in the sixteenth-century Jesuits Fonseca, Vasquez, and Suarez. "School" in the singular and plural was used by these writers for individual currents of thought, as it had been in the Middle Ages and early Renaissance, and in Fonseca for the totality of the Schoolmen. There need be no surprise, then, in finding Descartes refer to "l'Ecole," [11] in this sense, and Locke [12] and Berkeley [13] speak of "the Schoolmen." "Scholastic," in the wider sense of a person engaged in school activity, goes back to Theophrastus.[14] It has had a long and varied history.[15] From the free and easy connotations of "leisure" it passed to those of rigid school instruction. The latter undoubtedly provided the approach to the image with which the term "Scholasticism" was coined, occasioning the quip that Scholasticism has been named from its greatest misfortune.[16] At any rate, the use in French and Italian of the adjectival forms *scolastique* and *scolastica* as nouns for designating the teachings of the Schoolmen became current from the seventeenth century on,[17] and prompted the coining of the German *Scholastik* and the English "Scholasticism."

All that the history of the term shows, however, is that Scholasticism has a basic relation to the doctrines of the Schoolmen. But just what is the relation? And who are to be included under the notion "Schoolmen"? And what are the doctrines involved?

These three questions bristle with difficulties. The one with which to begin is obviously the second. Agreement upon at least some men who are to be called Schoolmen or Scholastics should be easy to reach. Possibly one could begin with John Scotus Erigena, or even go as far back as Boethius. But about thinkers from the time of Anselm and Abelard to that of William of Ockham there can hardly be any hesitation. They are commonly recognized as Scholastics.[18] Their writings can be taken ostensively as laying the ground for developing a tentative notion of Scholasticism. The problem of how other types that bear the name fall into relation with this basic notion could then be faced. These might parallel it, like Arabian and Jewish Scholasticism, or systematize it like seventeenth-century Scholasticism and neo-Scholasticism, or seek inspiration and guidance in it as does contemporary Scholasticism.

The basic task, accordingly, is to determine the type of thinking and the overall views that go to make up the body of doctrines that come down from those who are commonly recognized as Scholastics. Among them the most prominent are Thomas Aquinas, John Duns Scotus, and William of Ockham. Others that readily come to mind would be Anselm, Abelard, Peter Lombard, Alexander of Hales, William of Auvergne, Bonaventure, Giles of Rome, Henry of Ghent, Peter of Spain, and so on. As the frame of reference for the present inquiry is metaphysics, I will limit the concern to the metaphysical tenets and methods of these thinkers.

III

The fact that stands out most strikingly in the writings of these men is that they were theologians. Their prime intellectual commitment was to sacred theology. They engaged abundantly in metaphysical thinking, but either in the course of theological treatises or with quite evident theological interests in mind. In a word, they were thinking as theologians. Even a treatise like the *De Ente et Essentia* of Aquinas,[19] which can be read and is often read as a purely metaphysical discussion, indicates clearly enough the theological matrix in which its tenets were conceived. At the time of its writing Aquinas was engaged full time in commenting upon the theological *Sentences* of Peter Lombard. The reasoning in the *De Ente,* often succinct and hard to understand, is found developed at greater length and with primitive freshness in the longer articles of Aquinas' commentary on the *Sentences.* His distinctive doctrine of existence, upon which so much of the reasoning in the *De Ente* depends for its cogency, is nowhere explained in the short treatise. True, the *De Ente* does not offer itself as a discussion of existence, but only of essence and what exists.[20] But the fact that a treatise of this sort could be organized without any explanation of the way existence is known through the act of judgment, and of the radical primacy existence holds over essence, points tellingly to a different origin from the merely philosophical for the doctrines it presents. These necessary presuppositions, however, are found carefully thought out and developed in the course of the theological reasoning in the commentary on the *Sentences.* Does not this show clearly enough the soil from which they grew? Furthermore, preoccupation with theological questions of the day can readily be discerned in the discussions about the angels and the individuality of the spiritual soul in the *De Ente*.

What will this essentially theological matrix imply for Scholastic metaphysics as it interests us today? Will it allow the metaphysics to be genuinely philosophical? Will it require a theological approach to its tenets if these be accepted as legitimately philosophical in character?

These questions have been asked and discussed at considerable length during the past decade.[21] Perhaps the best way to illustrate the issues involved is to examine a particular instance. The instance just mentioned, the distinctive conception of existence in Aquinas, serves the purpose admirably. In his commentary on the *Sentences,* the theological order found in Peter Lombard is being followed. The mystery of the Trinity is first treated. Since it means three persons in one essence, it raises the question of the divine essence of nature. This, the Scripture as interpreted in Christian and Jewish tradition shows,[22] is existence. In the reasoning that follows, the proposition that God's existence is his quiddity is used without any proof and as though it called for none in the context. It was not new. It had been accepted before, but in a theological tradition.[23] Only later, and on particular occasions, does the commentary of Aquinas explain how existence is grasped by human intelligence,[24] and thereby lay the philosophical basis for showing the distinction between existence and nature in creatures and their identity in God.

What does such procedure imply? Does it not indicate that Aquinas was first led by theological meditation on a text from *Exodus* to conceive the nature of existence as the nature of God? The next step would be that the mark of a creature is to have a nature different from existence. This would require that the natures of things immediately knowable to human cognition be grasped in a way that does not reveal any existence whatsoever. Their existence would have to be apprehended in a different way by a different type of cognition. Had the genesis of the tenet that existence is originally known not through conceptualization but through judgment been purely philosophical in origin, one would have expected it to occupy a leading place in the procedure and to be the ultimate distinguishing characteristic to which all questions on existence are referred. Instead, it is mentioned only briefly on the occasion of dealing with other topics,[25] and is never made a fundamental consideration around which a whole metaphysical procedure might be organized. Although it may seem obvious after one has approached it through the theological medium of the Thomistic text, in point of historical fact there seems to be no record of its ever having been noticed before, and there is the fact that subsequent readers of Aquinas have consistently missed it when they approached the texts from a purely philosophical viewpoint.[26] It seems to be an exceptionally clear instance of Gilson's claim that to be understood the philosophy of Aquinas has to be approached via theology.[27] In the actual procedure of St. Thomas the crucial metaphysical role of existence as known through judgment makes its appearance as an end product rather than as a starting point.

Another instance is the reasoning that the spiritual soul has absolute being,[28] is a necessary being,[29] and can no more be separated from its existence than from itself.[30] If one approaches this reasoning in the light of the Scriptural assertion that man is made to God's image and likeness, coupled with the further conception that God is existence, one sees how an altogether special existential status is to be looked for in the spiritual soul. One is led to seek out and to find for it a different way of existing from that of nonspiritual things. But without the theological approach, would one ever arrive at Aquinas' way of reasoning in this topic?

After the basically theological cast of Scholastic thinking, perhaps the most outstanding feature from the viewpoint of metaphysical concern is its radical pluralism. The resultant surface phenomena have been noted often enough by hostile critics, with the conclusion that in Scholasticism everything is disputed and nothing ever settled. A close examination shows that the very starting points of the metaphysical thinking are different in the different writers. For Duns Scotus the starting point or first object of metaphysics is a common nature formally distinct from the thing's individuation.[31] The result is an entirely distinctive type of metaphysics. The distinction between God and creatures appears in terms of nature and individuation, insofar as in God nature and individuation coincide,[32] whereas the corresponding role in Aquinas is played by the identity of nature and existence. As a testing point of the radical diversity in the metaphysical thinking of the more eminent Scholastics, one might take their respective notions of a nature just in itself, since this is the basic object of human conceptualization. In Aquinas it has no being whatsoever,[33] in Duns Scotus it has the being that corresponds to the peculiarly Scotistic "minor unity,"[34] in Giles of Rome it has enough actuality to be known but not enough to exist,[35] in Henry of Ghent it has a characteristic being of its own that differs in a specially pertinent way from both real existence and cognitional existence.[36] The radical metaphysical pluralism in these various ways of conceptualizing natures is crystal clear. The philosophical pluralism in general seems to be recognized implicitly in Paul Edwards' *Dictionary of Philosophy* in not treating of Scholasticism under a single title, but rather referring the reader to its leading instances.

Yet this radically pluralistic thinking was presented in a common basic framework and basic vocabulary that may be called a "reanimated Aristotelianism." The division of all things into substance and the nine categories of accidents, the recognition of being and goodness as transcending the categories, the four Aristotelian causes, and the distinctions of matter and form and of potentiality and actuality were accepted and used everywhere. They were a skeletal structure that was given new and different philosophical life in each great medieval thinker. Needless to say, both vocabulary and conceptual framework were enlarged as progressing medieval thought introduced the sharp distinction between essence and existence, between common nature and the universal in its strict sense, the notions of precisive and nonprecisive abstraction, and other such non-Greek concepts, and explored the metaphysical implications of subsistence, personality, creation, and the like. Moreover, a particular thinker could find himself obliged by the intrinsic necessities of his philosophical notions to add an "epi-vocabulary" of his own, as may be seen for instance in Duns Scotus' "minor unity," "unitive containment," "haecceity," and so on. But all innovations presupposed the basic Aristotelian concepts and vocabulary. They were not at all meant to do away with or supersede the traditional framework. Rather, they were meant to build upon it and enlarge it according to progressing needs.

Another recognizable feature in these leading medieval Scholastics is their readiness and ability to use the work of other thinkers and incorporate it into their own. They had no hesitation in drawing upon whatever helpful elements they found in Aristotle, the Platonists, and the Arabian and Jewish writers. Often the items drawn from these sources were transformed into new meanings, and used to bolster new tenets that would have been incompatible with them in their original settings. Support for doctrines like creation and divine infinity can provide notable examples. The point at issue, however, is that the great Scholastics were able to look upon philosophy as a common heritage. They had the ability to absorb into their own thinking the best that they found in others, no matter how much they disagreed with the rest of the author's work.

Finally, metaphysics for these Scholastics was barred from any road to intellectual imperialism. It had to accept the status of one science among others. Despite its universal range in dealing with all beings, it did not have access to the causes by which the most important things for the theologians were to be explained.[37] In the Aristotelian framework it did not subordinate practical or productive sciences to itself, and did not give the particular principles of any of the other theoretical sciences.[38] It could hardly be regarded as the "root" from which the other sciences grew.[39] Rather, it was a science with its own field and its own methods. It was confined to its own work, and wholly unable to enter into the particular fields of any of the other sciences or to supervise their activities.

IV

These features of the Scholasticism found in its commonly recognized exponents in the Christian Middle Ages, although not enough for a satisfactory definition or overall conception,[40] should suffice for determining its role in regard to the metaphysical enterprise. The characteristics just considered show that Scholasticism has given birth to a number of different ways of metaphysical thinking. These ways were conceived in a theological matrix. They were the work of theologians forced to think metaphysically in dealing with their theological problems. With considerable labor the metaphysical insights may be traced to genuinely philosophical starting points in the works of the theologians, even though they are not presented there in the light of this philosophical organization. Once tracked to their philosophical basis, however, they are shown to be authentically metaphysical in character. They can be used as new inspiration to independent metaphysical thinking, as keys to unlock the doors to storehouses of new possibilities for metaphysical structures. But the condition is that they first be read as expressions of insights in theology, as part and parcel of an integrally theological effort.[41] Only then, as the experience of failures in the last few centuries makes abundantly clear, can their true operative force as metaphysical insights become apparent. To attempt to read them just as philosophy is to invite new failure, at least when one is first encountering them in their original habitat. They are found woven too thoroughly into the theological fabric to allow their genuine colors to be appreciated when they are roughly torn from their blending with the integral pattern.

Scholastic metaphysics today, accordingly, will consist in taking the genuinely metaphysical insights engendered by traditional theology and in developing and organizing them on the strictly metaphysical level. This will be the independent work of the present-day metaphysician himself. It cannot be attributed to the traditional theologian. The full responsibility for selecting the metaphysical starting points and for cultivating them to their full fruition lies with the present-day thinker. It cannot be transferred to the theologian. The new metaphysical structure has to stand or fall on its own merits.

From this viewpoint the radical pluralism of the Scholastic metaphysical enterprise should appear in clear-cut lines. Every new metaphysician, if he is doing genuine thinking, will put the contours of his own individual personality and his own unique background and upbringing into his philosophical work. Here as elsewhere in metaphysics each authentic thinker will develop conceptions that are not exactly matched by those of anyone else. Just as no two individuals have the same fingerprints, so no two may be expected to have the same metaphysics. But, just as fingerprints can be arranged in definite groupings on the basis of pertinent similarities, so there will be enough family resemblances[42] to bring under the one heading of "Scholastic" the many different types that find their historical origin in the traditional theology.

One common feature by which the members of the family may be readily recognized will be the traditional Scholastic vocabulary. It is inconceivable that a metaphysics presented in any other framework could lay claim to the title "Scholastic." The basic notions of substance and accidents, of nature and existence, and of efficient and final and formal and material causes are essential to the Scholastic tradition. It is not that the number of accidents need be placed rigidly at nine. Even Aristotle varies in the number according to the needs of the moment. Since the categories last named in the list of the ten depend upon relations, one can easily increase the list to suit one's purposes by increasing the number of relations. The point is, however, by and large the ten categories provide an obligatory framework of natures for Scholastic thinking. The exact number is not important. Nor can one always find a modern substitute for the traditional names. What modern term can replace "accident" as a designation for the nine categories? None has yet been found. How can the meaning of a "common nature" be conveyed by new terms like "abstract entities" or "metaphysical universal," except under qualifications that do away with the basic notions expressed by these phrases? Just as the basic Aristotelian vocabulary was increased by additions arising from medieval needs, however, so the present Scholastic vocabulary will always remain open to additions required by new developments. But this will have the character of an "epi-vocabulary," and not a radically new vocabulary or framework replacing the older one.

Furthermore, just as the way of metaphysical thinking born in the theological meditation of the Middle Ages was able to absorb what was advantageous to it not only in Aristotle but also in the Platonic and Arabian and Jewish writers, so Scholastic metaphysics today may be expected to have similar power and urge for intussusception of the best in modern philosophy. The osmosis can be genuine no matter how different the underlying structure or spirit of the current philosophies may be. Existentialism, phenomenology, linguistic analysis, and structuralism have much nourishment to offer it. Moreover, a certain amount of cross-fertilization is to be looked for, although the dominant characteristics will have to remain Scholastic if the new strain is to be regarded as continuing in the tradition. But there is no reason why the recessive characteristics should not be genuinely operative and make their own special contribution to the ongoing vigor of Scholastic life.

V

From all this it becomes quite apparent that Scholastic metaphysics is still very much a thing of the future. It is doubtful if up to the present there have been more than the very first beginnings of the authentic enterprise.[43] In what particular areas, then, has Scholastic metaphysics a distinctive contribution to make, a contribution that will justify its laborious pursuit in the foreseeable future?

One notable area is the epistemological concern with cognition and knowledge, truth and certainty. The Aristotelian heritage absorbed by Scholasticism held that cognition is to be explained in terms of being—the soul *is* in a way all things,[44] knower and known *are* one in the act of cognition.[45] Medieval Scholasticism developed this insight by investigating what the "in a way" was, and by explaining it in terms of intentional existence as contradistinguished from real existence. These metaphysical insights still wait application to the problems of perception that have risen from the controversies about sense-data and to the problems of knowledge that emerge from the various modern theories of truth. To see (it should be obvious) cannot be explained in terms of photography, and to hear cannot be understood as tape recording. The camera may garner in details more minutely than the retina, and the recorder more accurately than the tympanum. But the activity of the camera is not cognition. The camera does not see, unless you are speaking of its eye in a very metaphorical way. Nor does the recorder hear. Its activity is not cognition. Cognition requires explanation on an entirely different ground. Scholasticism, with its approach from the existential viewpoint, provides a promising basis for working out this explanation. Similarly, with regard to the truth and certainty of one's knowledge, an explanation in terms of existence seems required, and Scholasticism opens up an enticing approach here that philosophy can scarcely afford to bypass.

Another area is the philosophical demonstration of the existence of God. For a question that is so widely represented as having been decided definitely in the negative long ago, there is a surprising amount of current discussion about it today. The controversies of the last decade on the ontological argument still persist, and at present the old cosmological argument is being examined with renewed interest. The question is not precisely a religious one. Many sincere and deep believers in the existence of God have not the slightest interest in metaphysical proofs for it. Others may explicitly regard metaphysical proofs as almost blasphemous.[46] Yet there are others who earnestly seek an understanding of the conditions of their faith and are deeply appreciative of cool, rational certainty and insight in regard to the existence of God. Contemporary non-Scholastic philosophies are practically unanimous in renouncing the claim to be able to prove the existence of God with rational cogency and with positive understanding of what the nature of God is. There is no reason to doubt that these philosophies have a correct awareness of their own overall capacities, and of the type of conclusions that can be reached on the basis of their starting points. The various Scholastic metaphysics, on the other hand, expressly offer the possibilities for the demonstration of God's existence. These possibilities may be reciprocally exclusive, in the sense that if you accept the starting points of one you thereby cut yourself off from using the starting points of the others and the demonstrations based upon them. But they are there, in Aquinas, Henry of Ghent, Duns Scotus, and others, waiting for further exploration and development. In this area Scholasticism has much to offer in the future.

A parallel situation is found in regard to the rational demonstration of perpetual existence for the human soul. For non-Scholastic thought today the metaphysical arguments are regarded as invalid and as being of a type that would not be convincing even though they were valid.[47] The Scholastic sources at least claim positively to be able to offer cogent metaphysical demonstrations here, and accordingly invite sensitive exploration, clear understanding, and careful development from acceptable starting points to rationally unshakable conclusions.

Another area crying for exploration is the Scholastic notion of being as infinite, and the use of this notion as a nonconceptual basis for approaching current problems of freedom and subjectivity. Still another is the notion of human nature as involving intellect and will, which are capacities for an infinite object, yet including no power for attaining the object. The resultant "endlessness" of human nature provides an approach to facets that have been diagnosed as absurd or nauseating. Even the question of universals, discussed so often but continually recurring in modern philosophical literature and meetings, has still much enlightenment to obtain from a deeper study and more incisive application of medieval Scholastic thinking.

Do not these and other such avenues open out upon an extremely attractive future for Scholastic metaphysics? Matching these opportunities are the ever-increasing editions of the required source materials. Within five years there should be available a critical text of Aquinas' commentary on the *Metaphysics* of Aristotle, from the Yale center of the Leonine Commission. From its Spanish counterpart there should appear within about fifteen years a critical text of Aquinas' commentary on the *Sentences* of Peter Lombard. These two commentaries are crucial for probing his metaphysical thinking, and as yet they have not been available in critical form. Other Leonine texts, and critical texts of Duns Scotus and William of Ockham and a number of others are gradually being published. The necessary means for fruitful growth of Scholastic metaphysics seem promised for the foreseeable future.

The future, accordingly, appears bright. It is the prospect of a developing tradition that was given its contours in the great thinkers of the Middle Ages, that draws heavily upon the best in all preceding thought, and that will continue to inspire and guide new and creative efforts in the common metaphysical enterprise of Western thought and of world thought. It will be pluralistic and open, yet showing everywhere the family resemblances that will characterize it as Scholastic. It will not be dominant, or seek to dominate. It will represent in its pluralistic way a tradition of authentic metaphysical thinking alongside the others that bloom in the variegated garden of philosophical culture. Scholasticism asks nothing more for its metaphysics, but can be content with nothing less. Scholasticism *and* metaphysics are found in two partially overlapping circles. There is no need to separate them. The soil included in their combined embrace has been exceptionally fruitful in the past, and offers promise of an abundant harvest in the future.

NOTES

1. See address by Paul Weiss, published under "Announcements," *Review of Metaphysics,* 1968, XXII, 425–426.

2. "On trouverait difficilement dans l'histoire de l'esprit humain une notion plus controversée que le concept de scolastique." L. Gauthier, "Scolastique Musulmane et Scolastique Chrétienne," *Revue d'Histoire de la Philosophie,* 1928, II, 333.

3. ". . . et l'on peut dire qu'accablée sous plus de cinq siècles d'alluvions, l'ignorance de soi est le mal le plus grave dont souffre la scolastique." E. Gilson, "Les Recherches Historico-Critiques et l'Avenir de la Scolastique," in *Scholastica Ratione Historico-Critica Instauranda,* eds. H. Marinangeli and C. Recek, Rome, 1951, p. 142.

4. See L. Gauthier, "Scholastique Musulmane," 339–355. Cf. *ibid.,* pp. 230–232, and Maurice De Wulf, *An Introduction to Scholastic Philosophy,* trans. Peter Coffey, New York, 1956, pp. 57, 71. The translation of the latter work was made in 1907 under the title *Scholasticism Old and New,* Dublin and London, 1910.

5. See Carlo Giacon, *La Seconda Scolastica,* Milan, 1944–1950.

6. See J. E. Gurr, under heading "Protestant Scholasticism," in *New Catholic Encyclopedia,* s.v. "Scholasticism," 2. On the theology, see chapter on "Protestant Scholasticism" in A. C. M'Giffert, *Protestant Thought before Kant,* London, 1911, pp. 141–154.

7. See J. A. Weisheipl, "Contemporary Scholasticism," in *New Catholic Encyclopedia,* s.v. "Scholasticism," 3. Fr. Weisheipl includes neo-Scholasticism under this caption. One may be permitted to doubt, however, that the basic neo-Scholastic conception of a single philosophical "system" called Scholastic as canonized by De Wulf, is any longer contemporary.

8. There were no faculties of theology in the Italian universities. For references and a summary of the situation, see Paul Oskar Kristeller, *Le Thomisme et la Pensée Italienne de la Renaissance,* Montreal and Paris, 1967, pp. 42–47.

9. See De Wulf, *Introduction to Scholastic Philosophy,* pp. 51–52.

10. John Dewey, in Baldwin's *Dictionary of Philosophy and Psychology,* s.v. (1).

11. *Discours de la Méthode,* 4 (A–T, VI, 34.27); *à Mersenne,* February 25, 1630 (A–T, I, 117.20).

Cf. André Lalande, *Vocabulaire Technique et Critique de la Philosophie,* s.v. *Scolastique:* "Qui appartient à l' 'Ecole,' c'est-à-dire à l'enseignement philosophique donné dans les écoles ecclésiastiques et les Universités d'Europe du Xe au XVIIe siècle environ."

12. *An Essay Concerning Human Understanding,* III, 10, 8. "The Schools" (*ibid.,* no. 6; III, 8, 2; IV, 7, 11) and "scholastic men" (IV, 7, 11) are used by Locke in the same connection.

13. See index in *The Works of George Berkeley,* eds. A. A. Luce and T. E. Jessup, London, 1948–1957, IX, 187.

14. As reported in Diogenes Laertius, V, 37. For *scholastikos* in its basic sense of "leisurely" as inclusive of, yet wider in meaning than, the sense of *scholê* signifying a group engaged in school activities, see Aristotle, *Pol.* V 11, 1313b3–4.

15. See sketch in De Wulf, *Introduction to Scholastic Philosophy,* pp. 13–14. For information and extensive references to the use of *scholasticus*

and *schola* in Fonesca and Suarez, I am indebted to the as yet unpublished research of Professor John P. Doyle of St. Louis University.

16. See E. Gilson, "The Cultural Revolution of the Thirteenth Century," in *Spaulding Distinguished Lectures 1966–1967,* Durham, N. H., 1968, p. 16.

17. See instances given in Emile Littré's *Dictionnaire de la Langue Française,* s.v. *scholastique,* and C. Battisti's *Dizionario Etimologico Italiano,* s.v. *scolastica* and *scolastico.* In the Middle Ages the predominant notion of a *scholasticus* was that of an administrator of schools, with juridical functions. But even then the followers of a well-known theologian could be referred to as his "school"; ". . . fumant scolae plures in Francia et aliis terris per maxime a duabus caudis titionum fugantium, videlicet, Petri Abaiolardi et episcopi Gilliberti." Gerhoh of Reichersberg, *Liber de Novitatibus hujus Temporis,* ed. O. J. Thatcher, in *The Decennial Publications of the University of Chicago,* First Series IV, 1903, 82.4–5. In the Renaissance the notion of the schools as a distinct arena of intellectual activity and of the various "sects" as schools of the leading medieval theologians may be found: ". . . non in scholis solum, id enim fortasse laudaverim, utpote disciplinae exercitium, verum etiam in suggestis pro concione populari . . ." Battista Spagnoli (1447–1516), *Opus Aureum in Thomistas,* ed. Kristeller, in *Le Thomisme et la Pensée Italienne,* p. 138.12–14. "Et quia est dictu paene impossibile quam variae scholae, quam multiplices sectae profluxerunt, tres tantum memorabo. Henricus Guadanensis, Thomas Aquinas et Joannes Scotus videntur fuisse illustrium sectarum capita clariora." *Ibid.,* p. 163.14–19. *Familiae* (pp. 155.26–156.3) may substitute for *sectae.* In the last quarter of the sixteenth century the term "Scholastic" may be seen repeatedly as Bañes introduces his commentary on St. Thomas Aquinas. But for the followers of St. Thomas the term *sectatores* is used—Dominicus Bañes, *Scholastica Commentaria in Primam Partem Summae Theologicae S. Thomae Aquinatis,* ed. Luis Urbano, Madrid-Valencia, 1934, p. 2a. The word *schola,* on the contrary, is used for teaching activity in contrast to ornate writing: "Nota quarto, quam sit necessarium praeceptori Theologo, praesertim in schola dictanti, ab eloquenti ornataque oratione abstinere: quoniam id sine dispendio multi temporis fieri nequit: et scholasticorum argumentorum vim, ditionis mollities enervat." *Ibid.,* p. 7a. Quite apparent here is the opposition between the literary tendencies of the Renaissance and the didactic style that had become traditional in teaching theology. The polarization into two different approaches to theology marks off the "Scholastic theologians" as a "we" against a "they": "Unde immerito quidam diligentes Grammatici, qui Theologorum nomine gloriantur, Scholasticos irrident, quasi sacrarum literarum ignorantes; cum tamen ipsi multo sunt ignorantiores, non intelligentes Sacrae scripturae majorem utilitatem positam esse in dogmatum intelligentia. In quibus error multo perniciosior erit, quam in temporum et numerorum morosa computatione et Sacrae scripturae phrasibus observandis, in quibus omnibus pii Grammatici diligentia magis quam ingenio interdum Scholasticos Theologos superant: tametsi non desint ex nostris, qui in hac etiam parte plurimum valeant." *Ibid.,* p. 5b. In this setting, "Scholastic" qualifies meditations (Prologue, and p. 5b), *commentaria* (p. 2a), questions (p. 2b), doctrine and discipline (6b), arguments (7a), theology (7b), doctors (2b; 5b), theologians (5b), and is used as a noun (2a; 5a; 8) for the exponents of theology such as St. Thomas. Corresponding uses of "Scholastic" are seen in Gabriel Vasquez, *In Primam Partem*

Summae Theologicae, Venice, 1600, I, 1b; 12b–14a; 209b; and in the *Ad Lectorem.* In the latter, "docendo in Scholis" is found, and in the dedicatory letter "Scholis nostris" in the same sense, while "ex schola S. Thomae" occurs on p. 13a.

Is it too much to suspect that a conception like "in schola dictans" lurks behind the notion of "l'Ecole" as used by Fonseca and Descartes? The least that can be said is that the link between the many "schools" of thought in the Middle Ages and the grouping of them all under the one designation of *"the* School," like "the bench" or "the bar" in legal terminology, has not yet been satisfactorily established.

18. "These men, in fact, show very pronounced family resemblances." De Wulf, *Introduction to Scholastic Philosophy,* p. 46. It is interesting to note the use of "family resemblances" in English as early as 1907 for this purpose of grouping. For discussions of doctrinal definitions, and the failure to achieve one, see De Wulf, *ibid.,* pp. 10–46; 142–144; L. Gauthier, "Scholastique Musulmane," 334–343; H. D. Simonin, "Qu'est-ce que la Scolastique?," *La Vie Intellectuelle,* 1931, X, 236–241.

19. A discusion of the metaphysical characteristics of this work may be found in the "Introduction" to *On Being and Essence,* trans. Armand Maurer, 2nd ed., Toronto, 1968, pp. 7–27.

20. As appears beyond doubt in the opening chapter of the work, *ens* is understood in the sense of "a being," as found in some one of the ten categories.

21. E.g., Gilson, "Les Recherches Historico-Critiques et l'Avenir de la Scolastique," in *Scholastica Ratione Historico-Critica Instauranda,* Rome, 1951, pp. 133–142; A. C. Pegis, *"Sub Ratione Dei:* A Reply to Professor Anderson," *New Scholasticism,* 1965, XXXIX, 141–157; J. A. Oesterle, "St. Thomas as Teacher: A Reply to Professor Pegis," *ibid.,* pp. 451–466.

The problem here is not the same as the problem of a "Christian philosophy." Rather, it is the problem of how metaphysical reasoning can be raised above its own level and become theology. The problem of Christian metaphysics, on the contrary, is how the metaphysics can be genuinely Christian and yet remain philosophy.

22. "Contra, Exod., III, 14, . . . Hoc idem videtur per Damascenum, ubi supra, cap. ix, dicentem quod 'qui est,' maxime est proprium nomen Dei: et per Rabbi Moysen, qui dicit, hoc nomen esse nomen Dei ineffabile, quod dignissimum habebatur." *In I Sent.,* d. 8, q. 1, a. 1, Contra; ed. Mandonnet, I, 194. On the Christian tradition in interpreting the *Exodus* text, see C. J. De Vogel, " 'Ego sum qui sum' et sa Signification pour une Philosophie Chrétienne," *Revue des Sciences Religieuses,* 1961, XXXV, 346–354.

23. See E. Gilson, *Philosophie et Incarnation selon Saint Augustin,* Montreal, 1947, pp. 10–13; J. R. O'Donnell, "The Notion of Being in William of Auvergne," *Proceedings of the American Catholic Philosophical Association,* 1946, XXI, 157–162.

24. *In I Sent.,* d. 19, q. 5, a. 1, ad 7m; I, 489 (dealing with truth). *Ibid.,* d. 38, q. 1, a. 3, Solut.; I, 903 (dealing with divine knowledge). Cf. *In Boeth. de Trin.,* V, 3c; ed. Decker, p. 182. *ST,* II–II, 83, 1, arg. 3. *In IV Metaph.,* lect. 6, Cathala no. 605.

25. E.g., truth and divine knowledge in the commentary on the *Sentences,* mathematical abstraction in *In Boeth. de Trin.,* the first principle of demonstration in the commentary on the *Metaphysics,* and in *ST,* II–II, on prayer.

26. For further discussion and for references, see my book *An Interpretation of Existence,* Milwaukee, 1968, pp. 14–31, 132–134; and article "The Number of Terms in the Suarezian Discussion on Essence and Being," *Modern Schoolman,* 1957, XXXIV, 147–191. The temporal character of existence in sensible things, as contrasted with eternity in the divine existence, plays a crucial role in Aquinas' approach to the problem.

27. "Thomas Aquinas may well have first conceived the notion of an act of being (*esse*) in connection with God and then, starting from God, made use of it in his analysis of the metaphysical structure of composite substances." E. Gilson, *Elements of Christian Philosophy,* New York, 1960, p. 131.

28. *In I Sent.,* d. 8, q. 5, a. 2, ad 5m; I, 231. Cf. "per se absolutum esse," *ibid.,* ad 6m. ". . . in corpore acquiritur sibi esse absolutum." *In II Sent.,* d. 17, q. 2, a. 2, ad 4m; II, 433. ". . . esse absolutum habens." *Ibid.,* ad 5m.

29. See texts in T. B. Wright, "Necessary and Contingent Being in St. Thomas Aquinas," *New Scholasticism,* 1951, XXV, 442–462.

30. *De Pot.,* V. 3c; *Q. de An.,* 14c; *ST,* I, 75, 6c.

31. *Op. Ox.,* II, 3, 1, no. 7; ed. Quar., II, 229 (no. 235a). *Ibid.,* 3, 5, and 6, no. 10; II, 265 (no. 286).

32. ". . . ipsa natura divina *de se* est *haec.*" *Ibid.,* 3, 1, no. 9; II, 231 (no. 238b).

33. *De Ente,* c. III; ed. Roland-Gosselin, pp. 25.9–26.11. *Quodl.,* VIII, 1, ad 1m.

34. *Op. Ox.,* II, 3, 1, no. 7; II, 230 (nos. 235d–236).

35. See *Quodl.,* V, 3; ed. Louvain, 1646, p. 273a.

36. ". . . quoddam est esse rei quod habet essentialiter de se: quod appellatur esse essentiae." *Quodl.,* I, 9; ed. Paris, 1518, fol. 7r.

37. *In Boeth. de Trin.,* V, 4c; tr. Armand Maurer, *The Divisions and Methods of the Sciences,* 3rd ed., Toronto, 1963, pp. 44–45.

38. See my article, "The Aristotelian Conception of the Sciences," *International Philosophical Quarterly,* 1964, IV, 200–216.

39. E.g., "la *racine* de l'arbre philosophique." Pierre Aubenque, *Le Problème de l'Etre chez Aristote,* Paris, 1962, p. 50.

40. See *supra,* n. 18. These features get no help from the etymology of the word, and little if any from its history. The basic notion of leisure is hardly to the point, and the notion of school is quite indeterminate. From an epistemological viewpoint, "immediate realism" may characterize the medieval Scholastics, but not necessarily the neo-Scholastics. See E. Gilson, *Réalisme Thomiste et Critique de la Connaissance,* Paris, 1939, pp. 68–155.

41. *Supra,* nn. 21 and 27.

42. See *supra,* n. 18.

43. See my paper, "Scholasticism—Then and Now," *Proceedings of the American Catholic Philosophical Association,* 1966, XL, 7–11.

44. Aristotle, *De An.,* III 8, 431b21. Cf. 4, 429b30–31.

45. See *ibid.,* 7, 431a1–2.

46. See Gabriel Marcel, *The Mystery of Being,* trans. René Hague, London, 1951, Chap. II, p. 176; cf. p. 174.

47. "Even if the so-called arguments for the 'immortality of the soul' had argumentative power (which they do not have) they would not convince existentially." Paul Tillich, *The Courage to Be,* New Haven, 1952, p. 42.

Philosophical Analysis and the Future of Metaphysics

James W. Cornman

My task concerning the future of metaphysics is twofold: to consider metaphysics and philosophical analysis, and to consider metaphysics and language. It is clear that the subject matter of these two tasks is interrelated because philosophical analysis is analysis of language. In this paper I shall concentrate on philosophical linguistic analysis and metaphysics, and in the second paper, I shall, among other things, try to build on the results stated in this paper. Throughout both papers I will limit my interest in metaphysics to ontology—roughly, to theories of what there is, and, more particularly, to ontological problems, such as the mind-body problem, the problem of the external world, the problem of universals, and the problem of free will. I will not, then, be interested in the relevance of analysis and language to any other areas of philosophy such as semantics, logic, and epistemology. Nor will I be particularly interested in the relevance of the incipient science of linguistics to philosophy in general, and, in the first paper at least, I will not consider its relevance to ontology. For example, I will not consider Chomskian views about universal linguistic capacities of humans, which, somehow, are supposed to be capacities to internalize just those rules which the Chomskian theory of language uses to generate sentences.

What I shall attempt to do is to see whether it is reasonable to make modest predictions about the future of the relevance of philosophical analysis to ontology. I shall approach this task in an inductive manner, that is, based on recently past and present facts about various kinds of analysis and their relation to ontology. These predictions, however, will not be about what will happen, in the sense of what future analytic philosophers will do regarding ontology. This depends too much on who enters philosophy in the future and on which current vogues in philosophy will endure. It may be that rather neopositivistic interests will prevail, such as interest in axiomatic contextual definitions of quasi-logical operators, and interest in preliminary studies for a "future" science of linguistics. Nor would these be predictions about what will happen even assuming at least the present level of interest in ontology as exemplified by philosophers such as Gustav Bergmann, W. V. Quine, and Wilfrid Sellars. Rather, I will try to come to some conclusions about whether or not there are some fruitful ways to proceed in the future using some form of philosophical analysis to help solve or at least dissolve ontological problems. Because I wish such a prediction to be based on inductive evidence, much of the bulk of this paper will consist in stating the evidence derived from recent past and present uses of philosophical analysis to resolve ontological problems.

ONTOLOGY AND ANALYSIS IN THE TWENTIETH CENTURY

Logical Atomism, Reductive Analysis, and Ontology

The place to begin the search for evidence regarding philosophical analysis and ontology is with logical atomism. For our present purposes in this paper, we can construe this to be a theory with four components.[1]

(1) *A Tractatus-like Ideal Language:* A language structure modeled on the language of Whitehead and Russell's *Principia Mathematica,* containing extensional logical constants and uninterpreted primitive terms. It is, then, an extensional, truth-functional language structure.

(2) *The Method of Logical Constructionism:* The use of sentences containing certain primitive or undefined terms to give what are called "definitions in use" of other terms. A term is given a definition in use when each sentence containing the term is synonymous with a sentence containing certain other terms, but containing no terms synonymous with the term to be defined. This method as employed with logical atomism is used to provide definitions in use of all nonprimitive terms by the primitive terms

of the language structure once they are interpreted and included in the atomic sentences of the language. Atomic sentences are those sentences containing primitive nonlogical terms but no logical constants. All other sentences are to be logically equivalent to molecular sentences built from the atomic sentences using the logical constants.

(3) *A Theory of Reference:* Logical atomism has a particular theory about the relationship between language and what there is. This is the picture theory, which is roughly that there is a structural isomorphism between each atomic sentence and what it pictures or describes. For Russell, in addition, there was the principle of acquaintance which requires that the referents of primitive terms in true atomic sentences are entities with which we are directly confronted or acquainted.

(4) *An Ontological Theory:* For the logical atomists it is atomic facts that are structurally isomorphic with true atomic sentences. In addition, for a Russellian theory, because of its principle of acquaintance, these atomic facts are facts involving and only involving objects of immediate experience, such as sense-data. All other facts are supposedly reducible to these facts, corresponding to the way that all other statements are reducible to atomic sentences.

What is relevant for our purposes here is that the fourth component of logical atomism, ontology, is to be derived from the requirements of the first and third components combined with the results of the second, that is, the results of the meaning analysis of the nonprimitive terms. This kind of meaning analysis by means of definitions in use, which I have called the method of logical constructionism, and which is a central part of the method used by logical atomists to get from language to ontology, is essentially the reduction of the meaning of nonprimitive terms to the meaning of primitive terms. Because of this, I shall from here on call it "reductive meaning analysis."

One influential feature of logical atomism, which gave great impetus to a linguistic approach to ontology, and indeed to linguistic philosophy in general, and also elevated the method of meaning analysis to central importance in philosophy, was that it seemed to provide a way to settle ontological problems once and for all, and to do so by a kind of investigation peculiar to philosophy. It relies on philosophical investigations of logic and language. This seemed to give philosophy both a unique subject matter and method, which distinguished it from empirical sciences while allowing it to be scientific rather than speculative. Serious problems, however, arose for logical atomism and they have led to its decline and considerably lessened the likelihood that it will generate a future fruitful approach to ontology.

One problem is that, through no lack of trying, there have been few successful definitions in use of philosophically interesting terms within the framework of an extensional language structure. Terms such as 'nation' have not been analyzed in terms of sentences about individual persons; psychological terms have not been analyzed by sentences using only behavioral terms; physical-object terms have not been analyzed by sentences using only sense-datum terminology. And, as we have seen, without some such reductive analyses there is no way to proceed from language to ontology in accordance with the principles of logical atomism.

The second problem stems from a criticism by one of the original promulgators of logical atomism—Ludwig Wittgenstein—in the very book in which he stated his version of logical atomism, *Tractatus Logico-Philosophicus.* He claimed that statements about the reference of language, that is, statements about the relationship between language and reality are nonsensical. We can make statements about reality, as in science, and statements about language, as in logic, but an attempt to express the relationship between the two leads to nonsense. For one reason, the statement that atomic sentences picture atomic facts was seen to be neither extensional nor translatable into an "ideal" language. Consequently, of the four components of logical atomism we can at most state the requirements of an ideal language structure and the results of reductive meaning analysis. But all of these together, without a statement about reference, will not yield ontological conclusions. Indeed, this seems to leave philosophy to deal only with logic and meaning analysis. The impact of this problem helped pave the way for the next use of philosophical analysis that we shall examine, the use by logical positivists.

Logical Positivism, Meaning Analysis, and Verifiability

For the logical positivists, the only task of a philosopher, aside from being an historian, is to make language more clear and precise so that the likelihood of confusions resulting from language are lessened. This theory, then, rejects at least two components of logical atomism—the picture theory of reference and the resulting ontology. Positivists generally accepted the second component of logical atomism because clarification of language was thought to require meaning analysis. Not all, however, have accepted the first component. While Carnap and Bergmann have required analysis to go on within an "ideal" language structure and thus have had to face the first of the two unsolved problems confronting logical atomists, other positivists, such as A. J. Ayer, countenance definitions in use of ordinary terms in ordinary nonextensional language.[2]

There were, however, still problems confronting Ayer's positivistic analysis of ordinary language. First, even with the relaxed restrictions on meaning analysis—for example, the use of subjunctive conditionals—few significant analyses were achieved. There is the failure of Ayer's own analytic phenomenalism as he himself and Roderick Chisholm later showed, and the failures of analytic behaviorism also shown by Chisholm with his refutation of attempts to give behavioral analyses of belief-sentences.[3]

Second, there are two problems facing positivism's verifiability criterion of meaningfulness, which is its claim about a relationship between language and reality. The first problem is that the criterion is supposed to provide a way to decide whether any particular sentence is verifiable and thus cognitively meaningful, that is, whether it is either true or false of the way the world is. But no attempted formulations have succeeded. Each one, from Ayer's first attempt to the most recent, has resulted in a criterion either so broad that it allows obvious cases of nonsense to count as cognitively meaningful, or so narrow that it requires that many theoretical sentences of science are meaningless.[4] On the basis of this history of failures, it seems reasonable to conclude that no such attempt will succeed, and, therefore, that the verifiability criterion of meaning should be rejected.

It might be replied that the failure of any attempt to define 'empirical verifiability' is not sufficient to cast doubt on a verifiability theory of meaningfulness, because such a definition, although helpful for utilizing the theory as a criterion for deciding the meaningfulness of specific sentences, is not an essential part of the theory itself. Thus the theory might be plausible, although 'empirical verifiability' is not definable and perhaps even irremediably vague. The second objection to the criterion is compatible with the reply, for it states that the criterion is self-defeating whether or not 'empirical verifiability' is definable. This objection is that, if the verifiability criterion of meaningfulness is true, then the only sentences that have truth-value are analytic sentences and empirically verifiable sentences. Consequently, the criterion itself, if it is true, must be either analytic or empirically verifiable. But it is not analytic, because it is not self-contradictory to claim that some nonanalytic, nonverifiable sentences are true. Indeed it would seem that most people untutored in theories of meaning would reject the criterion as false because they think many religious and ethical utterances, among others, are true. Consequently, it does not seem to be a true generalization based upon empirical observation of the actual ways in which people use and respond to sentences. It seems, then, not to be analytic, and, if it is empirically verifiable, it seems to be false.

Some defenders of the criterion recognizing this problem have claimed that the criterion is a rule of language. It is, then, neither an analytic nor a verifiable statement. But it surely does not seem to be a rule that can be derived from the actual use of language, because 'true' and 'false' are, as a matter of fact, applied to many sentences which would have no truth-value according to the criterion. Other defenders have claimed that the criterion is not a rule governing the way language is ordinarily used, but rather a proposed rule for how language should ideally be used. Some of these defenders have justified adopting such a proposed rule by claiming that it is surely a necessary rule for a meaningful language of empirical science. But, although it may well be that the language of science should meet an adequate verifiability criterion, this provides no reason to think that any other meaningful area of language must meet similar requirements.

In short there is good reason to reject the verifiability criterion. It is acceptable only if there is reason to think that it is true of the way things are or that it is a justified proposed rule about the way things should be. But we have found no reason to accept it as a proposal and good reason to reject its truth, because, if it is analytic or empirically verifiable, as the criterion itself requires of all true sentences, then it is false. Logical positivism, then, like logical atomism, is faced with two serious problems, and thus it also seems that we should not turn to it for a clue to the future of ontology.

Conclusion About Meaning Analysis and Ontology

One difficulty common to both atomism and positivism, whether with the requirement that the analysis be done in ideal language or in ordinary language, is that no significant meaning analysis has proved successful. Consequently, there is inductive evidence that any linguistic approach to ontology which involves meaning analysis as an integral part is unlikely to provide a fruitful approach to ontology in the future. If, therefore, an analysis of language is to be helpful in producing ontological results it seems that it must be some kind of analysis other than meaning analysis. It is often thought that what prevents successful meaning analyses of expressions of ordinary language is its inherent vagueness. Those who wish to substitute an ideal language for ordinary language often justify the substitution by the claim that this corrects an important defect in ordinary language: vagueness. In addition, this reconstruction of ordinary language is often thought essential to the solution of many problems, including philosophical problems. Thus these philosophers can be said to consider meaning analysis as an ideal which cannot be reached because of the vagueness of ordinary language, so that it must be abandoned for what I shall call *reconstruction analysis;* other philosophers who reject meaning analysis turn instead to *use analysis.* It is time, then, to examine these two other kinds of analysis.

Reconstruction Analysis and Defects In Ordinary Language

Reconstruction analysis can be characterized as the linguistic method which in some way reconstructs certain of the rules governing the use of a given expression, thereby changing its meaning in order to achieve some purpose or other. In this kind of analysis the relation between analysandum and analysans is not that of synonymy, because the rules governing the use of one are not those governing the use of the other. In general we can say that the purpose of reconstruction analysis is to modify those rules governing the expression in question which are defective in some way, while preserving those rules which are not defective. Thus the ideal is to keep the meaning of the analysans as close as possible to the analysandum by reconstructing only those rules of the analysandum which are defective. Meaning analysis is, then, a limiting case of reconstruction analysis, the case where we can get rid of the defect by replacing one expression with another synonymous with it. One example of this is Russell's analysis of definite descriptions. But given that ordinary language is vague and unanalyzable, we cannot hope for synonymy, and therefore, in practice, meaning analysis reduces to reconstruction analysis.

Reconstruction analysis is to be used where we find that an expression we want to use for a certain purpose is in some way defective for that purpose, and we replace the defective expression with one that is not defective. If we make this replacement using meaning analysis, it would seem to be legitimate no matter what our purpose. This does not seem so obvious, however, if we use reconstruction analysis, because, at first glance at least, it does not seem legitimate to "reshape" an expression just enough to solve a problem we could not solve before reshaping it.

There are two basically different kinds of reconstruction analysis. The first is the kind of reconstruction we make when we draw a distinction between two or more senses of an ambiguous expression. Some expressions can be used in two or more different ways; the rules governing their use do not explicitly distinguish between the several senses. In such a case we would make explicit the different senses of the expression, thereby replacing the defective set of rules governing the expression by two or more sets of rules not defective in this way. Here the criterion of defectiveness is ambiguity. An example of such a use of *replacement analysis* to reconstruct a particular set of rules is the distinction made and utilized in symbolic logic between the inclusive and exclusive sense of 'or.' Such distinctions help to avoid certain confusions which might arise because of the ambiguity of 'or.' To avoid such confusions and to show where someone has gone astray because of such confusions seems to be the main, if not the only, purpose for doing this kind of analysis. It is helpful for any approach to any problem, but usually, as in our case, a method sufficient neither to solve nor to provide clues to the solution of the problem.

The second kind of reconstruction analysis has been called *explication.* Carnap explains that this kind of analysis, which is the

> task of making more exact a vague or not quite exact concept used in everyday life or in an earlier stage of scientific or logical development, or rather of replacing it by a newly constructed, more exact concept, belongs among the most important tasks of logical analysis and logical construction. We call this the task of explicating, or of giving an *explication* for, the earlier concept; this earlier concept, or sometimes the term used for it, is called the *explicandum;* and the new concept, or its term, is called an *explicatum* of the old one. . . . Generally speaking, it is not required that an explicatum have, as nearly as possible, the same meaning as the explicandum; it should, however, correspond to the explicandum in such a way that it can be used instead of the latter.[5]

An example of this kind of analysis is the explication of 'fish' by zoologists, as cited by Carnap. What the zoologists have done is to reconstruct the term 'fish' in such a way that such things as whales and seals are no longer called fish. The purpose of this explication was to make the term 'fish' more useful for the purposes of zoology; 'fish' had been somewhat defective in this respect. Whether or not the defect, however, was one of vagueness, as Carnap claims, may be questioned. Nevertheless, the rules governing 'fish' were changed to correct a defect, and the change affected the rules for the use of the term. Perhaps it is too restricting to limit explication to just that kind of reconstruction analysis which has vagueness for its criterion of defectiveness. It might be better to include all those kinds of analysis which have as their criterion of defectiveness anything but ambiguity, and have as their relationship between analysans and analysandum anything but synonymy.

As we have just seen with the word 'fish,' it is clear that there are purposes for which explication is justified. The question before us now is whether it is justified for the purpose of resolving ontological problems. As we have also seen, explication of a term is justified when and only when the term is defective in some way. We need, therefore, a criterion of defectiveness relevant to ontological problems. The only one that I can find to be relevant is the defect of misleading us about what there is, or ontologically committing us in undesirable ways. That is, only if ordinary language leads us to ontological commitments which are in some way undesirable is it defective in any way relevant to ontological questions. But a language by itself is not defective in this way, because no language by itself ontologically commits us in any way. As is brought out clearly by examining the four components of logical atomism, a theory of reference, that is, a theory that relates language to what there is, is also required. There is, then, no reason to think that language, by itself, misleads us about what there is. What often does mislead us is not language but some view or theory we might have about language, such as the 'Fido'-Fido theory of reference.[6] It is once we begin to talk and think about language as philosophers that we often become ontologically misled. It is not language which is defective but philosophers' views of language.

The conclusion, then, seems to be that ordinary language is not defective in any way relevant to the solution of ontological problems. Thus because explication is justified for a certain purpose only when the language is defective for that purpose, explication is not justified for the purpose of resolving ontological problems. Of course, this does not show that when reconstruction analysis is justified for some different purpose, it has no justified consequences for ontology. But even here I think it will not be relevant to deciding ontological issues. For example, it is often claimed that ordinary language must be clarified for the purposes of science, and that, once ordinary language is clarified adequately for a complete scientific explanation of what there is, scientific language rather than ordinary language will provide the best description of what there is. This type of scientific realism, however, which we will examine in the second paper, does not depend on successful reconstruction analyses. The origin of a set of terms, whether introduced as technical terms or constructed from ordinary terms, does not provide any reason for deciding whether that set of terms or some other provides a better description of something. Thus reconstruction analysis is not to be made relevant to ontological problems in this way.

Use Analysis and Nondescriptive Expressions

With the failure of meaning analysis and reconstruction analysis to provide linguistic keys to ontological problems, it might seem that philosophical analysis of language is not ontologically fruitful. Yet many think that the later work of Wittgenstein proves differently. Wittgenstein in his early years, as we have seen, subscribed to logical atomism, but, as we have also seen, he claimed that one of its essential components involves nonsense. In his later years he followed his own advice and gave up the approach to ontological problems by means of certain facts about language and a theory of the relationship between language and reality. He also gave up the idea common to atomists and some positivists that the language that we ordinarily use must be clarified for the purposes of philosophy by substituting an ideal language for it. Furthermore, he gave up the idea that meaning analysis can be applied to ordinary language in philosophically fruitful ways. The slogan, "Don't ask for the meaning, ask for the use," expresses this change in his position. One of his reasons for this change was rather dogmatized by some of his disciples into the view that all terms of ordinary language are family resemblance terms and thus are not amenable to meaning analysis. But Wittgenstein, as I shall interpret him for our purposes here, continued to agree with both the atomists and positivists that the way to approach and resolve ontological problems is through language. He agreed with the positivists that ontological puzzles could be dissolved without becoming involved in the ineffable, that is, in the relationship between language and reality.

Clearly, this is not the only way to construe the later Wittgenstein. He has also been interpreted, not as attempting to dissolve ontological problems, but rather as attempting to cure philosophers of the disease of being puzzled in such ways that they think there are ontological problems. The cure consists in getting philosophers to come to construe the uses of relevant linguistic terms in such ways that the terms no longer lead the philosophers into ontological puzzlement, nor into thinking that there are ontological problems. I am interested here in the first interpretation, because my view is that, even if we could in this way stop everyone from being interested in ontological problems, this would neither solve them, nor dissolve them, nor even show that no one should be interested in them, unless it is independently shown true that there really are no such problems, but misthinking makes it seem that there are.

One way to characterize the kind of analysis which has grown out of the later Wittgenstein is that it is the method which consists in showing logical similarities and differences between sentences of known logical kinds, and those of a different kind, whose logic is to be discovered. Once these similarities and differences are exhibited, general conclusions about the nature of the second set of sentences being examined are drawn. In light of these conclusions a new look is given to problems involving these sentences and quite often the problems are dissolved, or rather evaporate, because of the different way of looking at the logic of the sentences. To illustrate this method, I shall briefly examine attempts to employ use analysis to deal with three sentences: 'A is right', 'B raised his arm', and 'C is vain'. The purpose of these attempts is to show that although all three sentences are grammatically indicative, as are descriptive sentences such as 'A is blue,' 'B's arm went up', and 'C is blond', they are not themselves descriptive. I shall at this point merely explain the three attempts. How successful they might be will be discussed later.

The first attempt to be considered is that by P. H. Nowell-Smith, who is concerned with the problem of what kind of properties ethical properties are. Nowell-Smith, instead of trying to solve the problem, sets out to dissolve it by showing that terms such as 'right' and 'good' in their ethical use do not have certain logical features that terms expressing properties have. As a consequence, 'right' and 'good' do not express properties, and the problem about what kind of properties they express is dissolved. He does this by showing that, because there are important logical differences between indicative sentences such as 'x is right' and descriptive sentences such as 'x is blue', the former sentences are not descriptive, and as a result their predicates do not refer to properties.[7] In so doing, he is primarily attacking Intuitionists such as G. E. Moore, on whose view, claims Nowell-Smith, sentences such as 'x is good' are, like 'x is blue', descriptive, the primary difference between the two being that 'good' expresses a non-natural rather than a natural property. Such Intuitionists, then, seem to presuppose that 'good' and 'right' express some kind of property. Nowell-Smith, however, wishes to show that this is where they make their mistake.

The second example of use analysis to be considered here is an attempt to handle another problem which appears to defy solution, the problem of human action. It can be formulated in the following question: "What is the difference between someone raising his arm and his arm going up?" If, as the question presupposes, there is a difference, it would seem that there must be some difference between the kinds of events or states which cause the arm to go up in each case. Traditionally, there have been three different views about the unique cause which results in someone raising his arm rather than it merely going up. It has been thought that the cause of someone raising his arm is either some unique physical event (some unique brain process), or some unique mental event (an act of will or volition), or the person himself in some nondeterministic way. None of these three kinds of solutions, however, seems to be satisfactory. The first leads us into the problems connected with free will and determinism, the second into the problems for dualistic interactionism, and the third leaves us with a mysterious causal force which has been called "the self" but which, when we try to explain it, usually leads us back to one of the first two kinds of solutions and their problems.

H. L. A. Hart, like Nowell-Smith, however, looks at this problem in a different way. It is wrong, he believes, to talk about what certain expressions are supposed to refer to until we have found whether the logical features of the sentences containing those expressions are the correct kind for such a job. For Hart, although sentences such as 'He raised his arm' and 'His arm went up' are indicative sentences, they have quite different uses. While the second is used descriptively, that is, used solely to predicate some property of something, in this case the property of having his arm go up, the first sentence is not. It is used to ascribe responsibility to someone for his arm going up, rather than to refer to some event or process which differs in some way from the kind of event or process referred to by 'His arm went up'. Hart reaches this conclusion by comparing the decisions of judges with the sentences relevant to the problem of human agency; he finds many similarities between the two. He brings out the similarities by exhibiting the logical peculiarities of judges' decisions and then showing how sentences about human agency have many of the same peculiarities. In light of these similarities, Hart concludes that, just as a judge is not referring to a property someone has—is not describing him—when he gives his legal decisions, neither are we referring to something quite unique in a person when we use sentences such as 'He raised his arm'.[8]

For Hart, then, there is no problem connected with the difference between someone raising his arm and his arm going up because the question which formulates the problem presupposes that the two sentences 'He raised his arm' and 'His arm went up' describe two different situations and thus are both descriptive sentences. This is what Hart denies. Hart thus dissolves rather than solves a problem, in much the same manner as Nowell-Smith.

The third attempt concerns the mind-body problem. As generally conceived, there are three kinds of possible solution to the problem: body-no mind, mind-no body, and both mind and body. None of these three kinds of answers has been put forth satisfactorily. The first leaves us with the problems of materialism, the second with the problem of solipsism, and the third with solipsism plus some problematic kind of causation, whether the view be parallelism or interactionism. Is there, then, no more satisfactory way to approach this problem? According to Gilbert Ryle, there is. Instead of considering the problem in terms of minds and bodies, machines and "ghosts," Ryle suggests that we examine the words and sentences we use in our talk about such matters.

Essential to Ryle's position is his theory of logical categories. He thinks that philosophical problems such as the mind-body problem arise because philosophers have misconstrued the logical categories of the key phrases that are used to formulate the problems. A very common mistake is to construe sentences as belonging to the categories of reports and descriptive sentences, but only sentences with certain logical features belong to these logical categories. Other categories delineated in a like manner would be those of exclamations, laws, mathematical sentences, and poetic sentences. The sentences of each of these categories have certain logical features in common which the sentences of no other category have. It is at least one important task of a philosopher to show this.

According to Ryle, it is mistaken to think that when we use psychological-expressions we are talking in the same category as when we use physical-expressions, but instead we are referring to a radically different kind of substance, state of affair, or process, as a dualist would claim; nor are we talking in the same category about the same kind of thing, as identity theorists claim. Rather, we are talking in two different logical categories about one kind of entity—a person. Ryle's point is that all three traditional kinds of answers are wrong because they presuppose mistaken views about the logic of mind-sentences and body-sentences. These answers assume that questions about the relation of a person to his mind and the relation of his body to his mind are proper questions. For Ryle they are not. Furthermore, because the mind-body problem is essentially a problem about the relationship between mind and body, it presupposes that questions about this relationship are proper questions. If Ryle is correct, however, they are not proper questions and the mind-body problem is dissolved.[9]

An example of the technique Ryle uses to establish his thesis is the way he handles sentences such as 'A is vain'. For him this would be neither a sentence describing some mental states or episodes, such as feelings or pricks of vanity, nor one describing actual and possible behavior. As I have interpreted his position, Ryle would say that sentences such as 'A is vain' have a lawlike function and thus belong in the category of inference tickets rather than that of descriptive sentences. Thus 'A is vain' does not predicate a property of A as do sentences such as 'A is blond' or 'A is six feet tall'. It merely licenses us to make certain inferences about A's behavior.[10] In such a way Ryle attempted to handle mental-expressions in *The Concept of Mind.* If none refers to properties or objects either physical or mental, then it is wrong to ask about the relationships between mental objects and properties, and other objects and properties. Thus it is wrong to ask the questions which formulate the mind-body problem, and thus there is no mind-body problem.

A Problem for Use Analysis. The problem for Nowell-Smith, Hart, and Ryle as well as others who, like them, approach ontology by means of use analysis is that they move to a conclusion about the nondescriptive use of certain sentences which phrase the problems they are considering, from premises about the logical similarities and/or differences between these sentences and certain other sentences the use of which seems to be clear. They then use this conclusion either to solve or dissolve the relevant problem. But for all such arguments a certain sort of premise is needed, something like: " 'P' is used descriptively if and only if 'P' has logical features A, B, and C . . ." This brings up two related problems. First, there is the problem of showing why an expression used descriptively must have *any* special logical features. This involves justifying the claim that there are in the logic of a language symptoms of the kinds of things the expressions of the language refer to—a claim, incidentally, like the one the early

Wittgenstein made in 1916 when he said, "The way in which language signifies is mirrored in its use." [11] Second, if the first problem is solved, there is the problem of showing just what those special features are. Using the language of the Wittgenstein of the *Tractatus,* we can say that these followers of the later Wittgenstein must show, first, that some logical features of descriptive expressions are essential to their describing; and, second, just which features are essential rather than accidental. Can such claims be justified? They have not yet been justified and cannot be if the early Wittgenstein is correct, because to do so would involve us in the relationship between language and reality, about which we have seen that Wittgenstein claims we can say nothing. Consequently, use analysis fails to avoid the problem about the relationship between language and reality that we saw confronting both atomism and positivism.

Conclusion About Use Analysis and Ontology

We have found one advantage that use analysis has in comparison with any approach to ontology that requires meaning analysis. That is, there seems to be no problem in achieving the task of exhibiting logical similarities and differences in the use of linguistic expressions. But the evidence of past philosophical failures makes it dubious that the task of producing philosophically significant reductive meaning analyses can be completed. We did, however, find one problem facing use analysis which in its own unique form is the same kind of problem as problems facing both logical atomism and logical positivism. All three kinds of approaches to ontological problems by means of philosophical analysis require some claim about relationships between certain parts of language and reality, if they are to be relevant to resolving ontological problems, but no one has found a way to justify any such claims. Indeed, if Wittgenstein is correct, none can be justified. Thus, although use analysis avoids one type of serious problem facing logical atomism and logical positivism, it does not escape the other.

CONCLUSION ABOUT THE FUTURE OF ONTOLOGY AND PHILOSOPHICAL ANALYSIS

Based on the evidence briefly stated above, it might seem that it would be reasonable to be pessimistic about the future fruitfulness of philosophical analysis for ontology. Although optimism cannot be justified by the preceding evidence, I believe, however, that pessimism is premature for at least two reasons. First, we have not discussed all possible kinds of philosophical analysis, and thus, perhaps, all the evidence is not yet before us. Second, although Wittgenstein seems to think that the general problem concerning reference which is common to three of the approaches to ontology that we have examined is a fatal one, neither he nor anyone else has shown that it is. Indeed, in my book *Metaphysics, Reference, and Language* I claim that it is not fatal. Furthermore, even if it proves to be fatal and the linguistic approach to ontology by means of analysis must be rejected, it may still be the case that one thesis common to analytic philosophers is true, that is, that language holds the key to ontology. But that is the topic of my second paper and I shall delay until then any further discussion of whether some linguistic approach to ontology that requires analysis can avoid the Wittgensteinian problem, and whether there is some fruitful linguistic approach to ontology that does not require analysis. We should, consequently, also wait until then before we draw any additional conclusions, either optimistic or pessimistic, about the relevance of language and analysis to ontology.

NOTES

1. See B. Russell, *Our Knowledge of the External World*, London, 1914; and L. Wittgenstein, *Tractatus Logico-Philosophicus*, London, 1922.
2. See G. Bergmann, *The Metaphysics of Logical Positivism*, London, 1955; R. Carnap, *The Logical Syntax of Language*, London, 1937; and A. J. Ayer, *Language, Truth and Logic*, New York, n.d., and *The Foundations of Empirical Knowledge*, New York, 1955.
3. A. J. Ayer, *The Problem of Knowledge*, Baltimore, 1956, pp. 118–129; and R. Chisholm, *Perceiving*, Ithaca, N.Y., 1957, pp. 189–197 and 168–185, respectively.
4. See Ayer, *Language, Truth and Logic*, pp. 5–16; I. Scheffler, *The Anatomy of Inquiry*, New York, 1963, pp. 150–154; D. Makinson, "Nidditch's Definition of Verifiability," *Mind*, 1965, LXXIV, 240–247; and

J. Cornman, "Indirectly Verifiable: Everything or Nothing," *Philosophical Studies,* 1967, XVIII, 49–55.

5. R. Carnap, *Meaning and Necessity,* Chicago, 1958, pp. 7–8.

6. For more detail, see J. Cornman, *Metaphysics, Reference, and Language,* New Haven, 1966, pp. 148–160.

7. See P. H. Nowell-Smith, *Ethics,* Baltimore, 1954, chaps. 3 and 4.

8. See H. L. A. Hart, "The Ascription of Rights and Responsibilities," in *Logic and Language,* First Series, ed. Flew, Oxford, 1955, pp. 160 f.

9. See G. Ryle, *The Concept of Mind,* New York, 1949, pp. 167–168.

10. *Ibid.,* pp. 89–93, 116–125.

11. L. Wittgenstein, *Notebooks 1914–1916,* New York, 1961, p. 82e.

Process Philosophy and Metaphysics

William L. Reese

One could select from the history of philosophy a family of philosophers who might appropriately be termed "process philosophers" and their philosophies "process philosophies." And one might evaluate what he finds to be common to the philosophies thus selected. The systems in question would be realistic in tone, would feature categories of change and flux, and would have an event ontology rather than one centering in substance, for example. But if I, at least, were making the selection I am sure that I would find myself starting out from some one individual who seemed to me to deserve the name preeminently. And, this being the case, it would be more candid simply to let my preeminent case serve as the paradigm for all the rest. The instance of process philosophy which would for me initiate any such selective process, and which will hence stand for me as the paradigm in all that follows, is the system struck out by Alfred North Whitehead in *Process and Reality.* And I shall inquire about the future of process philosophy by asking about the viability of this effort.

The enemies of process philosophy simply leave Whitehead's system alone, maintaining a dignified silence about man's last best effort to frame a system of metaphysics in the grand manner. But Whitehead's friends have little disposition to leave the system alone. Each improves it according to his taste. We are given neo-Whiteheadian analyses in which we have Whitehead without God, Whitehead with substance reintroduced, Whitehead with Anselmic overtones, and Whitehead without feeling. Scarcely anyone interested in the system is content merely to accept it intact. Although I am drawn at times by one or another of these alternatives, I shall attempt in what follows to leave the system intact.

THE ROLE OF FEELING

Let me begin with the point most troublesome to many, that is, the selection of "feeling" as the most basic term in the analysis of the becoming of the events of the world. It is often held that this choice psychologizes existence. Whitehead's rationale, I take it, is that there is no other way of distinguishing the mode of being of an event in the present from the mode of being of an event now past. How does Whitehead make this distinction?

What exists in the immediate present has "subjective immediacy." Passage into the past entails a loss of immediacy and a gaining of both objectivity and relativity. It exists now as relative to another. Hence, we must contrast "subjective immediacy" with "objective existence for another." The actual is defined in these terms. "An entity is actual," says Whitehead, "when it has significance for itself." [1] In these terms every actual occasion is a pulse of self-significance, of appreciation, of appetition moving toward satisfaction. "Feeling" certainly fits the description, although in different events the feelings may be conscious, subconscious, or unconscious.

Whitehead believes that the only means of being something is to be something for oneself. This seems to combine Sartre's *en soi* and *pour soi*: the only manner of being in itself is to be for oneself. The only absoluteness in the world is the absolute of self-enjoyment. One might respond that some actual occasions are self-significant. How is it known that all of them are? It does seem forced, does it not, to claim that the electron orbits through adventures of self-satisfaction and appreciation? It does seem more natural, does it not, to view the electron as a center not of feeling but of force? In some simpleminded way we want to view an entity as needing a space, a time, and some mass or energy in order to be. So far as the simpleminded view is concerned, the electron is nothing whatever to itself. It is internally vacuous.

But the claim is that the electron cannot be internally vacuous. What we are leaving out of account is that space and time apparently can no longer be construed in a Newtonian manner. If space and time are not Newtonian, we cannot account for the being of a thing in terms of its location in space and time. The post-Newtonian or Leibnizian view is that space and time are somehow functions of events. I suppose this means that the space and time of the electron are defined by its relations to other things, and these relations have to be internal to the electron, since external relations cannot articulate the matter. I think the Leibnizian view also holds that the mass or energy of an entity requires that there be a qualitative internality in order for something to be to have mass, energy, and external relations. The point is clearer if we confine our attention to space and time. The Whiteheadian doctrine is very similar to the monadology of Leibniz but with a harmony determined through process rather than predetermined. The actual occasion of the electron in a given present moment is a node of world process, or the world from one perspective. At the very least, Whitehead's way of viewing the matter allows us to speak of that mirroring of the world which Leibniz sought, but could not consistently attain.

If the quantitative aspects of an event must be defined in qualitative terms, then we must accept some approach which allows a qualitative internality to characterize whatever there may be. Whitehead's manner of providing this qualitative internality is to hold that all events are consciously or unconsciously self-significant, appetitive, and capable of self-enjoyment.

Since Whitehead holds that the simpler occurrences are below the level of consciousness, and since he defines feeling as a prehension in concrescence, perhaps he is merely asking that an event have the ability we have requested to reflect the world into itself. Even though it may come to the same thing, I suggest that the Leibnizian language of mirroring has a greater palatability than the Whiteheadian language of feeling.

What must be retained is the programmatic contrast between "subjective immediacy" and "objective immortality," for in this contrast is situated Whitehead's manner of distinguishing the mode of being of the present from the mode of being of the past. What exists in and for itself exists as its own world with its own style of absoluteness and no direct contact with any other being. What exists for another is no longer anything for itself. It exists only in relation to others. There has been a withering away of its absolute for-and-in-itselfness. Its absoluteness has perished.[2] Its relativity has been born. Sartre contrasts the "for itself" with the "in itself." The Whiteheadian contrast is between that which is both "for and in itself" and that which is "for and in another."

The mode of being granted to the present allows us to utilize post-Newtonian modes of viewing time and space. The mode of being granted to the past captures quite adroitly the following set of insights:

(a) The intuition that, whether we are aware of the manner of its happening or not, it will be always true that what happened happened in a certain manner, when and as it did. The past cannot perish. It is hence in some sense immortal.

(b) The obvious point, which Whitehead works into subtlety, that contemporaneity must be defined negatively, and that our commerce with reality is always by means of the immediate past. Whitehead utilizes the fading of events into the past not only to provide an "elbow room" for contemporary events, but also to provide the context in which a single event can mirror the entire antecedent world. The point from which all of this begins is nothing more astonishing than the fact that there is a lapse of time in the movement of a sensation along the route of nerve cells to the brain, insuring that the report carried will concern the past. One might feel like arguing that this is merely a report on the nature of protoplasm, but that would not be accurate. The condition is more general, as in the case of starlight, for example. One is always reading the present from the past, whether in the case of stars or the situation of one's immediate neighbor.

Out of these distinctions Whitehead derives an argument for God. If it is the case that the past is immortal and that pastness means existence for another, and if only a small portion of the past exists for us in a usable manner, then this existence for another is either an existence of the total past for us in some minimal way[3] or it is an existence of the total past relative to an actual entity which is nontemporal in some respects, that is, to an ever-present, nontemporal occasion, the awareness of God. If we do not like the conclusion, then we must discover how to avoid it. We can reverse our decision that the past has objective immortality. But this denies a fairly widespread intuition about the matter. We can grant that the past is immortal, but hold that it is immortal to no one. This may be an option, although it would violate Whitehead's ontological principle. We cannot say that the events of the past are immortal to themselves, for that would give the past subjective immediacy, and transform it into the present. It would appear, then, that Whitehead's manner of handling the problem by making the past relative to God is close to being demanded by the initial distinctions he has made.

The category of feeling and the use of psychological process-type predicates allow him Leibnizian qualitative internality in his ontological units, and an interesting and possibly valid manner of understanding both the present and the past. The category and the predicates have a natural affinity, too, for what he wishes to tell us about the mode of being of the future, or the possible. Indeed, it seems clear that his explication of process generally takes as its pattern the psychological description of processes of human thought and feeling, including anticipation, conjecture, decision, and memory. Nor does it seem that he could have gained so much had he avoided the term "feeling."

THE ROLE OF ETERNAL OBJECTS

We come, then, to the admission of eternal objects to the system. Whitehead introduces them to account for the repetition of similars in our experience, to account for the fact that what is possible in one time and space may be possible in another. Beyond this he is interested in showing that the actualization of possibles is naturally cumulative, that the actualization of one possibility normally makes a new possibility relevant.

The first question is whether possibilities need to be given ontological status. On the ground that entities should not be multiplied beyond necessity it would be well if their admission could be avoided. Having granted a mode of being to the past, however, it is consistent with that decision to grant being also to the possible. For me, as for most, the decision to admit or to avoid the admission of this element occasions some inner struggle.

On the one hand, it does seem that in some sense Whitehead has given us a "slum of possibles," to employ Quine's expression. Indeed, Quine's famous article, "On What There Is," rehearses some of the problems. One paragraph attributes the view to a fictitious philosopher named Wyman:

> Wyman's slum of possibles is a breeding ground for disorderly elements. Take, for instance, the possible fat man in that doorway; and, again, the possible bald man in that doorway. Are they the same possible man, or two possible men? How do we decide? How many possible men are there in that doorway? Are there more possible thin ones than fat ones? How many of them are alike? Or would their being alike make them one? Are no *two* possible things alike? Is this the same as saying that it is impossible for two things to be alike? Or, finally, is the concept of identity simply inapplicable to unactualized possibles? But what sense can be found in talking of entities which cannot meaningfully be said to be identical with themselves and distinct from one another? These elements are well-nigh incorrigible.[4]

The well-nigh incorrigibility of the concept invites us to dismiss it. Quine ties the metaphysical mistake of too easily granting the reality of the possible to the act of naming what is not. In so naming intelligibility seems to require that the name refer, and in naming what is not we turn nothing into the name of something. And he solves the problem by doing something with naming. In the case of nonexistent things he calls for the kind of reformulation Russell used for definite descriptions. But this does not remove the problem of the ontological existence of the possible. One has avoided naming the nonexistent thing; but the reformulation clearly mentions other things, kinds of things. And the problem of possibility rises with respect to the instances of these kinds. In one sense the reformulation works not even with respect to definite descriptions. At times when I am naming, I am naming something which is not in the sense that it is not *yet.* It has not yet come to be, or come to pass, as we say. I am now thinking of its merely possible occurrence. When I envision on the basis of a given situation that a certain outcome is possible I clearly have a mental awareness of this possibility. But I do not expect my mental possibility to develop merely into a mental actuality. I expect this possibility to become an actuality in the world outside my mind. Hence, it would seem that I must believe, even as I envision in a mental way this possibility, that it is a possibility not only for my mind, but also for the universe. That is to say, the possibility of which I am aware seems to have ontological status; its manner of existence cannot be confined to my mentality.

Nor, for that matter, does it seem reasonable to situate possibilities within substantial entities, for then the relation of possibility to the interrelatedness of things is scanted. And one would seem to be committed to do with possibility what Leibniz did with his windowless monads, introducing some kind of predetermined harmony. Once again, the Whiteheadian way seems to have an advantage, possibility at least seeming to require a relation to the parts and wholes of things in such a way that to explicate it is to work with a mode of being relating in the most diverse ways to all that is.

But when we give the possible this status we at once engender the "slum of possibles," of which Quine spoke. It occurs to me that if from Whitehead's standpoint, or something like that standpoint, we could answer Quine's questions the slum might begin to resemble a proper suburb.

"How many possible men are there in that doorway?" The question is unclear. Does he mean: (a) How many men can jam into the doorway at a given time? Then he is asking about the kinds of experiment to which our students used to lend themselves prior to their discovery of social action. I would suppose that in one manner or another twenty or thirty possible men could jam themselves in a given doorway. Does he mean: (b) How many possible men could be in that doorway, given unlimited time? I would suppose that the answer to that question is: As many as you like, or perhaps an infinite number even though we have not yet had, nor can we have, an infinite number of men in the past, present, and likely future history of mankind.

"Are there more possible thin ones than fat ones?" If the question is (a) above, clearly there are more possible thin ones than fat ones in the doorway, perhaps as many as ten more. If the question is (b) above, then there are the same number of thin ones as fat ones.

Are the possible fat man and the possible bald man the same possible man? Again, it depends. It is possible. Since there are actual men both fat and bald, clearly it is possible that there be a man both fat and bald in that doorway; but it is likewise possible to have fat nonbald men, and bald nonfat men in the doorway. But I think this question is asking if there are levels of absraction among possibilities. Is it possible to have just a possible man, successfully represented either by a fat man or a bald man? There is something a bit iffy about this, but I would tend to interpret Whitehead's distinction between abstract and real possibilities as standing for this kind of distinction. The possible fat man and the possible bald man represent the same possibility taken abstractly; from a more particularistic standpoint, however, the two represent different possibilities.

Are no two possible things alike? This depends upon the answer to a prior question. Are any two actual things alike, in all ways except numerically? If not, then it would not be surprising should there be no two possible things alike either. One would suppose that possibilities might well be like the angels of Thomas Aquinas, each being its own *infima species.*

As for the question of identity, I would suppose that the whole point of eternal objects would be to help explain the identities and similarities of experience.

Taken one by one the questions of Quine seem not to be so incorrigible after all.

It is, very likely, however, easier to defend the notion of possibility from outside attack than it is to demonstrate the viability of a specific interpretation. Among the difficulties in Whitehead's rendering of possibility, one concerning perception is particularly troublesome to me.

Apparently it is the case, when I look at a red traffic light, that the quality of red seen by me is not identical to the quality of red seen by others—at least by many others. My evidence is my seeing the aberrant numbers in the color-sensitivity charts prepared to test such qualitative differences. In sense-datum language we would say that my sense-datum differs from yours. On some views we would say that the object has its own quality of redness. In this case, when I am seeing correctly, the red of my sense-datum matches the red of the traffic light. Perhaps the object, having no color in itself, stands as the cause of sense-data which vary in themselves according to differences of many kinds, including differences in the receptors of these data. In this case the object is the cause of various types of red and grey sense-data, although no meaning can be given to the claim that X is seeing the color correctly. In either of these analyses we are aware of appearances. In the cases of Locke and Kant an objective reality is posited lying behind these appearances.

Whitehead seems on the surface, at least, to provide us with an alternative to the language of appearances, and the consequent split between appearance and reality. Notice that the book is titled *Process and Reality;* it might well have been titled *Relativity and Reality.* The complex function which is the seeing of the red of the traffic light, involving among other things the traffic light and this particular seeing eye under this set of conditions, is the concrete event itself, one of the myriad events of which reality is composed. The precise quality of red I see is the precise eternal object ingredient in this event. It is simply commonplace that man is included in the world and not separated off from it. Each perceptual event is an instance of man and world. This gives us a situation radically different from the one in which human awareness is enclosed in a dark closet, attempting to decipher a perfectly inobvious world on the basis of sense-data presumed to have some resemblance to the world presumed to lie without.

But the difference entails the consequence that a person gaining a different quality of color from his perception of the same traffic light at the same time is part of a different event in which a different eternal object has been actualized—red, but a different red. A further consequence of the view is that these two events are members of different worlds. The Leibnizian principle of mirroring leads to the Whiteheadian principle of relativity with multiple points of reference, inheriting differently from the total past. My present awareness is a focal point shading back into a total world of other events. Your present awareness is a different focal point shading back into a somewhat different world. "No two actual entities," says Whitehead, "define the same actual world."[5] My awareness cannot collapse into your awareness. My present enjoyment or dissatisfaction fills my present moment. Your enjoyment, or whatever else, fills your present moment. In this sense there is a solipsism of the present moment. We come, then, by another route to the same point touched upon before, concerning the nature of the present.

The event ontology scores something of a triumph by putting us in touch with reality once again, and removing the temptation of asking the impossible question: How does the world look when we do not look? At least the question is impossible if it means: How does the world appear when it does not appear? But the penalty exacted by this direct knowing is a different kind of split —no longer between appearance and reality, there is a split among a multiplicity of intersecting worlds. It would be foolish to ask the color of the unobserved streetlight. We can, from the Whiteheadian standpoint, speak of the color of the streetlight for a standard observer, and this would appear to be enough.

But the things we say about what Locke taught us to call secondary qualities are not quite what we are encouraged to say about primary qualities. Descartes knew this, and so did Locke. Whitehead knows it, too, and it is his solution of the problem that we wish somehow to test.

Let me come to what puzzles me. In the same event of my awareness of the red of the traffic light—or I suppose it is the same event—I am aware that I am looking at a single traffic light. I know further that it has certain dimensions, although I do not know what they are without measurement. The point is that my measuring would take place in a subsequent event and yet I would tend to assume that the measurement can be referred back to the same light whose color I had earlier experienced. The point is that I am aware of some eternal objects immediately and directly in an event, and I am not aware of others even though they are also present.

To put the matter more dramatically, suppose that the perceptual event is the seeing of a red and white striped zebra. Once again, I am aware of the color, red; and I am aware that the terminations and beginnings of the color red provide stripes. The zebra would have no stripes were there no color. Hence, the eternal object, red, and the mathematical eternal object involve each other. Yet I am aware only of the former; as for the latter I have only a sense of numerosity, a sense perhaps, too, that the number is low, say less than two hands' worth of stripes, nothing more.

Is it consistent to say that reality is made up of events with nothing lying behind them, and at the same time to say that in perceptual events there are eternal objects present but not lying on the surface of the event, cut off from my present awareness? The statement uses the language of an underlying reality, which is at the same time denied.

It seems clear that Whitehead does allow something like the distinction of primary and secondary qualities. He distinguishes between eternal objects of the subjective species, such as color, and eternal objects of the objective species, such as time and space relations. One can go back to count the number of the stripes because the quantitative aspects of things are of the objective species and in a "public" world. Whitehead believes that extensive relationships provide us with a common world. Science is ". . . an important statement of systematic theory correlating observations of a common world. . . ." [6] The common world—he also calls it the public world—is in some ways more basic than the private worlds of individual events. It is the "systematic scheme of relatedness" [7] which makes vivid prehension possible. And since everything has got to be somewhere, and in relation to something, the extensive aspect of the world is a necessary condition of anything intensive.

What we have come to, of course, is the idea of the extensive continuum. The extensive continuum is involved in whatever occurs in any way. It is "the general scheme of extensive perspective which is exhibited in all the mutual objectifications by which actual entities prehend each other." [8] "The extensive continuum," he says, "is that general relational element in experience whereby the actual entities experienced, and that experience itself, are united in the solidarity of one common world." [9]

These statements seek to make consistent the notion of a public world, and the notion of a relativistic event ontology. For one thing we are told that there is this kind of consistency between extensive and intensive relations—that without the former we could not have the latter. I take it that the converse is also true, and that the extensive continuum is to be understood as a general nonatomized continuum of potentiality both extensive and intensive.

Let me cite the type of Whiteheadian statement leading me to believe that this is the case. In speaking of perceiving the world of contemporary actual entities he tells us that world

> . . . is objectified for us as "realitas objectiva" illustrating bare extension with its various parts discriminated by differences of sense-data. These qualities, such as colors, sounds, bodily feelings, tastes, smells, together with the perspectives introduced by extensive relationships, are the relational eternal objects whereby the contemporary actual entities are elements in our constitution.[10]

Here, then, we get the material we need in one context—the color of the zebra's stripes and the extensive relations which would allow us to count the stripes. Why is it, then, that I cannot know the number of the stripes as immediately as I know their color?

Whatever we do with this a puzzle is likely to remain. I believe it is Whitehead's view that both the red of the zebra and the number of his stripes come to us in the mode of presentational immediacy. "All exact observation," he tells us, "belongs to the mode of presentational immediacy."[11] Now what comes to us in this mode comes through an antecedent state of my body. In the present moment I read that state. I am aware of a number of red stripes. The eternal object of the subjective species, the red color, occasions no problem. The eternal object of the objective species, the number of stripes, perplexes me. Where is this eternal object in Whiteheadian terms? He says that eternal objects are where they are relevant. It does not seem reasonable to say that the eternal object of the number of the stripes is present in an antecedent state of my body when my awareness extends no further than the more general eternal object, numerosity. It does not seem to me reasonable to say that the eternal object of the number of the zebra's stripes is in the zebra, when the number depends on the contrast of red and white, that is, on eternal objects of the subjective species. Nor does it seem reasonable to hold that the zebra has an indefinite number of stripes until the stripes are counted by an observer capable of distinguishing red from white. In short, I cannot think of a reasonable alternative here.

And unless someone can help me rescue Whitehead from this situation I must conclude that I have come across a disorderly element in Whitehead's manner of ontologizing possibility. And Quine's desert landscape begins to seem attractive—but only as an alternative possibility.

THE INFERENCE FROM PERFECTION TO BEING

The final problem I mention concerns the family of philosophers with which to associate Whitehead's thought. One alternative is the Augustinian-Cartesian group. In this alternative it is valid to infer from certain kinds of perfection to certain kinds of being. The "cogito" argument and the ontological argument are the chief instances of this type of inference. The two arguments seem to go together. In whatever system of philosophy one of these arguments is valid, the other is also valid; and in whatever system of philosophy one is invalid, the other is likewise invalid.

We ask if Whitehead's thought belongs to this group. One might think that it does, and cite as support Whitehead's concern with relating value to ontology. But the role of value for Whitehead is not such that one can infer from value to existence. According to the "subjective principle" value requires a valuer, but Whitehead utilizes the principle to introduce his ontology of subjects whose satisfactions provide the valuations to which any talk of grades of excellence must relate.

One cannot turn to a treatment of the ontological argument in Whitehead, since it is not treated. The "cogito" argument is treated, but with some obliqueness in the exposition. He claims for Descartes, for example, "the greatest philosophical discovery since the age of Plato and Aristotle." [12] What is this discovery? (1) The substance-quality categories of experience "have lost all claim to any fundamental" role in metaphysics, and (2) "subjects enjoying conscious experiences provide the primary data for philosophy, namely, themselves as in the enjoyment of such experience." He finds in Descartes, that is to say, not a convincing "cogito" argument, but support for his subjectivist principle.

One reason that the great philosophical discovery is not the "cogito" argument is that this argument cannot be expressed in Whiteheadian terms. The "cogito" argument concerns the kind of evidence one's knowing gives of one's existence. Let us try to explicate this according to Whitehead's doctrine of propositions. A true judgment for Whitehead exhibits conformity between a proposition and an objectified nexus. The logical subjects of the proposition make up the nexus. The predicate of the proposition is constituted by an eternal object, simple or complex. One says "I think, therefore I am," and the claim of existence stands in the predicate place. It should, then, stand for an eternal object. But nowhere in Whitehead does one find a suggestion that "existence" could constitute an eternal object. Eternal objects concern everything but existence.

Indeed, when Whitehead does discuss the "cogito ergo sum" he suggests that ". . . each time he (Descartes) pronounces, 'I am, I exist' the actual occasion, which is the ego, is different; and the 'he' which is common to the two egos is an eternal object. . . ." [13] If the "he" is an eternal object, our logical subject turns out to be our predicate. One would suppose, then, that the true subject may be a kind of pronominal pointing to the existence of the cluster of qualities making up the ego.

In any case, it seems clear that in the Whiteheadian doctrine of propositions one cannot infer from predicates with qualitative characteristics—whether thinking, doubting, or being deceived—to *existing,* for the two kinds of statement have very different structures. For Whitehead, as for Kant, existence is simply not a predicate. And if the "cogito" will not work within this system, neither will the ontological argument, and for the same reasons.

One concludes that Whitehead's thought does not belong to the Augustinian-Cartesian family. It is not necessary to provide a family, of course, but I suggest that the coauthor of *Principia Mathematica* would not be uninterested in the consequences flowing from Russell's work, and in the logically and linguistically sophisticated analyses of the present time. As these analyses turn toward metaphysics, I believe that the relevance of Whitehead's thought to contemporary modes of analysis will become more evident. Some of the questions I have raised here will doubtless be reconsidered; their more definitive resolution will not, I think, occur by simple rejection of Whitehead's claims.

NOTES

1. A. N. Whitehead, *Process and Reality,* New York, 1929, p. 38.
2. *Ibid.,* p. 94.
3. This Whitehead allows, but the mode contains so much loss that it cannot be taken to be the solution to the problem.
4. W. V. Quine, "On What There Is," *From a Logical Point of View,* New York, 1963, p. 4.
5. *Process and Reality,* p. 102.
6. *Ibid.,* p. 502.
7. *Ibid.,* p. 389.
8. *Ibid.,* p. 118.
9. *Ibid.,* p. 112.
10. *Ibid.,* pp. 95–96.
11. *Ibid.,* p. 507.
12. *Ibid.,* p. 291.
13. *Ibid.,* p. 116.

Oriental Metaphysics

George Bosworth Burch

In discussing Oriental metaphysics I will confine myself to India, and in India I will confine myself to the Hindu tradition. Buddhist philosophy tends to be analytical rather than metaphysical, and Jain philosophy is outstanding in logic and ethics rather than in metaphysics. Of the four great Hindu philosophical traditions, Nyaya is oriented toward logic, Sankhya toward science, Yoga toward psychology, and Vedanta toward metaphysics. Vedanta means philosophy based on the Veda, which is the revealed scripture of Hinduism. As such it is analogous to Christian philosophy in the West, a melange of systems united by a common tradition, respect for scripture, and certain categories of thought, but differing in doctrine. As Christian philosophies agree in little more than accepting the existence of God and the soul, so the Vedanta philosophies agree only in acknowledging Brahman or the Absolute as the reality underlying the world and Atman or Self as the reality underlying experience. The dualist school of Vedanta philosophy is a theism distinguishing between Brahman as creator and everything else, including ourselves, as creatures. The so-called qualified nondualist school is a sort of pantheism seeing Brahman as the reality manifested in all things. The monist, or as the Indians, who like to put things negatively, call it, the non-dualist school, is an absolutism which asserts that Brahman is the only reality. This school, from its premise that Brahman is *the* reality, that is, the only reality, deduces, with Eleatic logical rigor, its two great principles, that the world, since it is not

Brahman, is unreal, and that the self, since it obviously is real, is Brahman. On the practical or religious side dualism teaches salvation by works, qualified nondualism salvation by loving devotion to God, and nondualism salvation neither by works nor love, both of which bind us to the illusory world, but only by knowledge, the necessary and sufficient way to overcome illusion. The goal of philosophy is to see the truth, and its motive is not wonder but escape from the sufferings which inevitably accompany the unfolding of error. For nondualism there are five steps of spiritual progress: first, the prerequisites of moral character, ability to distinguish reality from illusion, renunciation of the fruits of action, and strong desire for salvation; second, acceptance by faith of the Vedanta truths as taught by the Scripture or by the guru; third, rational understanding of these truths, this step being Vedanta *philosophy;* fourth, the meditation and way of seeing by which we come gradually not only to know but actually to see that the world is illusory; and finally, the sudden and irrevocable conversion of attention by which the illusion disappears, like waking up from a dream, or seeing that the snake which frightened you is really a rope. What happens to the people in the dream when you wake up? What happens to the snake when the rope is seen? If you can answer these questions, you can understand Vedanta.

Nondualist Vedanta is especially interesting philosophically because of its emphasis on reason. Although it is less influential outside of India than Buddhism or Yoga, it has often fascinated non-Indian metaphysicians. Its most famous teacher was the great ninth-century philosopher-saint Shankara, famous partly perhaps just because he popularized nondualism in a watered-down version compromising with common sense. He taught that the world, although not real, is not unreal either, but has a kind of reality, something like the phenomenal world of Kant, with whom he is often compared. During the intellectual dark ages of Moslem and British rule Indian metaphysical thought was suppressed, to the benefit of emotional nonmetaphysical religion. But the twentieth century has seen a renaissance of Indian thought, including philosophy, especially nondualist Vedanta, newly thought out and expressed in the English language which the conquerors had made the medium of education. Much of this has been restatement of the classical nondualism of Shankara, and here the most distinguished contemporary teacher is perhaps Professor Mahadevan of Madras. But there are also original teachers who, within the nondualist tradition, have departed radically from the system of Shankara.

I suppose that "the future of metaphysics" means contemporary trends, unless it is to be pure prophecy. I shall discuss two contemporary trends in nondualist Vedanta, established by Professor G. R. Malkani and the late Professor K. C. Bhattacharyya, philosophers very unlike each other. Malkani's originality might almost be called reactionism, since his philosophy, while departing from classical Vedanta, is in many ways like that of the fifth-century philosopher Gaudapada who is considered the founder of the nondualist school. Bhattacharyya, on the other hand, has introduced new ideas and new ways of thinking into philosophical thought. Both have many published works, and the works of both are difficult, but for opposite reasons. Bhattacharyya's writing is extremely obscure, because he says exactly what he means without compromising with idiom, using common words in an uncommon way. Malkani, on the other hand, writes such clear and fluent English that the reader risks being lulled by the simplicity of style into missing the profundity of content. Neither has many disciples at present, but I anticipate that their future influence will be great because of the intrinsic merit and power of their philosophies.

G. R. Malkani, now retired, was for most of his life director of the Indian Institute of Philosophy at Amalner, a tiny research institution in a remote town, where the integrity and austerity of the director's life matched the integrity and austerity of the philosophy he taught. He was also editor of the *Philosophical Quarterly,* and made it India's leading philosophical journal. He had an article in almost every issue of the journal and also published several books, all commendably short. I especially commend his *Philosophy of the Self,* recently reprinted in this country. There has been no evolution in Malkani's philosophical thought; he has never changed his views, and he has never doubted their correctness. He has only sought for greater clarity in expressing them. He once said that he has just one undemonstrated dogma, namely, the distinction between subject and object in experience. If you will concede that distinction, he is prepared to demonstrate rationally that the subject is real and the object unreal. These conclusions are simply the perennial doctrine of nondualist Vedanta. But in Malkani's teaching they are elaborated by corollaries and explanations which violate common sense but can be defended by reason.

First of these corollaries is *drishtisrishtivada,* seeing-being-ism, the theory that a thing is because it is seen—in plain English, subjective idealism. It is opposed to *srishtidrishtivada,* being-seeing-ism, the theory that a thing is seen because it is, which is the teaching of classical Vedanta. There are two kinds of illusion. A subjective illusion, like a hallucination or a dream, has no being other than its being seen by the person who has it. An objective illusion, like a mirage on the desert or an illusion created by a magician on the stage, although not real, is still objectively there, and is seen by anyone in a position to observe it, whether or not he is deceived into thinking it real, and is still there even if nobody observes it. According to classical nondualism God creates the world, not like the Christian God creating a real world but like a magician creating an illusion, and we see the cosmic illusion because it exists, unlike mere dreams. For Malkani this is quibbling. His two-valued logic generates a two-valued metaphysics in which whatever is not real is unreal. There is no ontological hierarchy among nonentities. It may well be that God created the world; Malkani would not deny that; but this statement has only cosmological, not metaphysical, significance, because God also is part of the illusion. The cosmic illusion, like any illusion, is only insofar as it is seen. The practical consequence is obvious. You get rid of an illusion as you get rid of a dream by waking up or get rid of a snake by seeing it is really a rope, without doing anything in the dream or without having to kill the snake.

A second corollary concerns the *jiva,* the individual self or subject who has the illusion. Malkani's theory is *ekajivavada,* one-individual-ism, the theory that the *jiva* is one, opposed to *anekajivavada,* the theory that it is not one, that is, many. *Ekajivavada* goes beyond Berkeley, who taught *drishtisrishtivada* but believed in a plurality of souls, although perhaps not beyond Kant, whose transcendental ego was not subject to the category of plurality applicable to phenomena. In a dream there are many persons but only one dreamer. Even classical Vedanta considers that individuality is the primary illusion, which is the source of other illusions when we falsely identify the self with the individual mind or body. But if individuality is illusory, there are no separate *jivas*. This also has consequences. In oral instruction Malkani asserts that he has no theory to teach but is willing to solve the pupil's problems, and will not speak until a question is asked. If the pupil has no problem, there is no need for discussion. If he has a problem, it can be solved, often by an analysis which eliminates the problem itself. But a problem must be a problem for somebody. A problem which never arises is no problem at all. A perennial problem in many religions is that of the opportunity or even obligation of the saved individual, buddha or saint, to be of help to those who are not yet saved, like Plato's philosophers going back down into the cave. Opposed answers to this separate Mahayana Buddhism from Hinayana, and Catholic Christianity from Protestant. The solution, as Malkani sees it, is that the problem of the saved individual's obligation never arises because no individual ever is saved, and no individual ever is saved because individuality is the very thing which we are saved from.

Another corollary is *ajativada,* non-origination-ism. The metaphysical answer to the question who made the world is that nobody made the world, because there is no world. "Like a dream, like a mirage, like fairyland, so is this world," said Guadapada. The whole temporal world, physical and mental alike, is unreal and illusory. But having illusion and release from illusion are themselves temporal, and so unreal. Illusion itself is illusory. Really there is no creation, no illusion, no world, no individual, no bondage, no release, and no freedom, but only Brahman. *Ekajivavada,* says Malkani, is the most satisfactory philosophical theory, whereas *ajativada* is the "last kick" of philosophy before silence, which alone can represent truth. The practical consequence of *ajativada* can be illustrated by the analogy of dreaming. If you dream you are pursued by a bear, you can run, but he may run faster. The best way of escape is to wake up, whereupon you will see that you are safe in bed, that there is no bear, and never was. But suppose you do not wake up; it does not make any difference; you *are* safe in bed anyway, whether you know it or not, and that bear cannot possibly hurt you. It is the same with the cosmic illusion. The goal of Vedanta is to attain freedom from illusion and realization of your identity with Brahman, which is described as absolute being, consciousness, and bliss. But suppose you do not attain this goal; it does not make any difference; you *are* Brahman anyway. There is no real freedom because there is no real bondage.

Finally, there is the very subtle problem of the relation between ignorance and error. A philosophy which teaches that experience reveals truth requires a theory of knowledge, but a philosophy which teaches that experience is false requires a theory of ignorance. Ignorance, which is negatively not seeing positive reality, and error, which is positively seeing negative unreality, are correlative; hence the problem, like the hen and the egg, of which comes first. Do we dream because we sleep or do we sleep because we dream? According to classical Vedanta ignorance is prior to error. Ignorance is the original and inexplicable fact, like the fall of man in Christian philosophy, which explains all our other troubles. The *jiva,* not knowing that he is the nondual Brahman, one without a second, falsely identifies himself with his illusory individuality, mind, body, and experience. Absence of truth leaves room for error, and one error succeeds another until ignorance is overcome. Malkani (if I understand him correctly) does not find this theory tenable. Error is prior to ignorance—not in time, but logically and causally. Ignorance may be a necessary condition of error, but it is not a sufficient condition to explain the particular errors we have. One error is caused psychologically by a preceding error, but there is no cause of error as such, either a rational cause, because it is error, or a psychological cause, because it is beginningless. The so-called cause of any thing is the cause of its coming into being, and a thing which never came into being has no cause. According to Indian categories of thought time is infinite, we have all existed from an infinite past, and our condition of being subject to error or illusion had no beginning, although it may have an end, indeed must have an end, else it would not be illusory. Error dominating consciousness drives out truth and so produces ignorance. The practical consequence is that the lover of wisdom who is seeking the Vedanta goal of freedom from error and realization of the truth that he is Brahman should concentrate on considering the illusoriness of the world rather than his identity with Brahman, a truth which he already knows both by scriptural authority and by rational understanding but still cannot intuit so long as he is bound by illusions. Only when I am free from illusions will the truth of my absolute being, consciousness, and bliss as the eternal Self shine forth, needing only to be freed from the veils of error which have concealed it.

We do not have to go to India to learn that the world is illusion. Our own philosophers, Plato and Kant, have taught us that. But we may have to go to India to find philosophers who take this seriously, with all its implications for theory and practice. Malkani has done three things for nondualist Vedanta: he has restated it in English, thus freeing it from the Sanskrit language with which it has been associated; he has set it forth systematically, instead of in the classical style of commentary on ancient Scriptures; and he has presented it in its most rigorous form. His presentation is strictly rational, with no appeal to the authority of Scripture, and as such can only be judged by reason. If it cannot survive rational criticism, it has no value. If it can, it does have value, at least to rationalists. It has no intrinsic dependence on the Indian culture in which historically Vedanta developed. If it is true anywhere and at any time, it is true everywhere and always.

The second metaphysician I wish to consider, K. C. Bhattacharyya, who died in 1949, has not been widely studied, because of the difficulty of his literary style, but some who have studied him, including myself, consider him the greatest philosopher of modern India. His many articles and short books were collected and published again in 1958 under the title *Studies in Philosophy*. As an example of his style let me read the concluding sentence of his book *The Subject as Freedom:*

> I am not introspectively aware of my actual introspective individuality but I am aware in my introspection into feeling that the self from which the feeling is distinguished may not actually introspect and may not even possibly introspect, that individual as it is as introspecting—individual or distinct freedom without being, it may be free even from this distinctness, may be freedom itself that is de-individualised but not therefore indefinite—absolute freedom that is to be evident.

This is difficult, but not impossible; the trick is to fathom the sentence structure, locate the antecedents of the pronouns, and have faith that what is stated is exactly what is intended. The intricacy of style is matched by the subtlety of content. Bhattacharyya's philosophy, although definitely within the tradition of nondualist Vedanta, is informed by his original genius, enriched by influences from non-Vedantic philosophy both Indian and Western, and presented in compact, irresistible logical chains of argument. This neo-Vedanta, as it has been called, is not a system but a way of thinking capable of indefinite development, and in Bhattacharyya's own writing it developed through three phases. To define the Absolute was his idea from beginning to end. In the first phase of his philosophy he defines the Absolute as *Indefinite,* in the second phase as *Subject,* and in the third phase as *Alternation.*

In his first phase Bhattacharyya defines the Absolute as Indefinite. This is in accordance with the doctrine, taught in the Upanishads, which are the philosophical portion of the Veda, that Brahman or the Absolute is best described negatively as not this and not that. His first book was a study of classical Vedanta, but the metaphysical view which it presents, as he himself says, is only "dimly traceable in the Upanishads" and not "completely brought out even by the commentators." It is, he seems to mean, what the Upanishads and Shankara would have said if they had thought it through. The principal non-Vedantic influence in the first phase was that of Hegel. Hegelian logic, he says, while it does not admit the indefinite but holds instead that dialectic necessity is creative, does not actually create the new category the necessity of which it sees, and this failure is an implicit admission of the indefinite. It would seem that Hegel, like Shankara, stated implicitly what Bhattacharyya states explicitly. There is nothing original, of course, in maintaining that the Absolute, since it is not limited and therefore not definite, is indefinite. But how can the indefinite be defined? Christianity has its positive theology which describes the ineffable God positively but figuratively and its negative theology which describes him literally but negatively. The former would be unthinkable for Bhattacharyya, who never speaks figuratively; there is not a single figure of speech in his collected works. And the latter would be equally unsatisfactory; his concern is to understand the Absolute, not to glorify it by rhetorically denying its limitations. To define the indefinite is a logical problem which cannot be solved in the categories of Aristotelian logic. It requires a dynamic dialectic, like Hegel's in spirit, but very different from Hegel's in substance, and, I might add, even more difficult than Hegel's to understand.

The principles of such dialectic are developed in the short article "Place of the Indefinite in Logic." Logic is an objective science dealing abstractly with the forms of everything thinkable. Its most basic distinction is between definite and indefinite. The indefinite cannot be discussed in categories applicable only to the definite, but only in such statements as, "The indefinite is not and is indefinite at once," statements which reveal the inadequacy of the various traditional logics. Against formal logic, these principles suggest the indeterminate form of doubt or ignorance beyond determinate affirmation or negation; against Hegelian logic, they point to unreason as an alternative to reason; against empirical logic, they consider objects of experience as determinations carved out of the indeterminate. Terms, separated from the surrounding indefinite by bounds themselves indefinite, may be understood either as being or as transition. Judgments are negations of the indefinite indifferently affirmative or negative. Inferences involve an alternation of static and dynamic aspects which reveals reason as essentially indefinite. The logic developed from such principles, unlike traditional logic, can be applied to widely different metaphysical theories, including the Vedantic assertion of the unreality of the world. We must reject the dogmatic assumption that knowledge must move toward more determinate truth. The logical impulse may be equally satisfied in getting rid of the limitations of definiteness. So far as logic is concerned, the Absolute may be either definite or indefinite. The metaphysical truth that the Absolute is the Indefinite is known not by logic but by revelation. But logic can make it intelligible, provided the logic includes the category of indefinite. Relation is possible only between definite terms. The indefinite cannot be related, cannot be subject or predicate of a judgment, and is not relative to anything. This, however, is mere logic, not an ontological proof of the actual existence of the indefinite Absolute. The purpose of neo-Vedanta is to understand the Absolute, not to determine whether it exists, which is logically impossible, and it is understood by understanding the logic of the indefinite.

Neo-Vedanta, however, like classical Vedanta, cannot remain satisfied with this quasi-negative conclusion, but seeks, if not any definite connotation, at least a definite denotation for the Absolute. The logical approach gives way to a psychological approach. The Absolute, as indefinite, cannot be any object of experience, but as the ground of all objects it is understood as the subject of experience. This is in accord with the Upanishadic formula *You're it,* more commonly translated *Thou art That,* an existential statement containing no nouns, adjectives, or verbs, and so no concepts, but only the personal pronoun *Thou* which indicates the person, the demonstrative pronoun *That* which indicates the Absolute, and the copula *art* which declares their identity. Realization of the subject as the Absolute involves two problems, the metaphysical problem of defining the subject and the psychological problem of being aware of the subject, and these twin problems of understanding the subject dominate the works of Bhattacharyya's second phase. The principal non-Vedantic influence in this phase was that of Kant. His interpretation of Kant, based on a thorough study of the texts in translation and formulated in a series of lectures, is highly original. He stresses Kant's thesis of "the transcendental ideality of time or the mental world, implying a distinction between self and mind," by which Kant's metaphysics is dissociated from the Augustinian and Cartesian dualism of mind and matter and affiliated to nondualist Vedanta, for which mind and matter are equally illusory as contrasted with the real self. But metaphysics cannot abandon its whole project by agnosticism. The thing-in-itself, which Kant considers unknowable, demands to be known, and therefore can be known—a kind of metaphysical analogue of Kant's "I ought, therefore I can." The Indefinite, which remains at every level of experience as a fringe not realized but demanding to be realized, is approached by the gradual inward realization of the subject. We advance in wisdom not by discovering new existences, for existence is obvious and does not need to be discovered, but by discovering new nonexistences, that is, by rejecting what we formerly thought to be existent. The principle of procedure is the identity of falsity and subjectivity. To put it in language more simple than Bhattacharyya would use, all objects are subjective, and the only thing which is objective is the subject.

But it remains to determine what the subject is. According to Bhattacharyya, the subject is freedom. The knowledge of the self or subject as freedom, which he considers a presupposition of Kant's transcendental philosophy, is the demonstrated conclusion of Bhattacharyya's book *The Subject as Freedom.* After an analytical study of the significant although meaningless word *I,* he develops a dialectic in which assumption of the subjective attitude leads to the successive rejection of the various modes of objectivity. The steps of this process include perception of environment, perception of the body, inner feeling of the body, knowledge by conscious nonperception of absence as a present fact, imagination, ideas, thought, feeling, and introspection. Actual introspection is pure knowing without content, although still as a distinct individual. Possible introspection is awareness of a subject beyond the individual actually introspected. At every step the subjective attitude appears as a demand for freedom from the illusory, and the elaboration of these stages of freedom shows the possibility of realizing the subject as absolute freedom. This demand is not fulfilled even in introspection, either actual or possible. But in introspection I may become aware that the self from which its content is distinguished may be free even from the distinction between my own actual introspection and others' possible introspection and so be de-individualized. This does not mean that the Absolute is indefinite—the doctrine of Bhattacharyya's first phase and the most profound conclusion possible in the objective attitude. The absolute self or subject, free from all distinctness, is still definite. The self or Absolute is not a thing having freedom but is freedom itself.

Granted that the subjective attitude leads to absolute freedom, we might still raise the question, why assume this attitude? Is freedom an end which justifies the subjective attitude as a means, or is the subjective attitude right in itself, with freedom a happy consequence? Cannot a case also be made for the objective attitude? This question leads to a consideration of the third and more comprehensive phase of Bhattacharyya's philosophy, in which freedom appears as the Absolute, but only as one of alternative forms. The concept of the Absolute as alternation is his most original and potentially fruitful contribution to philosophical thought. The principal non-Vedantic influence in this phase was that of Jainism. His treatment of this is no less original than that of Vedanta, Hegel, or Kant. The Jain philosophy of nonabsolutism has a seven-valued logic, the values being truth, falsity, indeterminateness, and their four combinations. According to the Jains this means that in any case each predicate may be asserted, not absolutely but relatively, in some respect. Bhattacharyya, however, interprets it as involving an alternation of values, and it is this which turned his thought toward alternation as a basic principle of metaphysics. In this interpretation of Jain logic he found a clue for comprehending the Absolute in a way at once more subtle and more profound than that given by the notions of Indefinite or Subject. His paper "Concept of the Absolute and its Alternative Forms" begins with the sentence, "Philosophy starts in reflective consciousness." This expresses his attitude toward philosophy, which needs no external motivation, either wonder as in the Western tradition or suffering as in the Hindu tradition, but is the natural activity of the human reflective consciousness. Reflection is awareness of the relation between subject and object, consciousness and its content. In the study of their relation the doctrines of the earlier phases, although not rejected, are transcended. The logic of the indefinite is still required, but the indefinite as such is considered a challenge rather than a position. The subjective attitude leads to the subject as freedom, but the objective attitude is also given equal consideration. There are three conscious functions—knowing, willing, and feeling. In knowing, content determines consciousness; in willing, consciousness determines its content; in feeling, they mutually determine each other. Knowing is truth; willing is freedom; feeling he calls value. Ordinary experience is a mixture of the three, but each can be purged of the accretions of the others and so become pure or absolute—absolute Truth, absolute Freedom, or absolute Value. These are incompatible and incommensurable, neither reducible to each other nor comprehensible under any higher synthesis, alternative absolutes.

This is an original theory of the Absolute, a novel metaphysics. But it is more than that. It involves a new logic and a new philosophical orientation. As such it can be considered systematically, on its own merits, without any historical reference to K. C. Bhattacharyya, who conceived it, or to the Vedanta tradition, which nourished it. It is a way of thinking with many applications. The principal category of conventional logic is negation: if a judgment is accepted, its contradictory is rejected. The principal category of Hegelian logic is conjunction: thesis and antithesis are conjoined synthetically. But the principal category of neo-Vedanta logic is exclusive disjunction: incompatible alternatives are both accepted, not together, which would be inconsistent, but alternatively. Truth, which is determination of experience by the objective reality, freedom, which is determination of experience by subjective will, and aesthetic value, which is mutual determination of subject and object by each other, are opposed ideals of life and if carried to perfection are incompatible forms of the Absolute. They cannot be synthesized or even harmonized, but neither can they judge one another, each being autonomous in its own function. Each rejects the others, but there is no transcendent ground for preferring one over the others.

The metaphysical consequence of the logic of alternatives is opposed both to conventional monism with its one Absolute and to conventional pluralism with its rejection of any Absolute. Neo-Vedanta teaches a plurality of alternative Absolutes. This is justified by its phenomenological basis. Metaphysics is conceived not as an analysis of Being, but as an analysis of experience, without any ontological prejudice. Bhattacharyya's neo-Vedanta, which is phenomenological and existential as well as Vedantic, offers suggestions for metaphysical speculation congenial to Eastern and Western philosophers alike, and may be expected to have a significant influence in the future of metaphysics.

Phenomenology and Metaphysics: Ontology Without Metaphysics?

James M. Edie

The phenomenologist's desire to have ontology without metaphysics is a bit like the Deist's thirst for religion without revelation and may be fated for the same end. In this book Gilson's famous observation that "Metaphysics always buries its undertakers" will, no doubt, be documented from many different philosophical standpoints. "Contemporary" philosophy, as distinct from "modern" philosophy, originated in the post-Hegelian contesting of metaphysics as a valid, or even meaningful, inquiry. This rejection of metaphysics is not specific to any one school of thought. Nearly all "contemporary" currents in philosophy—pragmatism, logical positivism, linguistic behaviorism, ordinary-language philosophy, logical analysis, phenomenology, existentialism, and now structuralism—owe their initial thrust as well as their popularity to audacious, catchy (and always oversimplified) anti-metaphysical postulates and slogans. We have been living in an anti-metaphysical age since the end of the nineteenth century.

There are signs, however, that the "contemporary age" of philosophy is now breaking up and, in its progressive disintegration, nearing its end. The logical positivists who began by claiming that metaphysics was nonsense have ended by recognizing that "To say that metaphysics is nonsense *is* nonsense" (Waissman).[1] Contemporary philosophy has, no doubt, greatly clarified (without going beyond) the problematic of Aristotle and Kant: metaphysical statements claim to give us knowledge of necessary and universal truths about reality (in its generality) which are neither pure analytical tautologies nor empirically verifiable synthetic statements about contingent matters of fact. If such statements are nonsense, then the statement that they are nonsense is itself also nonsense of the same kind. This has finally been recognized, and we are once again attempting to understand the nature of an a priori synthetic judgment of the kind which metaphysics, alone among the sciences, makes.[2] Although this negative conceptual clarification is probably the major contemporary contribution to metaphysics, I do not want to take up again here the problem of analytic and synthetic judgments, or the problems of formal and material a prioris. I will grant myself that the meaningfulness of synthetic ("material") a prioris applicable to experience (Kant) or discoverable in experience (Husserl) has been accomplished, and that metaphysical systems have at least this measure of general understanding, if not acceptance. This is, of course, especially important for phenomenology, because *in this sense* phenomenology, like Kantianism, is a metaphysics of experience even though it opposes all the "dogmatic" (that is, deductive) metaphysical systems of Greek and classical rationalism.

TRADITIONAL METAPHYSICS

But, in this paper, I shall be primarily concerned with a sense of metaphysics which is at once more general and more specific, namely, with metaphysics as that branch of philosophical reflection which deals with what there really is, that is, with the categories of being and reality.[3] It is more general because it deals with reality rather than with the meaningfulness of metaphysical statements; it is more specific because it restricts itself to making claims about "being" (and thus neglects the other transcendentals). This fundamental conception of metaphysics, which we owe to our common ancestors, Plato and Aristotle, is not so much challenged by phenomenology as reinterpreted and given a special and restricted sense. In this sense phenomenology never was as antimetaphysical as, for instance, logical positivism or linguistic philosophy (which believed that the metaphysical penchant could either be repressed without loss to the human spirit, or cured, as a condition of philosophical sanity). It is true that the word "metaphysics" never occurs under the pen of Husserl, but then it never occurs under the pen of Aristotle either, and it is equally true that, after 1907, Husserl designated phenomenology by the

Aristotelian name "First Philosophy." Phenomenologists, on the whole, prefer the word "ontology" to "metaphysics" and, in this way, are faithful to the Kantian revolution.[4] Husserl defines "ontology" as the *science of objects,* or "the a priori theory of objects as such." He likes Meinong's term *Gegenstandstheorie,* but feels that the "changed condition of the time" enables him to take to himself "the old expression Ontology."[5]

But before we embark on a discussion of the phenomenological definition of ontology, it is worthwhile noting that Husserl, at least, does not so much argue against traditional metaphysics (even to replace it with something else) as to bypass it, as just one more of the sciences of the natural attitude which, like the physical and behavioral sciences or the opinions of common sense, must be bracketed by the *epoche* and thus overcome through the phenomenological reduction. He seems to say that metaphysics, as the ultimate form of *scientia per causas,* remains, even in its most purified form, a science of the natural attitude. Metaphysical propositions (for example, taking a few at random from classical authors, *quodcumque movetur ab alio movetur, ex nihilo nihil fit, nemo potest supra seipsum, cessante causa cessat et effectus, natura non facit saltus, omne ens habet esse aut a se aut ab alio,* and so on), whether they be the results of empirical generalizations or postulates of reason, necessarily follow the various sciences (*ta meta ta physika biblia*) as their lawful and necessary extension. But even though it goes beyond physics, and even beyond "the physical," as Aristotle said, metaphysics remains caught in the same realistic attitude toward being as the other sciences, operating within the *natürliche Einstellung.* The value of traditional metaphysical systems is not, then, denied, and certainly not directly refuted, but metaphysics *as a science* in this sense, albeit the highest science, falls before the phenomenological *epoche,* which would, ideally, ground in transcendental experience those of its general principles, if any, which are valid. This view of metaphysics is also that of Heidegger, in *this* respect Husserl's disciple. Heidegger says that his philosophy has "overcome" (in the sense of "outgrown") metaphysics[6] because metaphysics has traditionally posed the question of being in an "ontic" manner. It has interpreted itself as *theiology,* the science of the highest in being, or of the highest being, "the divine," rather than as the ontological foundation of all beings and all sciences. Metaphysics and theology pose the question of the *Ursprung der Welt* in cosmological and causal categories; they attempt *to explain* the origin of the world, as an ontic and mundane reality, as a *kosmos* which would be the foundation and ultimate locus of all the categories. But phenomenology poses the question of the *Ursprung der Welt* in a more absolute and originary manner. It asks the question of how the world arises *as the world of human consciousness* beginning from the absolute and presuppositionless standpoint of actual present experience. It poses, beneath the problem of the *kosmos,* the problem of the *Lebenswelt* from which the cosmological explanations of science, metaphysics, and theiology are derived as well as second-order abstractions.

Metaphysics, as *scientia per causas ultimas,* thus has no privileged status in phenomenology; it is, in effect, replaced by a more fundamental science, namely, ontology (or, for Heidegger, *Fundamentalontologie*). This need not be replacement by cancellation; metaphysics is simply moved up to the level of ontic experience and seen *not* to be the most fundamental "science" of all. This is required by the return to experience (the *reduction*), which distinguishes the phenomenological method (like that of other radical empiricisms) from the "naive" and "mundane" conception of reality of the natural attitude. The transcendental attitude reveals a new and deeper sense of reality. Reality is now methodologically defined, through the reduction, as the correlate of consciousness. Phenomenology is based on the postulate that that which is real can be experienced and that everything which is experienced is, insofar forth, real. If there is an unexperienceable or strictly unknowable reality, it must be methodologically surrendered by phenomenology. No metaphysical entity, postulate, principle, or hypothesis can be admitted which cannot be reduced to experience. "What we cannot think," writes Husserl, "cannot be; what cannot be, we cannot think."[7] We must, of course, take Husserl's "think" here in its wide Cartesian sense (of thinking, knowing, willing, feeling, perceiving, imagining, and sensing); phenomenology replaces talk about *being* with talk about the *phenomenon of being,* because, in the last analysis, all *being* must be *phenomenon* or there could be no talk about it at all; it would fall into the unknowability and ineffability of nothingness. In this way phenomenology happily and effortlessly gets rid of a large number of the metaphysical categories and dichotomies (such as interior-exterior, substance-accidents, potency-act, appearance-reality, and phenomenon-noumenon) at the outset.

> Modern thought [Sartre writes] has realized considerable progress by reducing the existent to the series of appearances which manifest it. Its aim was to overcome a certain number of dualisms which have embarrassed philosophy and to replace them by the monism of the phenomenon. . . . There is no longer an exterior for the existent if one means by that a superficial covering which hides from sight the true nature of the object. And this true nature in turn, if it is to be the secret reality of the thing, which one can have a presentiment of or which one can suppose but can never reach because it is the "interior" of the object under consideration—this nature no longer exists. The appearances which manifest the existent are neither exterior nor interior; they are all equal, they all refer to other appearances, and none of them is privileged. . . . The obvious conclusion is that the dualism of being and appearance is no longer entitled to any legal status within philosophy. The appearance refers to the total series of appearances and not to a hidden reality which would drain to itself all the *being* of the existent.[8]

To say the same thing in the language of Husserl: "Object is everything and all that is." [9] What we discover, by a phenomenological analysis of experience, beginning with perceptual experience, are objects which polarize the selective and pragmatic attention of the experiencer. Neither sense-data (the explanatory postulates of empiricism) nor forms of judgment (the explanatory "deductions" of rationalism) are primarily experienced. The whole tissue of experience consists of constituted fields of objects (perceptual objects, imagined objects, thought objects, and so on), and thus "being" as the ultimate category is replaced by the category of "object" or "thing" (understood in the sense of "something").[10] We could, if we tried, find an intimation of this distinction in traditional metaphysics by developing the distinction among the transcendentals which Aquinas makes between *ens* and *res,* but, apart from the fact that this distinction is ambiguous in the texts of Aquinas himself, his successors have either taken *ens* and *res* as synonymous, or have not exploited this distinction in any phenomenological sense. There is, of course, the further and very important distinction that, whereas traditional metaphysics (and "ontology" as it was understood in the "dogmatic" ontologies of Baumgarten, von Wolff, and the neo-Scholastics) is a strictly deductive science proceeding from the intellectual cognition of *ens inquantum ens* to deduce *more geometrico* the properties of being as being, *ea quae sunt per se entis,* phenomenology, as a science of experience, rather than of being, can, of course, never be a deductive system like the classical metaphysical systems.[11]

PHENOMENOLOGICAL ONTOLOGY

According to Husserl, categories of meaning (in the double sense of *Sinn,* that is, unities of objective categorial "sense," and of *meinen,* that is, acts of judgment, *apophansis*) are universally and necessarily correlative to "categories of objects." Apophantic analytics or formal logic, as the purely formal analysis of logical grammar, of the logic of validity, and of the logic of truth, leads to the elaboration of the categories of formal ontology, or the science of objectivity in general. Formal ontology, based on the pure a priori categories of meaning, thus establishes the purely a priori science of being ("object") as a whole. Together, apophantic analytics and formal ontology constitute what Husserl calls the *mathesis universalis.*

> We take our start from formal ontology . . . which . . . is the eidetic science of object in general. In the view of this science, object is everything and all that is, and truths in endless variety and distributed among the many disciplines of the *mathesis* can in fact be set down to fix its meaning.[12]

Formal ontology, therefore, consists in the purely analytical study of the ultimate categories of objectivity, of what it is to be an object, or of "object-in-general." Formal ontology is followed by the analysis of the richer and more restricted regional ontologies, which are based more concretely on experience and which require, over and above the a priori analytics of formal logic, the instrumentality of a transcendental logic, or a logic of experience in a "material" (as opposed to a merely "formal") sense. The regional ontologies involve the discovery of invariant eidetic structures of various levels of experience which are "synthetic" or "material" and which apply the laws of objectivity as such to ever more concrete "regions" of experience. Thus, for instance, the phenomenology of perception will reveal the eidetic a prioris of the perceptual object as such; it will elaborate eidetic structures of experience which cannot be *deduced* from formal ontology, and which are, therefore, "material" or "synthetic" laws applicable only within a restricted domain (that is, the domain of the "physical," three-dimensional object perspectivally situated in intersubjective space) and not applicable to the whole of experience as such.

> The system of synthetic truths which have their ground in the regional essence [e.g., the essence of perception] constitutes the content of the regional ontology. The totality of the *fundamental* truths among these, of the *regional axioms,* limits—and *defines* for us—*the system of regional categories.* These concepts express not merely, as do concepts generally, specifications of purely logical categories, but are distinguished by this, that by means of regional axioms they express the features *peculiar* to the regional essence, or *express in eidetic generality what must belong "a priori" and "synthetically" to an individual object of the region.*[13]

Husserl's paradigm of a "regional ontology" is that of the perceptual object, and it is within the realm of the phenomenology of perception that he and his greatest disciples have made the most solid contributions. There is a theoretical as well as a practical reason for this, as we shall see presently. But I would like to pause here, now that we have at least this preliminary grasp of what Husserl means by defining ontology as the "science of objects," to complete our distinction between ontology as understood by phenomenology and traditional metaphysics. There is very little in Husserl's formal *mathesis universalis* (formal logic plus formal ontology) with its analysis of the concept of "object-in-general" (with reference to the subordinate concepts of "thing," "property," "relation," "substantive meaning" or "fact," "group," "number," "order," "part," "whole," and so on) which could not be given a place in traditional metaphysics. It is his conception of the various regional ontologies, which require a transcendental as well as a formal logic, that makes the critical difference. Transcendental logic is the analysis of the "objectifying" and "constituting" acts of consciousness, which is necessary to account for the world of objects actually experienced. Transcendental phenomenology is based on the discovery of the law of intentionality, that is, all experience is *experience of something,* a law which empirical psychology, for all its acuteness, was never able to thematize or "discover" because all natural experience always takes it for granted. Intentionality distinguishes conscious processes from all other kinds of processes in that they are ways of *having objects.* Since we have no access to being-in-itself except through the *phenomenon of being,* all being *quoad nos* is objectified and endowed with a meaning and value responsive to our theoretical and practical aims, needs, interests, goals, intentions, desires, and so on. Experienced being is the "world according to man" (Merleau-Ponty's phrase), a structured, objectified, intentional object, and this is why Husserl posed the problem of being in the language of "being in the world" [14] and gradually developed his thought in the direction of an "ontology of the *Lebenswelt.*" [15]

Phenomenology thereby replaces the ancient metaphysical category of "being" with the concept "world," or the "world of objects" (because to say "the world of objects" is to say the world as meaningful, as objectified, as structured by consciousness). Transcendental phenomenology discovers that "being" already always has a sense for consciousness, that it is the objective correlate of the processes of subjectivity which are the necessary and sufficient conditions of its objectivity. Perhaps the most striking contribution of phenomenology (in both its transcendental and existential forms) has been the elaboration of the notion of "world." This is not the Greek *kosmos,* an ordered and fixed totality of beings whose order and structure owes nothing to human consciousness, which is governed by "divine" laws to which the gods and men are subject. Nor is it the moral conception of "this world" of the New Testament,[16] the world of pride and concupiscence, the arena of sin under the reign of Caesar and Satan. Finally, it is not the world as the elaborate fabrication of a hidden metaphysical instinct in man, the "transcendental illusion," of which Kant spoke, which forces us to *think* a world which can never be experienced. The world, in the phenomenological sense, is the ever-experienced horizon of all objectifying acts of consciousness, the experienced coherence of all the objects presented in a given regional ontology, and, ultimately, the experienced concordance of the objects of all the regional ontologies within a coherent structure of experience. The world *as* world can never be given as an object in the strict sense (as *Selbst da*), but only as the field of contextual relevancy within which any given object is distinguished, as the ultimate ground within which all experience takes place. It is never a *given* totality but rather the always presupposed "presumptive" totality, the never completed but always more closely approached synthesis of all perspectives. It is our experience of the world, as the ground of any particular experience, that founds our belief (*Urdoxa*) that all perspectives, all objectifications, will ultimately be found to coalesce in a coherent structure. In short, the world is the ultimate and most global objective correlate of transcendental constituting subjectivity; it is the basis on which any given "object" can be identified and distinguished from any other and can thus acquire an "objective" sense.

No doubt the best way to describe "the world of objects" is to relate it to the various regional ontologies which are elaborated through the phenomenological analysis of the ways in which consciousness experiences objects and thus constitutes its *Lebenswelt.* This will also give us some clue as to how the various phenomenologies of perception (Husserl and Merleau-Ponty), of imagination (Sartre), of love and affectivity (Scheler), of embodiment (Heidegger and Merleau-Ponty), of will (Ricoeur), of reason (Husserl), and so on, could ultimately be fitted together. I will be guided in the following remarks particularly by William James, Alfred Schutz, and Aron Gurwitsch, all of whom have attempted to map, in a preliminary way, the geography of the regions of the experienced world in its correlation to consciousness. James preferred the term "Orders of Reality," Schutz spoke of the "finite provinces of meaning," and Gurwitsch prefers to speak of "autonomous orders of existence." [17] Since Gurwitsch has systematized the work of his predecessors, we can, without unnecessary ambiguity, follow his usages in the main, although in this discussion the terms "being," "existence," and "reality" are interchangeable terms.

All agree that the "paramount reality" (James's phrase) is the world of perception, and it is not accidental that phenomenology itself begins with the phenomenology of perception. We have become accustomed to credit Merleau-Ponty with the thesis of "the primacy of perception" because of his own *strong* version of this thesis, but, in germ, it is all there in James and Husserl before him.[18]

> Every science [writes Husserl] has its own object-domain as field of research, and to all that it knows . . . there correspond as original sources of the reasoned justification that support them certain intuitions in which objects of the region appear as self-given and in part at least as *given in a primordial sense* . . . and the *primordial* dator experience is *perception*. . . .[19]

It is in the elaboration of a phenomenology of perception that we discover the primary sense of "being" or "real object." The lived-time and lived-space of our corporeally embodied existence, perspectivally situated within a world of factually given physical bodies, gives us our primary experience of existence, and our primordial conception of "the world." This is the realm of fundamentally experienced and irreversible temporal synthesis (phenomenal time) on the basis of which we objectify our perceptual realities, other persons, and our own bodies as situated among others, our own past and the past of others, and on the basis of which we conceive the ideas of "objective" (standard) time and "objective" space. This is the inescapable world in which we live our lives, work, pursue our practical projects as citizens, as members of a family, or of a profession, and in which we die. Even when we are lost in the higher and "founded" regions of imagination, of categorial thought, or of scientific and philosophical theories, the perceptual world is always present in the margins of our consciousness as a perceptual imperative, as the inescapable place and time of our existence.

It is unnecessary, and in any event impossible, to recapitulate here or to discuss in detail the various structures of perceptual consciousness which have been elaborated by Husserl, Merleau-Ponty, Erwin Straus,[20] Gurwitsch, Schutz, James, and others. It is sufficient if we can distinguish this primordial level of experience from others (the regional ontology of perceptual reality). Nor can we hope here to give a complete map of the various orders of reality; it is sufficient to point out that man does not live only on the level of perception but also has experience of "objects" (taking "objects" in the wide sense given to the term by Husserl, as the correlates of experience) of different orders of reality: the past, the unreal, the imaginary, the ideal, the cultural, and so on. To take but two examples, schematically, we can distinguish the worlds of imagination (as the correlates of imagining consciousness),[21] and the worlds of categorial thought (as the correlates of thinking consciousness) from perception.

The objects of imagination are "unreal" when compared to the objects of perception, even though the worlds of imagination are all made of quasi-perceptual objects, possessed of their own specific temporality, their own specific thematic consistency, and so on.

> Worlds of imagination as exemplified by any epic poem, play or novel, may exhibit considerable complexity of events and happenings as inter-meshing with one another. The most diversified relationships may exist between personages involved; persons, human, divine, and even animal. . . . For a world of imagination to appear as *one* world, it must contain no contradictions, nor inconsistencies. . . . Contriving a world of imagination or, as in reading, following the imagination of an author, we proceed from phase to phase. At every moment of our imagining, whether productive or merely receptive, a certain phase of the imagined world appears as present and refers both backward to earlier phases and forward to later ones.[22]

The time of imagination does not correspond to perceptual time; we can relive the whole of the lives of the Brothers Karamazov in a few hours of our own lifetime; their world exists as a separate realm for the imagination which we can discover, leave, and return to—"as identically the same as imagined on a previous occasion"[23]—at will. In short, the worlds of imagination are not and cannot be perceived, and are possessed of a noematic consistency and coefficient of reality utterly distinct from the perceptual world, all the while being "founded" on perceptual structures which cannot ever be completely escaped but which can be manipulated by imagining consciousness so as to effect a veritable *metabasis eis allo genos.*

When we turn to the worlds of ideality, of categorial thought, and of the theoretical attitudes of consciousness, we discover "objects" (Husserl likes to use the more abstract term "objectivities" here) of a still different nature. Such "objects" are the purely ideal orders of logical systems, geometrical systems, number systems, and of scientific and philosophical theories, which constitute specific eidetic domains. Needless to say, we need invoke no Platonic *chorismos* to discuss such "objects," and there is no question of treating mathematical and conceptual entities as if they were perceptually real. Since every eidetic domain is considered as an autonomous order of existence, the sense of being and reality attributed to "ideal" entities must be defined in function of that particular contextual realm of experience.[24] It is in this sense of "being" that we can most easily distinguish phenomenology as a science of experience from traditional metaphysics. The status given to ideal entities is *just that* which accrues to them in experience; since we can live in the realms of ideality as effortlessly as we live in the world of perception, the realms of ideal relationships can be shown to have their own distinctive thematic consistencies, in this case essentially atemporal and unaffected in their objectivity by phenomenal time, and to be, as the correlatives of acts of thinking, "real" objects of consciousness. As such, ideal entities are subject to laws of logical validity, propositional truth, and so on, wholly independent of the laws which pertain to mundane perceptual reality. Thus the "reality" which we ascribe to them is of a different order, but for that reason no less "real" and "discoverable" *mutatis mutandis* than the objects of perception. In fact, it is here, in the treatment of ideal objects, that the true value of substituting the metaphysically neutral concept of "object" for the more naively realistic term "being" in ontology comes to the fore. The reality-status of objects of consciousness is totally in function of the acts of consciousness (perceiving, imagining, and thinking) in which they are experienced.

> To experience an object then means to apprehend that object within a wider context, the order of existence [regional ontology], having a certain systematic form of unity and continuity, in virtue of a specific constitutive relevancy-principle. Accordingly, when an object appears as existing, it presents itself as existing within a certain specific order.[25]

We are now, then, in a better position to define the phenomenological sense of "world." It is constituted of all the objects correlative to a consciousness which at the same time perceives, imagines, remembers, and thinks it, and so on. In order to elaborate this phenomenological notion completely it would be necessary now to pose (and criticize) the stronger form of the thesis of the "primacy of perception" which Merleau-Ponty has advanced concerning the interrelations of these various regional ontologies and the correlative phenomenologies of perception, imagination, and thought.[26] To argue this thesis we would have to show how all the "higher" levels of experience are "founded" on the perceptual (though irreducible to it), and how it is ultimately impossible to account even for perception without taking into account the structures of operating-imagination, operating-memory, categorial thought, and so on. These structures of experience which can and must be distinguished for the purposes of phenomenological analysis are not, in actual experience, ever separated *in actu exercito,* and the "world according to man," that is, the *Lebenswelt,* is the complex and interconnected structure which polarizes all of man's various powers at once. The least perception contains categorial structures and there is no perception isolated from the derealizing powers of imagination which accompany and surround it. Conversely, the most purified realms of irreality and ideality are never completely freed from their dependence on certain perceptual structures. But the discussion of this stronger thesis would take us in the direction of elaborating a complete phenomenological ontology of the *Lebenswelt* and away from our primary purpose of posing the question of the relation of phenomenology to metaphysics, understood (as we restricted it at the beginning of this paper) as *the theory of reality*. It has been necessary to provide this phenomenological excursus in brief outline even to pose our central question.

ONTOLOGY AND METAPHYSICS

With the concept of the orders of existence (or orders of reality) phenomenology is able to give a new sense to the concept of being, by translating it into "world of objects" experienced by consciousness. But, even granting this phrase its full phenomenological sense, the phenomenological theory of reality may seem to resemble, at least initially, certain classical metaphysical systems. The sense given to the word "reality" or "being" in the context of the various regional ontologies elaborated by phenomenology is not univocal, since each use of the term for a distinct regional ontology requires a *metabasis eis allo genos.* Yet, at the same time, these various domains of objects, taken as perceptual reality, the imaginary, the ideal, and so on, are not totally unrelated to one another since they all fall within the unified theory of "objectivity in general." Gurwitsch does not hesitate to speak the Aristotelian language of "unity by analogy" for the various senses of "reality" or "being" as applicable to the various regional ontologies. All objects are experienced as real, although not all exist in the same manner, and thus the concept of reality, as applied to the various orders of objects of experience, retains a unity which is not pure equivocity. Such a unity, according to Aristotle, requires a *proton analogon,* a primary sense with reference to which all the distinct but related senses of the term can be predicated. *To on polachôs legetai:* "Being," Aristotle tells us, "is predicated in many different ways," but it retains a unity of meaning because of the fact that in all its usages it retains a reference to one primary sense, *ousia.* Phenomenology, to be sure, does not and cannot speak the naively realistic language of *ousiai.* But, when it locates the primary sense of reality in perceptual objects and recognizes in the processes of perception the primary sense of objectification, on which all the higher orders of imagination, of ideality, and so on, are "founded," it translates into a new idiom a conception which is perhaps not totally and in every respect incompatible with Aristotle's fundamental insight regarding the concept of being.[27] According to this reading of phenomenology, the concept of reality (as an object of consciousness) is an "analogous" concept which derives its unity from the fact that the orders of experience thematized in the fundamental regional ontologies are all interrelated and founded on (although irreducible to) that primary experience of the real which is given in the structures of perception. Thus, phenomenology as a "science of objects" is more of a reinterpretation and restriction of traditional metaphysics than a rejection; it clearly does not rule out the question of reality or the investigation of the meaning of being from philosophy.

We have, up to now, however, given a one-sided presentation of the claims of phenomenology. The kind of phenomenological map of the orders of reality which we have outlined above is what Husserl, in his idealistic period, would have called a noematic analysis, and, although such an approach can be fully justified within transcendental phenomenology, it is far from the last word; in fact, it largely avoids and perhaps ignores the central phenomenological problem of the reduction to experience. It is turned toward the objects of experience and the a priori laws of their objectification, but leaves undisclosed the correlative subjective acts which "constitute" both objects and their a priori structures; in a strictly transcendental framework, *noematic analyses* must be supplemented by an *intentional analysis* which would take back each of the object-structures of experienced reality to their intentional source in "pure" transcendental consciousness.

To be sure, the orders of reality we have discussed always carried a reference within themselves to something more fundamental, namely, the subjectively experienced acts of consciousness which conferred upon them their particular index of reality. Phenomenology, in fact, gives a new sense to Kant's dictum that "Being is not a real predicate." The sense of the word "is" when applied to a given order of experience always, as we have seen, involves a reference to subjectivity, to subjective acts of perception, of imagination, of ideation, and so on, in terms of which alone the peculiar accent of reality proper to a given ontological region is conferred. But here we reach a more fundamental problem. Husserl, following Frege, insisted from the earliest pages of the *Logical Investigations* on the distinction between the meaning (that is, "objective sense," *Sinn*) of a proposition or experience and the factual (perceptual, imaginary, ideal) object in the world (*Gegenstand*) to which meanings are referred. This distinction between meaning and reference, within what he was later to call the noematic field, is a constant of his thought, and indeed seems essential to any phenomenology. In the *Sixth Investigation* he developed his, never retracted, intuitionistic account of the relations between "empty" meaning-intentions and their "filling" (or verification) in direct intuitive experience of the world. The world of fact, of direct intuitive experience of objects (of various orders) which are experienced as existing independently of consciousness, is not created or produced by consciousness but is found to be *immer schon da* prior to reflection, as the objective correlate of "passive" experiential syntheses which cannot be explained otherwise than by describing them.[28] This is what consciousness does not make. The sense of the early slogan *"zu den Sachen selbst"* is to emphasize this world-directedness of consciousness. The paradigm example of the experience of objects transcendent to consciousness is, of course, the perceptual experience of a physical object. The noematic *sense* of a given perceptual object has an ideal independence of the factual order and can be intended in temporally distinct and qualitatively different acts of consciousness (by a free variation in the imagination), *but* this meaning can be intuitively filled (verified) only in an act of perception in which the intended object is given "in person." Moreover, although perception gives us the best example of the distinction between sense and reference, the distinction holds good of other orders of experience as well. At the beginning of *Formal and Transcendental Logic,* Husserl shows that the ideal existence of logical entities is objective and independent of the multitude of different acts in which they are intended. We have here, therefore, a clear distinction between objects of consciousness, on the one hand, and the noetic acts in which they are intended (or "constituted") and, on the other hand, a further distinction between the objective, ideal meaning of any object and the instantiation of this meaning in actual experience.

This latter distinction is given a special importance in Husserl's later writings on transcendental phenomenology, when he interprets the transcendental reduction as the bracketing of all factual existence in order to preserve, as the proper phenomenological domain, only the ideally constituted meanings which come wholly from consciousness. In the *Cartesian Meditations* the world is reduced to "the universe of constituted *sense,*"[29] which is the purely a priori realm of transcendental constitution and into which no element of fact can enter or have any relevancy. Whereas earlier he had spoken of the correlativity of "fact" and "essence" and had treated perceptual and categorial intuitions as correlative processes, in his "idealistic" period he attempted to reduce the field of phenomenology to the experience of categorial or eidetic meanings exclusively and to rule out of transcendental experience, as irrelevant, all references to the fact-world transcendent to consciousness. Why he would want to do this is clear: only by ruling out the transcendent world of fact could one come to a completely clarified account of experience within (and without leaving) the "constituting" activity of consciousness. What consciousness "constitutes" is the *sense* of objects (and thereby brings about objectification under distinct essences, a priori types, laws, and so on). But why he cannot succeed in this enterprise is equally clear: what consciousness does not "produce" is the object itself, the perceptual, imaginary, ideal instantiation of the meanings constituted by consciousness. Every sense (essence, meaning) carries within it a reference to the object or complex of objects (the "state of affairs") of which it is the objective sense and which would be its intuitive verification in experience. But, if this is so, this prevents the total and sovereign "constitution" of the world, or of any particular object in the world, by consciousness alone. Consciousness is a necessary, but not a sufficient, condition of the experience of the object itself. In experiencing the world, consciousness, to be sure, "objectifies" (that is, confers meaning on, gives sense to) objects, but the world of objects drains consciousness out of itself and thus vindicates its ultimate transcendence to constituting acts. Perhaps we could best summarize this particular argument with reference to Sartre's reflections on the phenomenological notion of the phenomenon. Phenomenology attempts to overcome the dualism of appearance and reality by absolutizing the phenomenon, by incorporating reality itself into the phenomenon (since all being is experienceable and all experience is of being). But it is phenomenology itself which shows that the phenomenon ("object" as experienced) is only a "*relative* absolute." It is a *relative* absolute in an *objective sense* because it is, at any given moment, only a partial, one-sided, perspectival presentation of an object which is implicated in a "infinite" horizon of other possible experiences of the same object, and of other objects in the world; it is a moment in an experiential process which will never be completed.

> Although an *object* may disclose itself only through a single *Abschattung,* the sole fact of there being a subject implies the possibility of multiplying the points of view on that *Abschattung.* This suffices to multiply to infinity the *Abschattung* under consideration. . . . Thus the appearance, which is *finite,* indicates itself in its finitude, but at the same time in order to be grasped as an appearance-of-that-which-appears, it requires that it be surpassed toward infinity.[30]

Let us try to be clear. Since consciousness necessarily transcends itself toward a world of objects which it *is not,* a world of objects which it does not simply produce and which themselves "fill" and "verify" its otherwise "empty" meaning-intentions, the reality of the world as the ground of all experience poses, even within phenomenology, a metaphysical question, by which I mean a reality-question, which is not answered by an ontology defined as "the science of objects." This is because of the fundamental and primordial ambiguity of the concept of object as at once a meaning-structure (*Sinn*) and the *leibhaftig* instantiation of this meaning-structure in intuitive encounters with the real *in person.* The being of the world transcends the constitution of the meaning of the world as a necessarily transcendent condition of experience and thus requires the recognition of a sense of "being" or reality which is not itself "object" but the underlying reality-condition of the being of all objects.

But there is an even stronger reason for saying that transcendental phenomenology leads us necessarily toward a metaphysical question which it cannot solve with its own resources. If we return to the notion of the phenomenon ("object" as experienced), we will see that it is *relative* not only in the "objective" sense described above, but that it is also relative in a *subjective sense,* namely, in the sense in which the very concept of the phenomenon of being presupposes someone *to whom* being appears. This, says Husserl, is transcendental subjectivity, and he leads us back beyond the constituted senses of the various regional ontologies to the *acts* of consciousness which are the necessary ontological foundation of these senses. But, if this is so, we see that ontology, conceived as the "science of objects," is not coextensive with the realm of the real. Husserl had said that "Object is everything and all that is." But the acts of consciousness which constitute objects are not themselves objects, since they are the prior conditions of the appearance of objects. The subject is never an object to itself; even when consciousness objectifies its own acts, taking its just completed past acts as objects of reflection, this "objectifying" consciousness is not itself an object to itself but the "absolute" subject.

Husserl's own evolution in this regard takes us in the direction of an ontology of consciousness. In the *Logical Investigations* he spoke of consciousness as the flowing stream of experience in the nonegological manner of James and the empiricists. In the *Ideas,* the ego became an "ego-pole" as the formal reference of all conscious acts. Then Husserl begins to speak of the "absolute being of the ego" and, in the *Cartesian Meditations*, to endow the ego with "habitualities" sedimented within the ego which are transcendent to given acts of consciousness and which can be uncovered only by a "genetic" analysis of the ego's own personal history. Finally, he terms the ego a "monad," and discovers the insuperable difficulties for a purely phenomenological ontology in attempting to account for monadic egology through the theory of the constitution of sense. No doubt, the ego "constitutes" itself (as well as other selves, the world, and intersubjectivity in general) but it cannot *account for* its own constituting activity. Or, to put it another way: transcendental consciousness finds itself confronted with a world of objects which are the correlates of its acts of perceiving, willing, imagining, thinking, desiring, evaluating, and so on, and, by reflection, it discovers that it itself has constituted these objects "in their sense." But what transcendental consciousness cannot discover, by reflection, is the brute, existential (and, in our sense, *metaphysical*) fact that it must exercise its subjective acts of constitution in just these ways (that is, in perceptual, affective, imagining, thinking acts) and no others.[31] This is why Merleau-Ponty, who worked out the impasses of the *Fifth Meditation* in his phenomenology of embodiment, began by showing that the "complete reduction" to experience was impossible, and it is why Heidegger replaced ontology as a "science of objects" by a *Fundamentalontologie* of *Dasein*. The ego, no less than the world, thus must ultimately be given an ontological status and pose reality-questions which are not answered within the original conception of phenomenological ontology as a science of objects.[32] In the end, phenomenology cannot escape "the metaphysical"; it can only bracket it.

William James spent twelve years working out a "scientific" psychology (*The Principles of Psychology*) which, according to his original plan and intention, would be completely free of metaphysical presuppositions. And, when he was finished, he had to admit that the end product was a psychology into which "the waters of metaphysical criticism leak at every joint." [33] Husserl was more successful: the waters of metaphysics leak in only at the two extremes: on the side of the world and on the side of the ego. Everything *in between* is safe from metaphysics.

NOTES

1. The background of these remarks is Errol E. Harris, "The End of a Phase," *Dialectica,* March 1963, XVII, 23–47. This is the most convincing examination and refutation of the metaphysical foundations of linguistic philosophy known to me.

2. The article, "The Nature of Metaphysics," in *The Encyclopedia of*

Philosophy, ed. Paul Edwards, New York, 1967, by W. H. Walsh gives an extremely valuable summary of contemporary opinion on this subject.

3. No doubt this is a somewhat arbitrary limitation of the range of metaphysics; I am not in any sense denying that there are other acceptable and fully justifiable senses in which metaphysics can be taken.

4. I mean that "ontology" in a post-Kantian sense cannot be a deductive body of necessary truths but that it nevertheless deals with the primary categories in a manner to be explained.

5. Husserl, *Ideas,* trans. W. R. Boyce Gibson, New York, 1931, p. 68 n.

6. Heidegger, *Vorträge und Aufsätze,* Pfullingen, 1954, pp. 71 ff. Herbert Spiegelberg translates Heidegger's *Überwindung* of metaphysics in the sense of "getting over a painful experience." *The Phenomenological Movement,* The Hague, 1960, I, 290.

7. *Logische Untersuchungen,* Tübingen, 1913, vol. I, chap. 11. Cf. Marvin Farber, *The Foundation of Phenomenology,* 2nd ed., New York, 1962, p. xlv.

8. Jean-Paul Sartre, *Being and Nothingness,* trans. Hazel Barnes, New York, 1965, p. xlv.

9. Husserl, *Ideas,* p. 67.

10. *Formale und transzendentale Logik,* Halle, 1929, p. 101. Cf. Gaston Berger. *Le cogito dans la philosophie de Husserl,* chap. 3, p. 54, cited by Gurwitsch, *Field of Consciousness,* p. 167: "Ce qui s' opère, dans la reduction phénoménologique, c'est moins le passage de l'objet au sujet, que la prise de conscience du monde en tant qu' objet, en tant que phénomène—*qua cogitatum—il y a une categorie plus profonde* que celle d'être ou de non-être, c'est celle d'objet pensé."

11. Phenomenology can be neither deductive nor inductive but must employ the special techniques of eidetic intuition or *Wesenschau.* The justification of this procedure would take us too far afield; a good discussion of the phenomenological method as compared and contrasted with the ordinary "inductive" methods of empiricism can be found in Maurice Merleau-Ponty, "Phenomenology and the Human Sciences," in *Primacy of Perception,* ed. J. M. Edie, Evanston, Ill., 1964, pp. 64 ff.

12. Husserl, *Ideas,* p. 67.

13. *Ibid.,* pp. 77–78.

14. *Ibid.,* p. 51.

15. *Krisis,* The Hague, 1954, section 51.

16. Cf. Martin Heidegger, *The Essence of Reasons (Vom Wesen des Grundes),* tr. Terrence Malick, Evanston, Ill., 1969, pp. 49 ff.

17. Cf. William James, "The Perception of Reality," in *The Principles of Psychology,* New York, II, 283 ff; Alfred Schutz, "On Multiple Realities," in *Collected Papers,* The Hague, I, 222 ff; Aron Gurwitsch, *The Field of Consciousness,* Pittsburgh, 1964, pp. 382 ff.

18. For a discussion of the weaker and the stronger forms of this thesis cf. J. M. Edie, "Necessary Truth and Perception: William James and the Structure of Experience," in *New Essays in Phenomenology,* Chicago, 1969. We are here leaving out of account the strong form of this thesis and presenting it only in its weaker version, which would be accepted by all phenomenologists.

19. Husserl, *Ideas,* p. 51. I may be forcing Husserl here to say more than he means, since he is here speaking of the natural attitude, but this thesis is later incorporated into transcendental phenomenology without any change of meaning insofar as the primacy of perceptual consciousness is concerned.

20. Erwin Straus, *The Primary World of the Senses,* New York, 1963.

21. Apart from Gurwitsch, I have in mind above all Sartre's contributions to the phenomenology of the imagination in the *Psychology of the Imagination,* New York, 1949, and *Being and Nothingness.*

22. Aron Gurwitsch, *The Field of Consciousness,* p. 388.

23. *Ibid.,* p. 389.

24. *Ibid.,* p. 391.

25. *Ibid.,* p. 404.

26. Among others. We have said nothing in this paper of evaluating acts, love, affectivity, feeling, history, culture, religion, etc.

27. Cf. Gurwitsch, *Field of Consciousness,* pp. 410–411. In my remarks I go considerably further than Gurwitsch himself wishes to go. He, for instance, does not make the analogy between the various orders of experience with reference to perception as the *proton analogon.*

28. This interpretation is in accord with that found in Iso Kern, *Kant und Husserl,* The Hague, 1964, p. 298, and Louis Dupré, "Husserl's Thought on God and Faith," in *Philosophy and Phenomenological Research,* 1968, p. 204.

29. *Cartesian Meditations,* The Hague, 1960, paragraph 8.

30. *Being and Nothingness,* xlvii. As is customary in Sartre the term *Abschattung* here is used in a loose sense, as an equivalent for "object," rather than as the perceptual presentation of an object from one side.

31. In making these remarks I am not laying claim to any great originality. Robert Sokolowski has admirably advanced an argument similar to this in his masterful analysis of *The Formation of Husserl's Concept of Constitution,* The Hague, 1964, especially in chap. V, "Genetic Constitution." Sokolowski, however, stops short of the bald metaphysical assertions of this paper.

32. For many important insights into this question, I am greatly indebted to Mr. Garry Breckon, who is presently writing a doctoral dissertation at Northwestern University on "Edmund Husserl's Conception of Ontology."

33. William James, *Psychology,* New York, 1892, p. 467.

Toward a Neo-Neoplatonism*

J. N. Findlay

This paper does not propose to add to the mountain of scholarly comment on Platonism or Neoplatonism, a mountain growing at every moment, in a manner as emptily threatening, as the population of the world. Scholarly comment is excellent when directed to thought that is philosophically important by those capable of truly entering into it but it is idle and pernicious when directed to thought that is no longer a live option, or which is not capable of being made such by the philosophical commentator. Plato studied as a man monumentally mistaken, and taken in by verbal deceits from which he was only in later life recovering, and studied, moreover, by methods and on assumptions of which he would not have had the faintest understanding, is a Plato not worth studying, nor do such studies of him deserve philosophical attention. Plotinus and Proclus, likewise, studied as mere elaborators and embroiderers of middle-period Platonism, who may have had a fortunate or unfortunate influence on Christian theology, are similarly no fit object of philosophical attention, except, perhaps, as part of a "history of ideas." My paper is based on a lifetime study of Platonic and Neoplatonic texts, and of Aristotle's writings on Platonism, read in the original; but whatever value it may have rests solely on its capacity to enter into what may be called the "message" of these texts, and to make of this a "live," and indeed a contemporary, option. With this goes an inevitable tendency to pass beyond them at certain points, or to practice a speculative

* To appear in *Ascent to the Absolute,* George Allen and Unwin (Humanities Press), and included with their permission.

"filling-in" of them, a tendency never experienced by those to whom they are irrevocably dead.

I may say that in speaking of a "Neo-neoplatonism" I wish to imply both that Plotinus and Proclus understood Plato very deeply, far more deeply, in fact, than those who erect their own incapacity for system and their horror of mysticism and metaphysics into philosophical virtues. I wish to suggest that a profitable reading of Platonism is one that may criticize, but which will never fail to consider, their interpretations, which in my view erred, not so much by adding mystical touches to Platonism, as by an unmystical hardening and freezing of its outlines, so that Proclus's *Elements of Theology* reads like, and has even been admiringly compared to, a treatise on set-theory. And my own attempts at a deepening reinterpretation of Platonism and Neoplatonism will take the form, not only of relaxing this hardness, but also of certain borrowings from Hegel, borrowings which are not so absurd when we reflect that Hegel professed to have found all the secrets of his dialectic in Plato's *Parmenides,* and that he devoted almost as much space to the Neoplatonists in his *Lectures on the History of Philosophy* as he did to Plato and Aristotle. Hegel as a thinker may have been born in the dark forests of German subjectivism, but by the turn of the century he had advanced, we may say, into Attic sunlight, the Idea, with its impersonal Hellenism, having taken over the functions of the Transcendental Ego or other forms of involuted Germanic interior self.

I may say further, to conclude this introduction, that I shall not hesitate to be dogmatic and also to show prejudice. I shall be dogmatic because, although everything I say could be documented, such documentation would not persuade those who are determined to see only a reflection of their own nullity in the shining works of antiquity. And I shall be prejudiced, even to the extent of using abusive metaphors, since the best way to bring home the sense and worth of Platonism and Neoplatonism is to pit it against such inadequate types of thought as Aristotelian individualism, Germanic subjectivism, Semitic-Protestant theology, let alone extreme empiricism and certain forms of atomistic analysis. This is after all only what Plato himself did when he showed up Protagoras in the *Theaetetus.* But I am not really as prejudiced and as committed as I shall appear to be for the purposes of this paper. I hope by my efforts to put the reader into a metaphysical posture into which few genuinely enter, and by so doing to make clear what sort of thing such a metaphysical posture really is, and what profit and illumination can be found from this posture.

I may say, first of all, that the sort of metaphysic I am interested in, for the purposes of this paper, is what has been called a *revisionary,* as opposed to a merely descriptive, metaphysic, one that proposes to consider the pattern of categories and categorial commitments in terms of which the round of being ought to be envisaged, and can with most profit and illumination be envisaged, rather than that in terms of which it is actually envisaged, and which for some is embalmed in the most ordinary use of our words. I do not myself believe that there is any firm scheme of ultimate philosophical categories and principles to be discovered in what we unthinkingly say, or in the makeshift procedures by which we were taught the use of our terms. What we really think when we say things, and what was really put across when we were taught to say things, comes out only in our thinking, considered use of terms, when the stream of immediate idiom suffers an arrest, as it readily does even in the case of quite ordinary speakers, and when the hesitations and gropings latent in all our utterances and in all teaching are allowed to come to the surface. Ordinary usage suffices to pin concepts down and to put them on the table for scrutiny, but it is only when discomfort and puzzlement have done their modifying work that anything like an acceptable system of categories or rules can emerge. That firm categories and commitments and "criteria" can be found by examining unthinking usage is a view which unthinking usage itself disdains: it is a philosophical rather than an ordinary opinion, and its actual fruits, its multiplication rather than its removal of difficulties, have shown it up as misguided. And it is even more misguided from a point of view like our own, which believes that only *very deeply* reflected on modes of speech and thought can claim "correctness" in any truly significant sense, just as only deeply pondered and deliberated lines of action and decision can claim to be right or wrong. I shall not waste my time or yours pitting myself against a waning fashion: the categories and categorial commitments that we ought to accept are not those that we do, even after some thinking, accept, and much less are they those that are to be collected from an examination of surface-usage and of surface teaching-devices. They are such as have, when we try them out, a certain deep illumination, which is not only superior to that of surface-speech but also to that of many alternative forms of considered speech and conception. What the criteria of such deep illumination may be is, of course, a matter that can and should be considered, and it is one that I myself have fairly often written and spoken upon from the standpoint of "logical values." I shall not, however, discuss this matter on this occasion, but rather consider a special case of illumination. I shall assume that we all know an illuminating conceptual realignment when we encounter it, even though we cannot always pin down the criteria for such illumination.

What then is the immense revisionary reappraisal which distinguishes a Platonic categorization of the world from an ordinary one? We do not give the right answer if we say with Aristotle, who was probably excluded from the inner Platonic assemblies and who was certainly incapable of a full entry into Platonic thought, that it consists in setting up *beside* the things that we ordinarily acknowledge *another set* of supposedly explanatory or causative entities which merely add to the number of what we originally had, and do not make them more countable or otherwise easier to deal with. This is utterly wrong since the precise point of Platonism is that one does *not* leave undisturbed the ontological claim of the ordinary things of this world but dissolves it entirely, since it regards the so-called things in the world as things only in a qualified, derivative sense, while the only true things in the world, the only things that truly are or can be, are natures or characters such as being alive, being just, being equal, and so forth. To the ordinary or the Aristotelian mind these natures or characters are things parasitic upon the individual things that exemplify them or instantiate them, they exist *in* the latter or are descriptive *of* them, while the individual things have no such dependence upon these natures or characters, but simply include them as their appanages. To Platonism, however, this ordinary view of things is completely misguided: it is the things of ordinary experience which are in truth parasitic upon the true things or forms, and which are merely the multitudinous reflections or instantiations of these true things and nothing in themselves at all. We must learn a new talk in which "being just" and "the just itself" are the truly substantival locutions while expressions of instantiation here or there, or now or then, merely qualify or modify such substantival locutions. And we must learn a new predication of such truly substantival locutions of themselves, which gives rise to no difficulties as long as it is not confused with the old predication which is merely the converse of instantiation. The inversion we are describing is abundantly spelled out in the *Republic, Timaeus,* and elsewhere, but never really got through to Aristotle, although it sufficed to make him a tortured dualist, one who believes in ordinary individual things and *also* in species or natures which in a paradoxical manner tell us *what* these individuals are—one would have thought that the plain answer to the question is that they are these or those individuals—and by buttressing his half-held individualism made him reject at least the *generic* universals to which Plato had given the same status as the specific ones. And the *other* categories of quality, quantity, and so on, are then all declared with satisfaction to be parasitic upon being in the primary sense, whether this last be that of the species or the individual. In this tortured ontology, which is rather a long worry than a definitive doctrine, we have strong indirect support for the basic positions of Platonism.

The basic strength of Platonism lies, however, in its appeal to our imagination, our understanding, and our sense of values. It appeals to our imagination since it recalls us from the dull identification of objects and the dull recognition of them as being thus and thus circumstanced, to the more colorful, immersed entry into their character and situation, which is in a sense the background possibility that identification and factual determination presuppose. It is by the generic content of our references and assertions that they manage to hit targets, and such content is soon seen to be a more interesting and fundamental thing than the dull targets that it enables us to hit or the mere fact of hitting them. Nothing is more insignificant than who or what a thing or person is and whether or not it or he is really thus or thus circumstanced, although it is of the most immense concern to all but the grossest dullard *what it is* to be this or that sort of thing or to be thus or thus circumstanced. Our understanding likewise speedily moves to the insight that, while we may be inclined to look in the direction of particular embodiment for a paradigm of what is, we soon find that we cannot successfully pin down such particularity in its purity, or identify *it* in varying contexts and occasions. All that is substantial, invariant in it is a pattern, a character, a set of suches which we hail and name on every occasion of their appearance. This character or pattern is all that we can grasp and handle in thought on many occasions, and introduce to and consider with others: the existence of an individual seems to be no more than the fact that certain identifiable, recognizable universals are instantiated and reinstantiated. The identity of such universals, so far from being a derivative, metaphorical sort of identity resting on resemblance or what not, reveals itself as in truth the paradigmatic sense of identity, to which all other senses of identity merely add complications or overtones. Only by practicing the Platonic inversion can we justify science and scientific knowledge, which would be quite impossible if we had to plumb individuals exhaustively or to make illegitimate extensions of what was true of them to other individuals similarly qualified. Our sense of values, moreover, as pervasively present in the intellectual as in any other sphere, makes us feel that what is standard, graspable, light-giving, or directive is not any and every mixed state or condition but only certain privileged sorts of state or condition, which stand out from others, and about which and between which other unprivileged states or conditions cluster and have their nearer or further place. The intelligible world is rendered intelligible by certain *prime* universals from which other universals *derive* their intelligibility. Equality as such is such a prime universal from which unlimited possibilities of greaterness and smallerness are divergent; being a whole number would be such a prime universal which further specifies itself in the countless precise numbers between which lie all the less savory possibilities of fractional divisibility whether rational or irrational; and justice or right dealing is likewise such a prime universal from which the infinite forms of the devious, the inequitable, and the shifty make their departure. (Our examples are, of course, Platonizing rather than textually Platonic.) And the prime intelligible states are thinly distributed and of some specially marked out type as opposed to the unnumbered states which lie between them or which deviate from them, and over which they give us intellectual or moral mastery. There is good ground, then, for inverting the normal individualistic view and for making so-called individuals, with all their deviant specificity, into mere variations upon standard patterns, parasitic on standard patterns as the latter have wrongly been thought to be parasitic on them. They are the roughage, the barnacles that a Form accumulates in the process of instantiation. Forms in Platonism are then no more a luxurious duplication of being than individual substances are a luxurious duplication in the metaphysic of Aristotle. In the latter metaphysic, qualities, relations, times, places and so on, have being only in the secondary sense of being how, toward what, when, where, and so on, primary substance is: in the Platonic metaphysic so-called individuals only have being as localized manifestations or near-manifestations of universals. The substance, the οὐσία, of the world, does not then lie in shadowy instantiations, but in the fixed, definite, changeless essences by which the shadows are cast, and of which they are merely the projections. That we give proper names to such projections does not make them into proper entities.

The ontology of Platonism is therefore an ontology of a thinly spread system of prime patterns, with a less confidently accepted set of interstitial patterns which deviate from these first and which are held in place by them. But to be a true ontology it must somehow include the half-being of the Forms' instantiations in the Forms' own being, and not merely place the latter alongside of and outside the former. They must depend on the Forms, be outlying appendages and offshoots of formal natures, they must in no sense be there independently or as of full right: to hold otherwise would be to Aristotelize both Forms and instances. We here see the meaning of a doctrine darkly obscure to Aristotle and to most modern commentators: the doctrine of the causality of the Forms. In an individualist ontology it is the merest confusion to ascribe some character of an individual to some independent, paradigmatic source: as Aristotle remarks, someone *like* Socrates could come into existence whether Socrates existed or not. But in a Platonist ontology instances of ø-ness are parasitic upon ø-ness itself, and it is only because there is a ø-ness itself that there can be localized sharings in it. It might be thought, and rightly thought, on Platonist principles, that this involves the being, in some sense of "being," of a universal recipient of instantiation, a repertory of "places," in which instantiations can take place, and in a sense be "individuated." Such a repertory is, of course, provided by the universal recipient, the enigmatically conceived Space of the *Timaeus*. But the *Timaeus* talks enigmatically about this recipient because it wishes to avoid giving full-scale ontological status to it: the recipient is even less real than the form-copies which flit in and out of it and which it seems to individuate. The recipient is in fact no more than a name for the multiple instantiability, the variously localized manifestability of the Forms, and this, it may be held, is of the Forms' essence, even if outlyingly so; it is a side, an aspect of the being of the Forms themselves. So much is this deeply accepted that talk of form-copies as entities distinct from Forms is comparatively rare in Plato: it is Proclus who first separates the unparticipated Form from its participated instance. Plato adheres in the main to a doctrine of "real presence": it is the Form *itself* which is present in its participants, and which makes them what we recognize them to be. And we may hold that the first part of the brilliant argument of the *Parmenides* is nothing but a warning against treating the instantiations of Forms as truly separate entities which have it in their power to rend apart the Forms of which they are dispersed "presences." Multiplicity of "presence" and diversity of location of the same "presence" are, we may say, part and parcel of what it is to be a Form, its extensional as opposed to its inner, intensional aspect: in neither case do we have to recognize genuine entities other than Forms. And a Form's genuine self-predication or being itself, while being in a sense the paradigmatic source of its connection with self in its instances, is none the less to be distinguished from the latter, and so will not give rise to an infinite regress. So much we may opine is to be understood by the doctrine of the Forms as causes: their instantiation is after a fashion an outlying phase of their being. And if it is still felt that there is something merely metaphorical about this doctrine, then we may remember that the Forms specify the Good, and that the Good is said, in more than one well-known passage, to lie behind the being and structure of the world of becoming, a doctrine also expounded, with much mythic detail, in the *Timaeus*. All this shows how seriously Plato took his formalist ontology, and how dynamic a role he gave to his Forms. If the Forms are the only things that there ultimately are, then whatever is done or undergone must in the last resort be done or undergone by *them*.

The Platonic ontology, of course, not only extends downward from Forms to their instances: it also extends upward from Forms to their supreme source. Distinct Forms are plainly specifications of Forms more generic, and generic Forms all specify a final transcendental Form of Unity or Goodness, which is not so much a specific Form as Formality or the Formal Status as such. Plato does not consider all the complications which might stem from the fact that Forms, although in some sense all falling under one ultimate super-Form, might none the less specify it in quite different ways, and so differ radically in category, and make differing contributions to the whole notional economy. Nor does he fully elucidate the "dialectic" by means of which the architecture of the world of forms must undoubtedly be established. It seems plain, however, that at a fairly early stage in his thought, this dialectic took the form of a preliminary mathematicization or Pythagoreanization of all the types and characters of things, and a subsequent properly dialectical attempt to show all these mathematical differentiations to be the deducible specifications of the principle of Unity or Goodness itself. The first phase was dianoetic or mathematical, and in some way involved the reduction of all qualitative distinctions, including those of psychology and ethics, to relations and proportions of numbers: the second stage, the properly dialectical, was to provide a complete *philosophy* of all these numbers and relations of numbers. As regards the first stage, it is by no means unintelligible to ourselves that being water, or earth, or air, or wood, or gold, or purple, or angry, or intelligent, or a man, or a dwarf-star, or an electron are all basically a matter of specific proportions or quantitative measures; this is the creed of modern science, for which we need not here argue. And that even the *values* of action, life, and theory have a basis in number and measure is a view that many have found appealing. The *Republic,* the *Timaeus,* and the *Philebus* as well as other writings make plain what Plato understood by the reduction of Forms to Numbers, no matter how little Aristotle was able to make of his doctrine. And once the requisite numbers and numerical relations are arrived at, and consolidated as the "hypotheses" of the sciences, it becomes the task of Dialectic Proper to show how they all "proceed" from the basic form of Unity or Good.

The main lines of this procession are not in doubt: they involve the imposition of Unity or Limit on a "recipient" characterized by a hydralike multiplicity of dimensions and by an indefinite capacity for quantitative excess. Just as the world of instances presupposed a recipient which is in the end no more than a name for the multiple instantiability of the Forms, so the world of Forms presupposes a recipient which is no more than another name for the quantitative specifiability of the Super-Form beyond them. The two recipients are in fact one and the same,[1] as Aristotle engagingly tells us in *Metaphysics* 988a and as we can see from meditating on the *Philebus*: both are principles of indefinite quantity, variously specified as a many and a few, a more and a less, a long and a short, a broad and a narrow, a deep and a shallow, a quick and a slow, a hot and a cold, an acute and a grave, and so on: a principle or principles which, in association with a principle of Unity or Limit, can "generate" all cases of quantitative pattern, all the "Forms" that there can be. This second, transcendental recipient principle is, however, as much parasitic upon the principle of Unity in the world of Forms as it was in the world of the senses. It is completely mastered and molded by the latter. It can in fact be held to be no more than a name for the inherent specifiability of absolute unity, its necessary descent into an unending range of distinct quantitative patterns. All these doctrines, so mystifying to those who have never advanced beyond the notion of a set of disjoined, piecemeal universals, largely associated with Socratic virtues, and who have failed to see that Plato's whole endeavor was to *unify* the possibilities of being into one single, systematically ordered picture, assume comprehensibility when Plato's endeavor, and its Pythagorean background, becomes clear. This endeavor, obviously lies behind the *Republic* as much as any, later, reported teachings. And it may be argued that the second half of Plato's *Parmenides* is nothing but a semi-jocose, literary statement of this endeavor, in which the two transcendentals of Unity and Unbounded Quantity play an elaborate game with one another, sometimes making interesting nonsense in their apartness, and sometimes joining in fecund union to generate the mathematical dimensions of being, sometimes revealing their categorial character by remaining indifferent to flat denials of their own being, sometimes by making use of such denials to pull the house of reason down. And the dialogue ends in a superb sentence which whatever else it may be is not meant to express a *reductio ad absurdum* but Plato's deepest sense of the meaning of the world: that Unity both lies apart from, and also is necessarily present in, all the possible, incompatible variety that there can be in the world.

Plato's deepest intentions plainly also involved the development of a theory of mind which was no mere excrescence on the theory of Forms, but part and parcel of the latter. Even in the *Republic* the same specification of Goodness that generates the universe of Forms generates the possibility of states of mind that take cognizance of them, the two being in fact merely sides of one and the same process, while in the *Sophist* and also in the *Parmenides* and the *Philebus* [2] we have the recognition of a universal mindfulness and livingness, Zeus's kinglike life and mind, which in a sense pervades the whole realm of Forms, and expresses its living unity, its interconnections of relevance, and its paradigmatic realization of Active Intelligence as such. This mindfulness and livingness is, of course, not to be confused with its instantiation in our soul or in any other soul: it is the pattern, the eternal Idea of the latter. But it is *present* in our souls and their activities as other universals are present in their instances, and such presence must, as in other cases, be part and parcel of its being. The intermediate, observer soul of the *Phaedo* must therefore plainly have its own representation in the formal world that it contemplates, and we therefore find in Plato a beginning of the distinction between the noetic and the noeric, betwen infinitely diversified objectivity and the subjectivity which is correlated with it, which was to be developed by Proclus, and perhaps carried still further by Husserl. In their doctrine of Νοῦς the Neoplatonists merely worked out what was plainly implied by Plato, and those who find their elaborations unnecessary are those who have not understood what Plato was basically intent on: not the construction of a set of isolated conceptual meanings, but of a whole map of the intelligible universe of possibilities seen from the standpoint of a paradigmatic intelligence that can compare and integrate them all. This living thought-map is also plainly conceived to be the source of such wisdom and insight as seeps down into our souls, and it certainly seeped down, in curiously coarsened form, in the Aristotelian doctrine of the Active Intelligence.

I have been very Neoplatonist in my interpretation of Plato and I can therefore be much more brief in my appraisal of the Neoplatonists. Plotinus, I consider, very strangely combined the capacity to work out the plain implications of Plato in endless scholastic detail, with an originality which some would connect with his mysticism, although I myself would connect it with his new line of logic. While I would criticize Plotinus for his scholasticism, which at many points gives undue fixity to the thoughts of Plato, I would admire him for his logical innovations. I shall try to make plain what I mean on both of these heads. As regards the first, it is characteristic of Plotinus that he accepts and canonizes a feature of Platonism in respect of which it is least strong, that he practically turns a difficulty and a weakness into a principle of explanation. This kind of inversion is a device of philosophers at all times, and often leads to an illuminating change of perspective, but in the case of Platonism it embalms and hardens its worst features. In Platonism there is plainly a certain necessity in the procession of "lower" principles from "higher" ones: there is a certain generosity in the higher genera, a freedom from "envy," which insures their communication to lower orders of half-being. There is, however, a pervasive suggestion that necessity does not amount to need, and there is a faint air of misfortune and discredit, even of guilt, in the descent into instantiation. The happiest and purest of philosophers may have to serve an apprenticeship in the cave, but the best state for them will be one where they are able to contemplate Forms shorn of all perturbing instances. In Plotinus necessity without need becomes a central principle of explanation, and it becomes a theorem that the *less* one requires anything beneath one or dependent on one, the *more* will one spawn such interior dependents. One becomes like a tropical fish dropping infinite seed into the waters without concern or interest, or like a narcissistic woman coldly inspiring an infinity of unrequited passions, and the like. The conception is as strange as it is unedifying: it explains by nonexplanation. It is as if one sought the cause of some great social movement in the fact that no one wanted it and that nothing led up to it.

There is, moreover, on reflection, nothing specially august, nothing σεμνόν, in the removal of instances: being a goat-stag is not of surpassing interest in that nothing fulfills such a description. While what is unexemplified, for example, perfect circularity, *may* be of surpassing interest in view of the constant approximations to it, its lack of illustration none the less represents a poverty, a defect, and a life spent among uninstantiated universals, or in ignorance of their instantiation, would be as dull as a life spent in conversing in uninterpreted calculi. And what is true of instantiation is likewise true of specification: being numerous is interesting and exciting since such an infinity of specific numbers fall under it, being beautiful is august since it can be carried out with such typical variety, and so on. No one denies that there is an élan, a fascination, in steeping oneself in Number or Beauty. But despite the appeal of the Genus, and the dubious cogency of modern rejections of self-predication, it is *in* their instances and *in* their specifications that universals live, and the most profound immersion in an essence as such involves a sidelong awareness of *possible* species or instances.

None the less it is precisely such a shearing of the generic from the specific which Plotinus systematically practices, and what is for many a sign of his admirable remoteness from "pantheism." Unity Itself is simply Unity Itself, of which nothing whatever can be properly predicated: we are back in the half-truth of the first hypothesis of the *Parmenides,* regarding which the Platonic interlocutor remarks that he does not think it can be true. We proceed thereupon to the infinitely rich field of the specifications of Unity Itself, the Forms or cases of Being, of which the Shepherd, to use a Heideggerian phrase, is Intelligence or Mind as such, the omnipresent, eternal possibility of thinking which at all points matches the variety of what can be thought. But this noetic-noeric realm derives its richness, not so much from the Unity lying above it, as from *its own* attempts at a hermeneutic applied to that inscrutable Unity. It is, moreover, a realm given over to "eternity," which means, despite protests as to its livingness, that all in it is frozen into lifelessness. An unchanging, perfect intellectuality confronts a perfect round of unchanging intelligibles. The lesson has not been learnt that the preciousness of the eternal lies in its revelation through, and in contrast with, the changing. And while Plato showed some disposition to find an interstitial place in his Form-world for the ignoble, the botched, and the deviant, Plotinus admits none but Forms of prime lineage, so that his noetic assemblies become rather like the star-studded gatherings of some hostesses, wholly dazzling, quite without contrast, and not a little dull. If the descent to what is individual has a reflection yonder, there is nothing that reflects a descent to the ignoble. Of course, beneath this realm we have the realm of Soul, where living thought and action occurs, and where there is also stimulating decline toward the sensory. The realm of Soul is, however, responsible for its own fun, even if its fun may be an attempt to mirror in the servants' hall the frozen aristocratic relationships above. And below Soul lies Nature, creative without caring to create, lost in admiration of a life of thought which in its turn cares nothing for it. I shall go no further. I have deliberately exaggerated the curious unilateralism of Plotinian concepts, so as to bring out their deep perversity. They satisfy certain instincts of self-prostration, but they do so at the cost of systematically affronting our understanding.

At once, however, we come to another side of the Plotinian coin: its profound and living logic. In the system of Plotinus there is literally no work for the ordinary notion of diversity to do. Things are in a sense other than one another, but such otherness never excludes a deeper identity. The realm of pure intellection does not merely lie outside of the Supreme Unity: it aspires toward it and is in a sense always in touch with it. And the objects of intellection and the intellect which contemplates them are not mutually exclusive: each is in a sense the total intellectual system, even if with some special emphasis. The logic of systematic interpenetration has never been more sublimely stated than in some of the Plotinian accounts of the intelligible world. And the realm of Soul, with its changeful temporality, does not merely lie outside of the realm of intellect, but aspires toward it and enters into it: eternity becomes fully significant through its pervasion of time. In the same way Nature in its blind creativity is in its own fashion practicing the contemplation practiced yonder by Soul and by Mind. Not only in the realm yonder is "each all, and all all, and the glory infinite," but "everything yonder is also here." There is nothing remote and alien even about the Supreme Unity: He is what we find when we enter most deeply into ourselves. In this magnificent denial, that of diversity as understood in formal logic —which of course some will not find magnificent at all—Plotinus removes the disadvantages of his system: the scholastic hedges melt away, and the lifelines to the Absolute become open. We have achieved the thought that is characteristic of philosophy as opposed to that of the dianoetic sciences. If we turn from Plotinus to Proclus, the other great διάδοχος of Plato, much the same is true. The scholasticism is at times almost more preposterous in its rigidity, but there is also a great overriding of the firm distinctions drawn. There is a stress on the immense *power* or *might* of the higher hypostases, a might proportional to their approach to simplicity, and on the manner in which this might is outpoured as a sort of providential care over the lower reaches of creation. We are moving into a region where Aquinas will afterward construct his theology, where the infinite variety of mind and body will exist "as if conflated" (to quote Dante) in the simplicity of God.

All that we have said does not, however, affect the fact that there is something unsatisfactory about this whole Neoplatonic restatement of Plato: there is an imperfect fusion between its structure of unilateral dependence and the deep identity which pervades all its hierarchically ordered members. It has no real, no understandable procession comparable to the moment of return which is so emphatic in it. To continue the Platonic succession further one must move over the centuries to early nineteenth-century Germany where Hegel, newly emancipated from the subjectivism of Kant and Fichte and from the darkly neutralistic Spinozism of Schelling, suddenly took up the Greek thread and became Plato's greatest διάδοχος. Greek thought had, we may say, a renaissance on that remote German soil, in the Walpurgis midnight of German romanticism, much as Greek aesthetic sensibility had reflowered in the *Iphigeneia* of Goethe and the poems of Hölderlin. Hegel's following of Plato is evinced in his choice of the *Begriff,* the Notion, as his categorial Absolute, of which the Idea is the mature phase: the former being a principle of Universality which also declares itself in Specificity and Individuality, while the latter further embodies the Livingness and the Mindedness in which Universality declares itself supremely. In this new Germanic Platonism the defects of the old Platonism and Neoplatonism were cunningly removed: the Kantian interest in the empirical, and the Fichtean interest in the concretely moral, and the Schellingian interest in the natural had all made their precious contribution. Individualization, Instantiability is a "moment" of the *Begriff* to be set beside its Universality and its Specifiability as something organically part of it and without which it would not make sense. And the *Begriff* has, further, all the causative, dynamic quality which Plato only halfheartedly attributed to his Forms: objects in the world develop and behave according to the *Begriff* which is instantiated in them. In the Idea, furthermore, the mature form of the *Begriff,* all the patterning of conscious experience which had been excogitated by Kant, Fichte, and

Schelling becomes part and parcel of the *Begriff*. The *Begriff* essentially divides into a subjective and an objective phase: it involves, on the one hand, interior subjectivity, ready to impose universals on, or to extract them from, a preexistent objective order, and, on the other hand, an objectivity, ready to have such universals imposed upon it, or extracted from it. And what emerges is the necessary accommodation of the one to the other: the Idea is not merely Intellection as such, or Intelligible Objectivity as such, but Intellection finding itself in Intelligible Objectivity, the Idea of a thinkingness which both involves and overcomes objective otherness. What Plotinus had worked out in his account of the intelligible world, and what went back to Plato's account of the Form of Good as a source both of knowable universals and of their knowability by minds, thus received a final working out, and not, be it noted, as some external reflection upon it, but as something demanded by and developed out of its structure.

We may further see in the Hegelian *Entaüsserung,* or self-alienation of the Idea in Nature and finite Spirit, a mature form of the Neoplatonic emanation, and of the Platonic metaphors from which this was derived. The Absolute Idea releases its moment of *Besonderheit* or Specificity, which is also its moment of intuitive sensuousness, in the spatiotemporal order of Nature, much as the Demiurge, the Ideas conceived as agency, is responsible for projecting images of the Forms into the impassive medium of Space. The *Entaüsserung* of Hegel has, however, this great superiority over the emanation of Plato and Plotinus, that it is *needed* as well as necessary: without a descent into instantiation, an embodiment in actual instances, whether natural or spiritual, the Idea would die from very need, like the God of Angelus Silesius. Hegel sees that it is only by being exemplified in specific and individual forms that the Idea can be the unifying peak and center of the whole system, and that it can return to itself, not in empty ecstasy, but in the truly mystical experiences of artistic creation, religious worship, and philosophical illumination. The two systems have the same teleological structure, but in Hegel the teleology works both ways: not only does Nature aim at Soul, and Soul at Intellect, and Intellect at the supraintellectual Unity, but the Hegelian Idea also fulfills itself in the total logical system of concepts and categories, and the latter fulfills itself in the conscious experiences of spiritual beings, and these last require the natural, corporeal order in which they can embody themselves and out of which they can gradually develop their interior life. And not only does Hegelianism incorporate the Other in the most intimate being of the Idea, as Plato does too in his conception of the Great and Small, the indefinite materiality which is part of the being of the Forms, but it also incorporates the whole hierarchical arrangement and movement of the system in its supreme Category. The Hegelian Idea gathers up in itself the whole ideal dialectic of the logical categories, and the whole real dialectic of Nature and History: in all that issues from it we have only itself.

We suggest accordingly that it is in Hegelianism that Platonism finds its highest fulfillment: in an Idea developed into an ideal world of specific conceptions, arranged in an order, not merely of generality, but of inclusiveness and surmounting of opposition, and terminating in the idea of a subjectivity which truly meets itself in and through a matching objectivity, such an Idea being, moreover, inseparable from an actual carrying out in the ordered array of natural forms and the living, developing, historical consciousness of men. I do not, however, wish to suggest that the fulfillment is all on one side, and that the Germanic Platonism absorbed and resumed all that had been excogitated at Athens and Alexandria and in the Roman Campagna. For the Germanic Platonism suffers from a deep fault which the passing years have made all too evident: it is too entirely this-worldly, too tied down to place and to period, too deeply reliant on actual arrangements in which we can no longer trust. It rightly sees in Nature and History the eternal strategy of the Idea, but it is misguided in thinking that the whole of this strategy can be dug out here, and that, moreover, in the trivial span of centuries that we call "world history." We live, moreover, in a period full of menace, not merely of the relatively supportable menace of the destruction of Spirit by Nature, but of the intolerable menace of the destruction of Spirit by Spirit, which accords ill with the optimistic teleology projected both by the Platonic Form of the Good and the Hegelian Idea. It is not a question of interstitial evil, parasitic upon goodness, and bound to wither away through its own inner contradictoriness, but of evil so mighty that it seems likely to destroy all in destroying itself. It is here, I think, that we should take seriously, and not as a mere myth, the otherworldly prospects offered us by Platonism and Neoplatonism, the prospect of a spectrum of states leading from sensuousness and corporeality and this-world immersion to an increasing attenuation of these things, until we end in the pure enjoyment of the total gist and sense of the world, and of the supreme Unity in which that gist culminates. Even if the noetic order is as much dependent on instantial existence as the latter is dependent on it, it may still represent a genuine and specific type of experience and being, characterized by interpenetration rather than diremption, which mystics experience from time to time without always fully understanding its peculiar logic, but which we may hope to experience more perfectly when we lose our present bodies. Now I shall discuss what I shall call the "cortical predicament," a predicament which I regard as the source of most that is most darkly miserable, but also of much that is most radiantly glorious, in the human condition.

The Orphics who inspired the Pythagoreans who inspired Plato saw the source of man's problems in the body: σῶμα-σῆμα—the body is a tomb. I do not myself believe that there is anything wrong about having a body: I should be very sorry not to have one. A body enables one to express oneself palpably, to be there for one's friends, to illustrate meanings in a manner in default of which they would not be meanings at all. Our misfortune is not in having a body, but in having the sort of body we do have, incorporation in which is the very essence of cave-life, of existence "down here." For the bodies we have are not tenanted solely by ourselves: they are dense with a population of other tenants and a noisy and scrofulous batch of tenants at that. Sometimes it is really remarkable that we can hear ourselves speak. There are the innumerable cells and organs, doing their work consciously or unconsciously, but certainly not by any grace of *our* direction, and there are the lower-grade atoms and molecules, no doubt grumbling at being subordinated by organic order at all, and having their grim revenge in the final triumph of death. I myself —for I am a hylozoist and an animist—believe that all these beings have their own life and consciousness. I believe, further, that this conscious life is in some ways superior to our own. They are less cut off from environing objects which have not the distanced character for them that they have for us: they are less cut off from one another. Solipsism and scepticism about matter are not possible at their level, since the diremptions that make these kinds of theory possible do not exist there. And I believe that they enjoy undoctored sensations in a manner that some philosophers have thought that we ought to or once did: the sensational life of the retina, for instance, must be positively famous. We, however, like a lot of fainéant aristocrats fallen on evil times, live in a true ivory garret in the grey matter beneath the skullbones. Here ready-made views of things are handed up to us, with interpretative slants put upon them by our minions and not at all by ourselves. Our minions likewise manage to filter that living past that we always carry about with us, and decide what we shall, in our ivory garret, be able or unable to bring to mind. In some inscrutable fashion, the revival and use of our past has become bound up with certain cortical excitations, much as a lecturer's power to give a lecture may be bound up with certain often silly, poorly set-down notes. These minions have the power, after a fashion, to separate us from ourselves, and in old age effectively do just this. Who has not witnessed the pathos of some elderly friend or parent groping for words and meanings, which the decay of a cerebral transcript has rendered inaccessible? Worst of all, these grey minions, who as intelligences grasp little, and as grey cells grasp nothing whatever, have managed to corrupt philosophers into believing that it is *they* who do all our referring and inferring and understanding and abstracting and remembering and deciding and loving and hating and so on, and that our categories and norms are built into *their* structure. Whereas all these beliefs are not merely false, but categorially absurd: if the grey cells are considered merely as grey cells, no one can attach even the slightest sense to such beliefs, and they merely create an asylum of ignorance and pseudo-explanation worse than any believed in the heyday of the soul. To be crucified in the cortex is, among other things, to be subject to all the problems of philosophy, for cortical life means precisely that we can never fully document or authenticate or explicate all that we know and remember and understand. If the cortex thus makes philosophy and all the other great rational enterprises possible, it remains arguable that the perfection of these enterprises will lead us beyond the cortex. We shall then have bodies, as long as we want them, but they will be our own bodies, pejoratively called shades, that will express our every whim and stirring; we shall have a concentrated, gistful grasp of things remote and complex that will not need to be spelled out in laborious inferences or explorations, and we shall be able to share one another's feelings at will in a manner which will make solipsism a laughable superstition. All this has been described in some of the most unforgettably gorgeous passages in Plotinus, and it is all much too good not to be true. And it makes it possible to believe in an ultimate, overall coincidence of Goodness and Being, and so lends credibility to the Platonic-Hegelian metaphysic that we have been considering. That this is the best metaphysic may be a matter of inherent logic, but will none the less be best seen in connection with the facts; and the totality of facts, that it orders, and many of these facts will not be accessible until the cortex and its deceits have been laid aside. If anyone wishes to pursue these topics further, I shall refer him to the sixth chapter of my *Transcendence of the Cave* which deals with "Otherworldly Geography." This chapter contains the whole message of my Gifford Lectures on Cave-life, but it is inconspicuously placed in an obscure part of the volume, as I feared that it would otherwise prove a grave source of intellectual scandal. It has in fact been misunderstood, and I wish here to say that it is based neither on speculation nor clairvoyance, but purely on philosophical argument. If you are interested in that argument, I must refer you to the peccant chapter.

I wish, in conclusion, to say something about the religious value of the metaphysic I have been elaborating, a question important for me since I regard religion as the most embracing of the rational enterprises, one that engages the heart and the will as well as the mind. I give it as the verdict of my feeling that only a Form, something basically universal, although uttering itself in the individual and the specific, can be truly adorable, can in any way deserve the name of "God." One cannot rationally worship this or that excellent thing or person, however eminent and august: only Goodness Itself, Beauty Itself, Truth Itself, and so on, are rationally venerable, and to bow one's knee to an instance is to commit idolatry. And whatever philosophers may say of the fallacy of self-predication, it remains plain that an αὐτοεκαστόν, or each thing itself, is what it is more ultimately and absolutely than the instances which exemplify it: it is in fact the inexhaustible source from which instantiations flow and of which they necessarily fall short. And the various prime αὐτοεκαστά all cohere together and form a single rounded ideal as is not possible in their instances. All this is something which the Jews, with their fine sense of idolatry but imperfect theology, only dimly perceived, but which was always perfectly plain to Plato, who may therefore be hailed as the father of all rational theology. And we may be glad that the deceit of a Syrian monk enabled this wisdom to fertilize the West, which could take from a bogus Areopagite what it would never have taken from Proclus. Of the deceit of this monk one may say: *O felix culpa quae tantam ac talem nobis tradidit theologiam.* It was this Platonic theology which is responsible for the note of deep rational liberalism that one repeatedly encounters in Aquinas. And perhaps it even influenced John XXIII, when he said that the Russians, however much they might deny God, could never free themselves from the values and the influence which were from God Himself. Without this Platonic infusion we should all be foundering in the semidarkness of such as Kierkegaard. It will be plain that I am a prejudiced person, and that I do not admire many things that many others admire. But I remain spiritually in orbit about quite a number of very different luminaries, even if my central sun remains Platonic.

NOTES

1. It is perhaps wrong to identify the two recipients: the one instantiates and the other specifies, and they are analogous rather than the same.
2. *Philebus,* 30d.

Part II

METAPHYSICS AND THE DISCIPLINES

The Levels and Objectivity of Meaning

James M. Edie

It is an underlying or "hidden" premise of this paper that a given phenomenological analysis, if it is properly completed, leads necessarily to ontological questions.[1] The phenomenology of language (or expression, or meaning—taking "meaning" as a verb as well as a noun) leads necessarily to the question of the ontology of meaning. But this is an underlying or "hidden" premise which we shall, in this paper, attempt to hide by applying some strict phenomenological brackets to all the possible Platonic and Meinongian ghosts which the reader may sense lurking in the shadows, in order to focus on the meaning of language in an ontologically neutral sense. We shall begin by distinguishing three levels of meaning in language, without claiming that these present us with an exhaustive catalogue or map of all the meaning-functions of speaking.

IMMANENT MEANING: LANGUAGE AS A PHONOLOGICAL SYSTEM

Merleau-Ponty has, perhaps more clearly than any other phenomenologist, and certainly better than Husserl, orchestrated the first level. His philosophy of language was, in this respect, inspired by Saussure and structural linguistics, and to some extent shares its defects.[2] The great achievement of structural linguistics (in the work of persons like Saussure, Jacobson, Trubetskoy, Hjelmslev, and so on) was to discover, just on the surface level of the taxonomic analysis of language, that a given linguistic system (*langue*) follows strict syntactic and paradigmatic regularities which can be formulated in terms of phonological and morphological rules distinctive of that language. These rules are more basic, more "automatic," and more "impersonal" than the syntactical rules which govern the use of language for the purposes of representing meanings, expressing attitudes, or addressing oneself to another. They are discovered simply by the analysis of empirically given languages taken just in their "objective" aspect of historically given data, as something to be described, as it is, without reference to any higher function or purpose it may have (such as, for instance, in the *intention to speak*). To take language in this empirically neutral way as a "natural" object, is to take it, in the words of Saussure, as *langue* and not as *parole* (or as the actual utilization of a given language by a speaker for the purposes of signifying, naming, expressing something, and so on). *La parole* is a speaker's *use* of a given language here and now for purposes of expression. But, in order to speak, the speaker must be in possession of a *langue,* and this language is an already instituted and available system of phonological, morphological, and syntactical rules which (logically) preexist any present and actual use of the language by an individual speaker.

If we isolate *language,* then, as a finite and closed system of phonetic elements (phonemes, sound segments) which follow certain highly restrictive phonological rules (according to sequence patterns, complex plays of oppositions, arrangements into forms or morphemes, and so on), we find that language exists, in the first instance, beneath the level of speech as a highly organized system independently of its use to signify anything other than itself. The phonemes (or as is now preferred "sound segments") which constitute the various restricted phonological systems permitted in any given natural language have no meaning in themselves. This is to say that they are not truly *signs,* and, on this level, the ancient Aristotelian definition of language in terms of the *sign-meaning* or *sign-thing signified* dichotomy has no application. The sound segments which constitute a linguistic system refer to nothing extralinguistic; they signify only themselves and their relationship to all the other elements of the given language. Each phoneme takes its place in the phonological system as an element sufficiently distinct to be distinguished from all others in the same system and capable of being related to others according to a system of phonological rules which apply only within the system and refer to nothing outside the system itself. In other words, each phoneme takes its place in the phonetic system as the *diacritical element* necessary, according to rule, to distinguish each "form" and eventually, in combinations, each word from another.

The morphological rules according to which morphemes and words distinguish themselves from one another as arrangements of sound segments according to such rules constitute the "structural system," which defines a given language and distinguishes it from any other. (Saussure: *Le langage n'est pas une substance mais une forme.*) Each element in the system, and ultimately each word, must be defined in terms of its relation to all the other elements of the system, and this is why it is unnecessary to look for the meaning of words—on this level—in anything transcendent to the system itself. The linguistic convention which defines a given language institutes itself as a meaning insofar as meaning is understood "structurally," that is, as a system of phonological and morphological rules. This is also why a language cannot be learned "by parts" but must in some sense be learned "as a whole," that is, because the elements of a language have no sense (and make no sense) when separated from the distinctive rules of combination which hold throughout the language globally.[3] A language, as *langue,* is, then, a finite system of word-sounds arranged according to "diacritical" variations and regularities necessary and sufficient to distinguish each word from every other and permit it a place in the system. The only *meaning* of language, on this level of analysis, is contained within itself. As Saussure used to like to say, language is "un système où tout se tient." Approached just as a morphological system based on phonological rules, language carries its meaning wholly within it; it has an *immanent* meaning distinctive of its own style, of its own intonation, of the peculiar play of distinctive propositions which distinguish it from every other as *one* way, among many, "to sing the world."[4]

There is here no "deep structure" of language; we are on the phonological surface which distinguishes each natural language from every other as a highly selective and restrictive use of sounds (chosen arbitrarily from among the much vaster phonetic possibilities of our natural speech mechanisms as such, that is, all the sounds the human organism *can* produce), all of which refer to themselves and one another through their value in use (*valeur d'emploi*) in a systematic manner. Thus, although sometimes very great in number, the words which constitute the lexicon of any natural language are a finite system of words formed according to the "closed" phonological rules of that particular language, all of which are definable in terms of other words taken from the same lexicon. Though the number of words capable of being formed in accord with the phonological style of a given language is indefinite, and may appear as an "infinity" with respect to the two or three score phonemes used for their production, we know that the vocabulary of no natural language is actually infinite and that it is "closed" in a manner analogous to and determined by the phonological system. Both on the level of morphemes and on the level of words all the forms of a given language refer to and presuppose one another in fixed ways.

It is this aspect of language which enables us to understand the intralinguistic or "syncategorematic" functions of words.[5] Taken categorematically, a word is "paired with" and refers to something other than itself, that is, a meaning, a thing, a mood, and so on. But there seem to be many words which do not refer to anything, as, for instance, the word "to" in the sentence *She stoops to conquer,*[6] or the interrogative particle *ne* in Latin,[7] or the syncategorematic words for conjunction, negation, disjunction, and so on. Some linguists say simply that such words have no meaning,[8] but it would be better to say that their meaning is "immanent" to the linguistic system itself. They *do* have meaning insofar as there are clear grammatical rules for their use, and their omission results, in a given language, in ungrammatical sentences. But it is not only that such words have an intralinguistic function, that is, they take their meaning from the place they hold in the system as a whole, but that *all* words have something of this immanent function of deriving their meaning from the positions they are *able* to occupy according to the rules of the given language. Thus Merleau-Ponty can write: "Each word *has* meaning only insofar as it is sustained in this meaning-function by all the others. . . . For a word to keep its sense it has to be held in place by all the others. . . ." [9] We reach here the most important contribution of structural linguistics to the theory of meaning. Merleau-Ponty has, perhaps better than anyone else, brought this aspect of language to the fore in his studies on the learning of language and in his argument for the "immanent," "gestural," and "affective" meanings of words (which are, at the same time, as he sees it, arguments *against* the possibility of a universal and eidetic grammar for all languages).[10]

Both Saussure and Merleau-Ponty like to say that words are defined less in terms of their "meaning" (which would require taking them as signs) than by their "value" in usage (*valeur d'emploi*).[11] In his remarks on babbling in children, and on the "inner speech" of adults (which is but a continuation of childish babbling),[12] Merleau-Ponty is especially sensitive to what we might call the sound-sensuous meanings of words, the meanings which are not yet distinguished from the phonological patterns themselves but which are realized precisely in the verbal gesticulation of uttering sounds and noises in rhythmic and patterned forms. This is perhaps similar to what mystics like Boehme referred to as "the language of Adam"—the "sensual speech" (*die sensualische Sprache*) of self-expression which takes place beneath the level of the concept and the idea.[13] There is a meaning immanent to language, writes Merleau-Ponty, of which conceptualism and intellectualism know nothing (or which they have forgotten): "The meaning of words must be finally induced by the words themselves, or more exactly, their conceptual meaning must be formed by a kind of subtraction from a *gestural meaning* which is immanent to the word. . . ." [14]

> And elsewhere: There is a languagely (*langagière*) meaning of language which effects the mediation between my as yet unspeaking intention and words, and in such a way that my spoken words surprise me myself and teach me my thought. Organized signs have their *immanent meaning,* which does not arise from the "I think" but from the "I am able to." [15]

The word, taken just as an element within the language of which it is an integral part, is a "sign" not of *something else* but of all the other "signs" which constitute the language as a whole, and, if they are then taken to allude to the world, it is as a global whole, all together, that they serve to make the whole present to our thought. On this level, but only on this level, the cultural relativism of a Benjamin Whorf makes sense and we can agree with Merleau-Ponty that no language is completely translatable into another because at least one thing, namely, the meanings of the phonological system itself, must be left behind in any translation. This discovery of the importance of the "immanent," "affective," or "existential" meaning of words—a meaning which is not "rendered by" but which "inhabits" words—[16] is at once one of the greatest originalities in Merleau-Ponty's contributions to the phenomenology of language and the source of his misunderstanding and denigration of the more "logical" and "grammatical" discussions of language by Husserl, particularly insofar as these involved the project of discovering "grammatical universals" common to all languages.[17] It led him into the kind of exaggeration we are accustomed to associate with Wittgenstein on another level: "The word is a *tool, defined by a certain use,* without our being capable of formulating this use in an exact conceptual formula." [18] Merleau-Ponty is, on the whole, more concerned with the process of learning a language and with what Chomsky calls "linguistic competence" in its dumb, prereflexive sense than with describing and distinguishing levels of meaning; he is more concerned with the "miraculous" emergence of words within a preverbal and even nonverbal process of oral gesticulation (governed by rules unconcerned with and insufficient to account for meaning in any categorial sense), that is to say, with the primary phonological systems of speech, than with the syntactic and semantic structures which endow words with "objective" and "ideal" meaning. He writes:

> . . . we can no longer consider the learning of language as an intellectual operation of reconstituting meaning. We are no longer in the presence of two entities (the expression and its sense) the second of which would be hidden behind the first. Language as the phenomenon of expression is constitutive of consciousness. To learn to speak, in this perspective, is to coexist more and more with the milieu. To live within this milieu, for the child, is an incitement to appropriate language and thought as its own. . . .[19]

But precisely because the primary phonological systems according to which we speak necessarily reach their culmination in *words,* it is impossible to limit the discussion of what language *means* to the immanent and intralinguistic structures of phonology. With the emergence of words, meaning becomes dependent on syntactic (and semantic) rules and structures which are not accounted for by phonology and morphology. With the word, language becomes a semeiological system, which is to say that it is endowed with the function of standing for, indicating, or referring to something other than itself. What the higher systems of syntax and semantics bring into play is another "miraculous" human ability, the ability to take something for something else, to analogize (the elemental and all-pervasive function of higher intelligence which the associationists spoke of in terms of "association" and which Husserl called simply "pairing," *Paarung*). It is, hopefully, unnecessary here to vindicate once again the distinction between "meaning" and "reference" which has so often, beginning with Saint Anselm's dialogue *De Veritate,* been discovered and then forgotten by philosophers. We accept the distinction in the Fregean (*Sinn, Bedeutung*) and Husserlian (*Bedeutung, Erfüllung*) sense.[20] To say that language is a semeiological system is to say, in the most general way possible (so as to avoid, for the present, otiose controversies), that words are "paired" with meanings (or "carry" meanings) and/or objects of reference in the real world which would instantiate or verify such meanings. We find, then, a double transcendence of language as "sign" of something else, and we *ipso facto* distinguish the word-sound (or written mark) from what it *means* as well as from what it denotes, or "names," or refers to.

TRANSCENDENT MEANING: FROM THE SEMEIOTIC TO THE SEMANTIC

With the recognition that word-sounds carry (are "paired" with) meanings, we necessarily operate the passage from the conception of linguistics as a science of elements interrelated in a closed system to the conception of linguistics as a science of usage according to rules of syntax for the purpose of signifying something transcendent to the semeiological system itself. The primary, although incomplete, elements of syntax are *words* which must be arranged according to strict syntactical rules *in order to* make sense. Such rules are the necessary, although insufficient, rules of sense. All this is hardly new and hardly worth restating. But I would like to refer here to two remarks concerning *words* inspired by Paul Ricoeur's now fairly celebrated polemic with the structuralists, which is his most recent contribution to the phenomenology of language.[21] He says that "the word" is both "much more and much less than the sentence." Both remarks are important for our purposes. The word is evidently "less" than the sentence (and this is *the* fact about "mere words" which has been recognized since the earliest philosophies of language), because it is destined to take its place in a sentence. The only complete unit of meaning is the sentence within which words are syntactically ordered. Even in cases where men seem to speak in words rather than in sentences, such as the first words uttered by the child,[22] or ejaculations (like "Splendid!" "Bravo!" "Fire!" and so on),[23] or other shorthand and elliptical forms, such words are *understood* as sentences. Words, as such, have no functions apart from their functions within sentences and the incomplete grammar of the "parts of speech" (of the verb, the noun, the adjective, and so on) which we find in grammars has meaning only in function of the *only complete* syntactical unit—which is the complete sentence. Nevertheless, the word, the compound word, and the subordinate phrase have meaning, although always incomplete meaning, independently of sentences, which is to say that they are "signs" (of meanings, of things), and thus, as opposed to the elements which compose them, carry meanings which point beyond themselves, meanings of which they are only arbitrary and conventional symbols, which appeal to the usage of language with the intention *to speak* (*la parole*). They are, as Ricoeur rightly says, at the "juncture of language and speech" (*au carrefour de la langue et de la parole*).[24]

It is just here that the word, although less than the sentence as a constitutive part of the sentence, is "more" than the sentence in its ability to fix meaning and to "outlive" the sentence. The only complete and unitary expression of meaning is achieved in the properly formed sentence (as a grammatical arrangement of words); the sentence is thus normally the only full unit of thought and, as such, as we shall see, enjoys a certain independence from the words which compose it. But, at the same time, our sentences are highly transitory, passing, rapid happenings or events. They are what happen to words. We scarcely ever fix our sentences permanently in our minds or remember them. If we wish to remember them, we must deliberately "memorize" them. We learn vocabularies of words but not vocabularies of sentences (except for the most standard and stock phrases of a language). Words, on the contrary, represent sedimentations of more incomplete but more readily available meanings; they outlive the sentence which quickly dies (and as Ricoeur says: "means to die"); they get defined in dictionaries and can be stored in our cultural space in a way sentences (with exceptions perhaps for some of the very greatest) are not.[25] The most illiterate peasant cannot speak without some explicit awareness of the words he is using, but he can and does speak without any thematic awareness of the rules of grammar according to which he is using his words in sentences. Words provide us with the sedimented lexicographical possibilities of our language and put the whole past history of our language at our present disposal. Ricoeur argues, in an interesting way, that the word is the primary instrument (though of itself it is incomplete for the expression of meaning) of the passage from the semeiotic level to the semantic level. For, just like the phonemic "sign" in a given linguistic system, the "word," as such, has no meaning; it is a "sign" differentiated by a conventional rule from all the others and, as "sign," that is all it is. It does not tell us, of itself, of what it is the "sign." So far as the linguistic system itself is concerned (as *langue*), its "meaning" is wholly outside it, arbitrary; it is but one more phonetically and morphologically distinct element in a closed system of mutually interrelated elements which holds its distinctive value in the system from the fact that there are clear (infrasemantic) rules which differentiate it from all the other "signs" or elements of the system. As an element in the semeiotic system, the word is only "virtually" meaningful; it must be animated by an intention which comes from outside the sound-system as such to take on meaning. But, at the same time, it is the word which can be "paired" with meaning, which can be thought and uttered and thus take on semantic value within the actual production of a meaningful sentence, because all sentences are composed of nothing but words. It is in this operation that its ambiguity is revealed: that which was a "mere sign" becomes the vehicle of "meaning." We owe new and great words, charged with new meanings which enrich the possibilities of our language and our thought, to the original and "new" uses of words by poets, philosophers, creative and inspired minds. The sense of the word "belief," for instance, will never again be the same for a literary man as it was before Hume made it a fundamental category of philosophical discourse; a great mind impresses itself on us through giving words distinctive and new senses, but, at the same time, these senses and these words remain without effect on the laws of syntax and grammar as such; the laws of syntax can swallow up and accommodate any words which have been and may be invented; they remain on a higher and different plane of abstraction and generative power. We can pose problems of "universals of grammar" and an "eidetic of language" on the level of syntax which we cannot pose on the level of the word.

The sentence is, then, what we do with the words we have learned; it is our attempt to grasp and express a meaning which has been left to us in the words of our language, and ultimately to use these words in new ways and give them new senses. The sentence is the creative moment which never employs just the same words in just the same combinations and with just the same sense twice. Sartre, with his fine sensitivity to the nuances of verbal creativity, writes:

> It is within the sentence, in fact, that the word can receive a real function as a designation; outside the sentence the word is just a propositional function . . . entire sentences, commonplaces, do not, any more than words, pre-exist the use which is made of them. . . . To understand the word in the light of the sentence is *very exactly* to understand any given whatsoever in terms of the situation and to understand the situation in the light of the original ends. . . . In order for words to enter into relations with one another, in order for them to latch on to one another or repulse one another, it is necessary that they be united in a synthesis which does not come from them. Suppress this synthetic unity and the block which is called speech disintegrates; each word returns to its solitude and at the same time loses its unity, being parcelled out among various incommunicable meanings.[26]

And Merleau-Ponty writes in the same vein:

> I understand or think I understand the words and forms of French; I have a certain experience of the literary and philosophical modes of expression offered me by a given culture. I express when, utilizing all these already speaking instruments, I make them say something they have never said. We begin reading a philosopher by giving the words he makes use of their "common" meaning; and little by little, through what is at first an imperceptible reversal, his speech comes to dominate his language, and it is his use of words which ends up assigning them a new and characteristic signification. . . . I say *I know an idea* when the power to organize discourses which make coherent sense around it has been established in me; and this power itself does not depend upon my alleged face-to-face contemplation of it, but upon my having acquired a certain style of thinking. I say that a signification is acquired and henceforth available when I have succeeded in making it dwell in a speech apparatus which was

> not originally destined for it. Of course the elements of this expressive apparatus did not really contain it—the French language did not, from the moment it was established, contain French literature. . . .[27]

We may oversimplify somewhat, but I believe we will not falsify the central insight contained in these passages if we locate the central phenomenon of language *as speech* (that is, in its *actuality* as opposed to its *virtuality* as a *system*) by saying that language is *a speaking to someone about something.* This tripartite Husserlian schema, although in need of interpretation as a formal invariant of language, has taken on a new importance in the debates between structuralists and phenomenologists at the present time.[28] Language cannot be exhaustively accounted for as a closed, structural system of rules precisely because it involves the intention and the need to apply such rules in a movement which points beyond them (1) toward the ideality of meaning, of what we use language to say, of "the meant," and (2) toward the things in the world about which we are speaking, toward those realities to which our meanings apply and which verify them. Moreover, language is the means by which we address ourselves to others and express our moods, feelings, desires, commands, prayers, whims and so on (in what Husserl called "non-objectivating" or "non-presentational" acts). Thus language, which can be considered as a closed system of signs or symbols governed by fixed rules on the semeiotic level, on the semantic level necessarily refers to something other than itself (and thus, in a peculiar way, participates in the self-transcendence and reflexivity of consciousness itself). This is true of language not as an inert, cultural institution (*langue*) but as the act of speaking (*la parole,* the "speech act"); the level of semantics, or meaning in the proper sense of the term, is reached at the moment when what was a virtual possibility of expression becomes an act of expression, when a choice among all the possibilities of the system has been made and others thereby excluded, when a new and actual combination of words takes place in a sentence.[29] Language in this sense is the means used by the subject to come to himself and to direct himself toward something beyond himself. Moved to the semantic level, the semeiotic system becomes a subject who speaks to another. This is the level of the institution of meaning as such, of creation and actualization, when hitherto unused possibilities of discourse are uttered and understood. The originality and importance of Noam Chomsky's "transformational generative grammar" is rooted in this discovery: that the only role of the "system" is to serve creative speech, that *langue* is subservient to *parole* and is absorbed in it, that what must be explained by a linguistic theory is the possibility of forming new sentences within the fixed rules of syntax. This creativity alone will give us *sufficient* explanation of "linguistic competence."

> The central fact to which any significant linguistic theory must address itself is this: a mature speaker can produce a new sentence of his language on the appropriate occasion, and other speakers can understand it immediately, though it is equally new to them. Most of our linguistic experience, both as speakers and as hearers, is with new sentences; . . . the class of sentences with which we can operate fluently and without difficulty or hesitation is so vast that . . . we may regard it as infinite. Normal mastery of a language involves not only the ability to understand immediately an indefinite number of entirely new sentences, but also the ability to identify deviant sentences and, on occasion, to impose an interpretation on them. . . . It is clear that any theory of language that neglects this "creative" aspect is of only marginal interest.[30]

The originality of "generative grammar" is that it goes beneath the surface-level phonological analyses of the structural-linguistic conception of language to an examination of the more abstract rules of syntax, which alone allow us to pose the question of "meaning" in a full and complete sense—on the level of the sentence.[31] By posing the question of "universals of grammar" Chomsky gives a new sense, although he nowhere takes cognizance of this, to Husserl's phenomenological project of a pure logical grammar. Whether he can ultimately do more than this is not certain, because in its very program "transformational generative grammar" encounters a *paradox* of language which cannot be solved on the level of syntax, that is, language is able to incarnate the living meaning-intentions of original speakers in their creative production of ever-new sentences according to syntactic rules which themselves remain invariant and "universal" (deep-structures) beneath the surface of ordinary speech.

SEMANTIC OBJECTIVITY

We have up to now discussed briefly, and distinguished, three levels of meaning in language: (1) the phonological level of meaning immanent to the semeiological system as such, (2) the emergence of sense and reference from within the semeiological system when words become *signs* of something transcendent to the system, and (3) the completion of this process on the level of semantics proper in the formation, in actual speaking, of sentences which constitute complete, full units of meaning.[32] Henceforth, we shall only be concerned with the third level.

We may well sympathize with Chomsky and others who find it impossible, at least in the present state of human nature, to distinguish the borderlines which distinguish the syntactic from the semantic rules which govern the constitution of meaning.[33] One way to settle the question, at least for purposes of discussion, would be to follow the distinction which Husserl elaborated in *Formale und transzendentale Logik,* namely, that the laws of syntax which formulate the *formal* a prioris which govern the possibility of the formation of sentences are not sufficient to enable us to produce meaningful sentences. The *formal* a priori laws of "pure logical grammar" provide us with *necessary* and universal, but not *sufficient,* conditions for the sense and meaning of sentences; these laws of pure grammar (*reine Formenlehre der Bedeutungen*) must be supplemented by more particular rules specific to the various "material regions" of meanings, which enunciate *material* a prioris governing the contextual relevance of the words within a sentence to one another. As is well known, Husserl discussed this problem with reference to his distinction between nonsensical propositions and countersensical propositions (*Unsinn—Widersinn*). For instance, if the formal laws of grammar are not observed (according to which, for instance, only predicates can be predicated of a substantive), we get such "heaps" of words as: *Brown squirrel is and, If however wants tomorrow, King but where seems anyway,* and so on. Such heaps of words are meaningless because they violate purely formal laws of syntax. But the strict observance of the formal rules of syntax is not, just of itself, sufficient to guarantee that the sentences formed in accord with them will be meaningful. Pure grammar does not rule out such formulations as: *All squares have five corners, This algebraic number is blue, Blue plus one equals three, Portugal is not diatonic,* and so on. Such formulations violate no law of formal logic or grammar; the substantives are substantives and the predicates are predicates, but these expressions are nevertheless countersensical because they violate laws of material or "regional" relevance which require that the words which are put together in sentences must, at the very least, be intrinsically related as belonging to the same region of discourse. A sentence like "Portugal is not diatonic" is devoid of meaning because one cannot legitimately affirm or deny of a country a musical status of this sort.[34] The laws which would enunciate the *sufficient* conditions for a sentence to have meaning must, therefore, be more than merely "formal"; they must take into account the material meaning-content of the words used, and this can only be done by distinguishing "contexts" or "regions" of meaning, each with its own specific "synthetic" a prioris. This alone, to be sure, does not tell us very much. It tells us only that there are semantic laws of "context" which cannot be reduced to the purely formal structures of syntax. But, nevertheless, such a distinction does at least enable us to isolate "the syntactical" (*das Grammatische selbst*) from all other meaning-conditions, and thus to situate the project of a "pure logical grammar." Insofar as the transformational grammar, which is being elaborated by Chomsky and his school, is concerned with "universals of grammar," even if it should succeed in its task, it will not be able to provide us with the sufficient conditions of meaningfulness. Precisely because grammar is concerned with "the universal" structures according to which sentences are formed, it cannot govern the particular contexts within which words are used in living and new ways in the act of speaking.[35] In order to do *this* semantic (as opposed to merely syntactical) considerations must be brought into play.[36]

One could, without injustice, interpret the whole progression of Husserl's philosophy of language, from the *Logische Untersuchungen* to *Erfahrung und Urteil,* as an attempt to articulate this distinction. The fundamental correlation in his thought is that between "categories of meaning" (or signification) and "categories of objects," between judgments about experience and their foundations in experience. In his studies on pure logical grammar he posed the question of the necessary conditions of the possibility of propositions and elaborated the formal a priori conditions of judgment; in his studies on transcendental (that is, phenomenological) logic he attempted to provide examples of the material or "synthetic" a priori conditions of meaningfulness (within the various regional ontologies) which, through experience, specify the purely formal study of "objectivity in general." To pursue Husserl's work along this line would be the only proper way of providing a complete justification (which would be, at the same time, an illustration) of the distinction between syntactic and semantic objectivity which we are invoking. For the purposes of this paper, however, I propose to take a less technical and, at the same time, less rigorous route. But I believe it is possible to illustrate what I (and I trust Husserl did also) mean by the "objectivity" of meaning (that is, the synthetically objective, semantic a prioris which rule the understanding of sentences) through a reflection on a more recent piece of philosophical analysis by William P. Alston. Alston qualifies the theoretical observations he develops in Chapter Two of his *Philosophy of Language* (on "Meaning and the Use of Language") as "pioneer work." [37] This qualification is justified and remains valid even if we are able to impose a phenomenological interpretation upon it—of which I fear neither he (nor Husserl) would approve.

But we are, after all, now becoming aware of the possibility that what Wittgenstein did when he took contemporary philosophy around the "linguistic bend" was to turn it back in the direction of Kant, and that the "linguistic turn" involves, in its method, at least a limited "transcendental turn" as well.[38] I am using the term "transcendental" here in a restricted, but authentically Kantian and Husserlian, sense: namely, the search for *the necessary conditions of the possibility* of something being the case, whether on the level of the formal analysis of meaning-structures, or on the level of the analysis of the material conditions applicable to a given region of objectivity. If, in addition, the necessary conditions of the possibility of acts of consciousness should turn out to be necessary conditions for the possibility of objects (and of their correlative meanings),[39] then we would have operated a *complete* transcendental *revolution.* I am not suggesting, of course, that anything like this is in the offing. Even the restricted claim that linguistic philosophy has taken a "transcendental turn" in the minimal sense may be asserting too much (and it certainly goes beyond anything which can be established in this paper), but *this much* at least may be helpful, if only to indicate the bias behind the observations which follow.

Wittgenstein's "battle against the bewitchment of our intelligence by means of language" issued in a program of defining the meaning of words by their *use*. But, at its inception, this program was beset by an instructive and almost insurmountable ambiguity. When we say that the meaning of a word *is* its use, we may mean that it is a specific kind of human behavior which operates according to "rules" (if we are logically and rationalistically inclined) or "regularities" (if we are more stringently empiricist) which delimit the field of the possible occurrences of such a word, both by giving us rules for all the possible instances in which it could actually occur in speech and by excluding all the rest. Such rules (or regularities), for any given language, are quite complex and it is unclear in the Wittgensteinian literature whether primary emphasis is to be placed on the phonological (or structuralist), on the syntactic (or transformationalist), or on the semantic levels. The question must be: how is a word "used" to make sense, how is it effectively brought under a rule at all? And how does our knowledge of the rule (that superordinate category which defines all the possibilities of the actual "use" of a given word and which can only laboriously be discovered by philosophical analysis) give us the *meaning* of the word? After all, we already know how to *apply* these rules even though we have no *explicit knowledge* of them. Stated in this way, the problem is not essentially different from that posed by Kant in the *Critique of Pure Reason* when he found that, since experience and concepts are heterogeneous, a *schematism* and a theory of use (*Gebrauch*) was necessary to show how it is possible to put a thing (an experience) under a rule (concept) at all.[40] This is something that occurs in ordinary experience effortlessly prior to any reflection about it. We know, therefore, that it is possible. What we do not know is exactly *what* we are doing when we perform such elaborate acts as speaking a language, and thus making sense. This is why we need theories: to bring to the level of fully reflexive and discursive awareness what we already know (*in actu exercito*) but cannot say (*in actu signato*).

On this subject the Wittgensteinians seem to present all the possible shades of doctrine from the extreme linguistic behaviorism of a Paul Ziff to openly intentional and psychological interpretations of usage (Hampshire, Strawson). Wittgenstein himself seems to vacillate between the two extremes.[41] Therefore, his cryptic dictum, *the meaning is the use,* is in need of interpretation, and Alston gives us an interpretation which puts Wittgenstein in touch with a tradition he was not thinking of. (The Wittgensteinian revolt against traditional philosophy must be tempered by the realization that, in some instances, the tradition stood on solid ground, which is not to say that the disciples of Wittgenstein will necessarily bring about the renaissance of German Idealism.)

We must be content here with really making no more than a suggestion. We stated above that the "semantic" conditions of meaning are distinguished from the merely "syntactic," in that they are situational or contextual in nature. We must, therefore, return to the primary context of language which is that of *someone saying something about something to someone.* Let there be a *speaker, what* he says, a *thing* about which he is speaking, and a *hearer.* What is essential to *meaning* in this situation? Not the *thing about which* the speaker is speaking, because we have already separated meaning from reference. Not the *hearer,* because the speaker could be speaking to himself or to a "putative" listener (a dummy, or a distracted or deaf person).[42] What is *essential* is that there be a *speaker* and that he *say something* (express a meaning). Or, since we are concerned only with the *essence,* that there be a *speech act* (meaning-act) and *something said* (meaning-content). To be sure, such an act always takes place within a wider context of behavior, in terms of which it is understood, but just *what* it is that is to be understood, the *meaning* of the behavioral act itself, must be distinguished from everything else. This is what Husserl called the *meaning-content* of an act of expression, and what Alston, following J. L. Austin, calls the "illocutionary" force of the speech act. And since, as Alston says, "the concept of an illocutionary act is the most fundamental concept in semantics and, hence, in the philosophy of language,"[43] it is appropriate to attempt to distinguish the illocutionary act from what it is not. It is above all what "constitutes sameness of meaning"[44] in terms of the "illocutionary act-potential" of sentences which are otherwise distinct. If the illocutionary value of a given word or a given sentence did not change when another word or another sentence were put in their places, they would have the same meaning. It is to be distinguished from the "perlocutionary," that is, from all the effects (and intentions to produce effects) which the speech act may carry with it incidental to its meaning but intrinsically unrelated to the meaning as such. The illocutionary-perlocutionary distinction is similar to the distinction Husserl made between the ("objective") presentational character of an act of meaning and all its nonpresentational aspects.[45] For instance, while I am speaking I may either deliberately or inadvertently cause my interlocutor to realize that I am tired, or happy, or exuberant, or depressed, that I want something, that I am interested in something, that I value something, and I may, by addressing my wishes, commands, pleas, whims, or requests to him, get him to do something, and thus bring about an external change in him and in my environment. These *effects* of language, and their source in my own lived, psychological dispositions, as they are experienced in acts of consciousness, lie outside the meaning of *what* I am saying when I am saying something. It is indeed true that every nonpresentational act (wish, command, commendation, evaluation, and so on) must have as its basis a presentational act ("an illocutionary act can be a means to a perlocutionary act, but not vice versa"),[46] but it remains that the felt desires or moods it may convey to my hearer and the external effects it may produce are distinct from such presentational meanings as such.

Before proceeding, let us briefly recapitulate what we have discovered up to now. (1) The *meaning* of a sentence must be distinguished from the words which compose it taken in isolation. The same meaning can be expressed in any number of different verbal forms, in the same or other natural languages, and the fact of the translatability of languages into one another (through transformational rules of various kinds) shows that sentences enjoy a specific distinctness, as units of meaning, from the words that compose them. In translating from one language to another we do not isomorphically render each element in one language into the other but translate the meaning of one sentence into another. (2) This *meaning* must, furthermore, be distinguished from my own psychological acts which accompany its expression; my sentences may *convey* my inner psychological states to another but they do not *mean* them since the same meaning can be expressed at other times, when I am contented and pleased with myself and not only when I am gloomy and depressed as at the present moment, and so on. Meaning is essentially free of all the indexical, egocentric, or, as Husserl would say, "occasional" circumstances which escort and accompany it. (3) Furthermore, the meaning of my sentences may produce external effects on my milieu and on other persons, but the *meaning* of a sentence is not exhausted in the effects it may cause; the same meaning may at one time be causally very potent and at another without any effect ("overt response") at all (if, for instance, I am addressing an idiot). Ideas "whose time has not come" are without effect. (4) We are, furthermore, assuming that it is unnecessary to repeat in this context that meanings are not simply things referred to or the act of reference, and that they are not mental images or clear and distinct ideas open to introspective inspection "within" the mind.[47] (5) Finally, we know that, although the expression of meaning requires a phonological system and a syntactical system as its necessary conditions (and that there *are* purely phonological and syntactical levels of meaning), these are not sufficient to account for meaning, for, otherwise, we would not be able to explain how the normal speaker is able to understand perfectly well the *meaning* of ungrammatical sentences garbled on the tongues of illiterates or foreigners who have not yet learned all our linguistic conventions. There seems to be no meaning-ambiguity in such sentences as *We was robbed, He don't live here no more,* or *Boss-man likeum Turkey-shoot* on the semantic level even though such expressions clearly violate syntactical and morphological rules.

How then are we to establish just what a sentence *means* (its illocutionary force) over and above these aspects of its "environment"? Alston proposes that we accept a vaguely "behavioristic" approach by specifying "the situation of utterance as a determinant of meaning" in terms of "what speakers are doing when they use language."[48] This *turn to the "speaker"* (which has been strangely absent from most behavioral theories and is Alston's important innovation) must distinguish between the bare "situation in which the speaker operates" (the conditions we have been enumerating) and "what the speaker is doing in that situation." This *Wendung zum Subjekt,*[49] to be sure, falls far short of Husserl's turn to meaning-intending acts and the discovery of transcendental constituting acts of consciousness. For Husserl it makes no sense to speak either of "meaning" or of "object" except in terms of the structures of subjectivity to which and for which objects are objectified and thus receive meaning. But we cannot expect this much; we are content, as we stated above, with a limited transcendental turn, and, in effect, Alston takes this turn when he attempts to explain the meanings of sentences, in that which is strictly "illocutionary," by showing that we must list the semantic conditions which make the sentence produced by the speaker meaningful *just as such,* without reference to any other behavior than that of just saying something. Husserl, also, did not turn to the experiencing subject in order to *reduce* meaning to the *psychological acts* of the subject but to show that objective *meaning-contents* ("the meant as such") can occur only for a subject. Language does not speak all by itself; it speaks only when it is used by a subject. The meaning of language is thus always a function of some *use*. The essential thing, for our purposes here, is to distinguish the properly linguistic sense of use from an infrahuman behaviorism, on the one hand, and psychologism, on the other. The *meaning* of an expression is itself "objective," according to Husserl, and must be delineated by an eidetic analysis which will result in thematizing the a priori conditions necessary for the possibility of such an expression to have such a meaning.

Granted that the analysis of the meaning of sentences is not something which can be accomplished in one fell swoop, that sentences can frequently have more than one meaning (all of which *can,* nevertheless, be clearly distinguished from one another given sufficient time), that there are levels of meaning, and that there are various levels of generality on which meaning can be specified, and so on, Alston gives a sample of what he means by specifying the conditions of an act being an illocutionary act by listing, for instance, the conditions necessary in order to understand the meaning of a simple request to open a door.[50] If we ask someone to "Please open the door," such a request implies, among other conditions of intelligibility, that (1) there be a particular door to which attention is directed, (2) that the door is not already open, (3) that it is possible for the hearer to open that door, (4) that the speaker wants the hearer to open the door, and so on. Now, we can say that if any one of these conditions is not satisfied, there is something wrong with making such a request on the part of the speaker. That these meaning-conditions primarily concern the sentence as uttered and meant *by the speaker* is clear from the fact that they are necessary conditions only of what he *means* and are not necessary conditions of the performance of the act requested. Whether or not the hearer obliges the speaker is irrelevant to the *meaning* of the request. What is not so obvious, but which is nevertheless true, is that these meaning-conditions are also semantically "objective" with respect to the speaker.[51] They do not require that the speaker effectively mean what he asks, but only that he *mean to say* what he asks. It is true that the speaker is the one who expresses the sentence and, therefore, it is to his situation that we turn to understand what he means. But there are cases in which a speaker can discover what he really means only by speaking (which is the reason why the psychological intentions of the author of a sentence are not the *only* criterion of its meaning).[52] For instance, suppose the speaker did not really want the door to be opened, and was just testing his interlocutor to see if he would obey (as in boot camp). This does not at all mean that the fourth condition listed above ceases to hold for this expression; the *meaning* of the expression requires that this condition hold. It is the sentence which *means* in this case, and the speaker can always be brought to recognize this, even though what the sentence he utters *means* may be irrelevant to his peculiar intentions in uttering it. In an extreme limit-case such as would occur, for instance, if the speaker, after requesting me to open the door, were then to evince shock and surprise that I did so by saying something like "But, I did not mean that!", then we would rightly say either that he did not yet understand the meaning of the sentence, even though he himself had produced it, or that we were confronted with a pathological case. Since rules of semantics are rules, they can be broken like any others, but this does not alter their "ideal," "objective," and necessary character. The speaker who does not understand the meaning of his sentences can be led to see just why what he said in this language means just this and can mean nothing else (by listing a priori semantic conditions). In short the speaker *must* (is obligated to) know what his sentences mean under pain of expressing only nonsense. This is not a psychological but a semantically objective obligation that affects him not as a moral person but as a user of this language. He is, willy-nilly, governed by a priori laws of contextual consistency and coherence of which he is not the master, although he is the only user.[53]

We stated at the outset of this discussion that it would be impossible to produce more than a sample illustration of what we mean by the semantic "objectivity" of meaning in this paper. The background for speaking of "objectivity" in this connection at all is, of course, the work of Edmund Husserl. But it would seem that the kind of behavioral-conceptual analysis of meaning being pioneered by Alston, although it speaks a different language, can be interpreted in an eidetic sense. By vindicating the "objectivity" of meaning as something necessarily constituted by a subject, but which follows essential, a priori laws not reducible to psychological experience, we have said and implied nothing, as yet, regarding the ontology of meaning. If one takes seriously the distinction between sense and reference, it becomes pellucidly clear that meaning is not some entity like a perceptual object, or an image, and that the phenomenology of thought has a specificity which distinguishes it from the phenomenology of perception or the phenomenology of the imagination. Thought deals with "idealities," by which one need not mean "another realm of things" similar to perceptual objects or imaginary objects, but rather, in the case we have been discussing, *necessary conditions of possibility*—conditions of meaning which are, for thought, as inescapable and "objective" as the physical objects over which we stumble in the real world are for perception.[54] No further claim is made, in this paper, about the ontological structure of the world which is experienced as the transcendental field of application of such idealities.

NOTES

1. See my other paper, "Ontology Without Metaphysics?" in which I develop the phenomenological conception of ontology and its relation to phenomenolgical analysis of perception, imagination, thought, etc. Phenomenology does not exhaust itself in staring at the phenomena, as some unkind critics have suggested, or at least it ought not to do so. The only purpose of employing a phenomenological approach is to secure a basis on which to answer the primary philosophical questions. I believe that phenomenology does provide the basis for an ontology of meaning, by accounting for the "ideal" structures of objective experience.

2. The principal defect of structural linguistics is its denigration of

syntax and universal grammatical structures independent of the various phonological systems of natural languages and its ignorance of "deep structures" even when these apply to phonology itself; in Merleau-Ponty this becomes a blindness to the significance of Husserl's contributions to "pure logical grammar" and his unconscionable attempt to interpret the later Husserl as having abandoned this program. Cf. my article "Can Grammar Be Thought?" which will appear shortly in a volume from the Northwestern University Press to be entitled *Patterns of the Life-World.*

3. On this point we find agreement among Merleau-Ponty, Chomsky and transformational grammar, and structural linguistics: all three assert that language must be learned "as a whole."

4. "If we consider only the conceptual and delimiting meaning of words, it is true that the verbal form—with the exception of endings—appears arbitrary. But it would no longer appear so if we took into account the emotional content of the word, which we have called above its 'gestural' sense, which is all-important for poetry, for example. It would then be found that the words, vowels and phonemes are so many ways of 'singing' the world, and that their function is to represent things not, as the naive onomatopoeic theory had it, by reason of an objective resemblance, but because they extract, and literally express, their emotional essence. If it were possible, in any vocabulary, to disregard what is attributable to the mechanical laws of phonetics, to the influences of other languages, the rationalizations of grammarians, and assimilatory processes, we should probably discover that . . . the predominance of vowels in one language, or of consonants in another . . . do not represent so many arbitrary conventions for the expression of one and the same idea, but several ways for the human body to sing the world's praises and in the last resort to live it." *Phenomenology of Perception,* trans. Colin Smith, New York, 1962, p. 187.

5. I do not mean, of course, that this is the only, or even the primary, way in which the categorematic/syncategorematic distinction is to be understood, but that this gives a first idea of the "immanent" functions of words within language itself. See note 36 below.

6. Cf. Ronald W. Langacker, *Language and Its Structure,* New York, 1967, pp. 71 ff., my example.

7. Cf. Noam Chomsky, *Cartesian Linguistics,* New York, 1966, p. 41.

8. Langacker, *Language and Its Structures, loc. cit.*

9. Maurice Merleau-Ponty, "La conscience et l'acquisition du langage," *Bulletin de Psychologie,* November 1965, p. 256. I am certainly not suggesting, as Gilbert Ryle has, that *all* words are *only* syncategorematic expressions ("Meaning and Necessity," *Philosophy,* 1949, p. 71), but only that something of the "immanent" meaning—a holding within the system —which is an exclusive characteristic of syncategorematic words, is to be found in a less exclusive way in all words.

10. I believe that Merleau-Ponty is mistaken in this, and that the existence of phonological meaning does not in any way inhibit natural languages from realizing within themselves universal grammatical structures of the kind spoken of by Husserl and now the object of investigation by transformational grammarians. Cf. "Can Grammar Be Thought?" referred to above. Chomsky argues, it seems to me on sound bases, that even the more general and abstract rules of phonetics lead one to suppose that there may be universal structures common to all languages even here. Cf. Noam Chomsky, *Language and Mind,* New York, 1968, pp. 33 ff.

11. Ordinary language "is never composed of absolutely univocal meanings which can be made completely explicit beneath the gaze of transparent constituting consciousness. It will be a question not of a system of forms of signification clearly articulated in terms of one another—not a structure of linguistic ideas built according to a strict plan—but of a cohesive whole of convergent linguistic gestures, each of which will *be defined less by a signification than a use value (valeur d'emploi).*" Maurice Merleau-Ponty, *Signs,* trans. Richard McCleary, Evanston, Ill., 1964, p. 87, italics mine.

12. Merleau-Ponty, "La conscience . . . ," pp. 229 ff.

13. Cf. Norman O. Brown, *Life Against Death,* New York, 1959, p. 72, and Merleau-Ponty, "La conscience . . ." p. 252: "The original form of language would thus be a kind of chant. Men would have sung their feelings before communicating their thoughts. Just as writing was originally painting, language was first a chant which, through later analysis, became a linguistic sign; it was through this original singing that men discovered their power of expression."

14. Merleau-Ponty, *Phenomenology of Perception,* p. 179.

15. Merleau-Ponty, *Signs,* p. 88. my italics.

16. Merleau-Ponty, *Phenomenology of Perception,* p. 182: ". . . spoken or written words carry a coating of meaning which sticks to them and which presents the thought as a style, an affective value, a piece of existential mimicry rather than as a conceptual statement. We find here, beneath the conceptual meaning of words, an existential meaning which is not only rendered by them, but which inhabits them, and is inseparable from them."

17. Husserl considered the first level of formal logic to consist of a study of "the grammatical" as such, i.e., the conditions of possibility of the existence of sentences. This study, which he later expanded to the framework of a "pure logical grammar," remained an important part of his phenomonological archetectonic, although after *Formale und transzendentale Logik* (1929) he made no further contributions to it. See "Can Grammar Be Thought?" cited above.

18. Merleau-Ponty, "La conscience . . . ," p. 253.

19. *Ibid.,* p. 242.

20. Since one cannot treat of everything in one article, I am presupposing a basic acquaintance with the texts of Husserl. He treats of the distinction between sense and reference especially in the First, Fifth, and Sixth Investigations of the *Logische Untersuchungen;* for Frege see, principally, "On Sense and Reference," in *Translations from the Philosophical Writings of Gottlob Frege,* eds. Peter Geach and Max Black, Oxford, 1960, pp. 56 ff. Frege referred to "meaning" as *Sinn* and its "reference" as *Bedeutung.* Since the words *Sinn* and *Bedeutung* have the same meaning in ordinary German, Husserl took them as synonymous and uses them to express "meaning"; he used terms like *Gegenstand, Objekt,* and *Erfüllung* to express "reference."

21. Paul Ricoeur, "La structure, le mot, l'événement," first published in *Esprit,* May 1967, was republished in *Man and World,* February 1968, pp. 10–30, and *Philosophy Today,* Summer 1968, pp. 114–129.

22. Cf. Merleau-Ponty, "La conscience . . . ," pp. 230 ff.

23. "As a matter of fact, it has not been sufficiently observed that a work of the mind is by nature *allusive.* Even if the author's aim is to give the fullest possible representation of his object, there is never any question as to whether he is telling *everything.* He knows far more than he tells.

This is so because language is elliptical. If I want to let my neighbor know that a wasp has gotten in by the window, there is no need for a long speech. 'Watch out!' or 'Hey!'—a word is enough, a gesture. . . ." Jean-Paul Sartre, *What is Literature?* trans. Bernard Frechtman, New York, 1965, p. 62.

24. "Dans le dictionnaire, il y a seulement la ronde sans fin des termes qui se definissent en cercle, qui tournoient dans la clôture du lexique. Mais, voici: quelqu'un parle, quelqu'un dit quelque chose; le mot sort du dictionnaire; il devient mot au moment ou l'homme devient parole, ou la parole devient discours et le discours phrase." Ricoeur, "La structure," p. 25.

25. ". . . it often happens that we find ourselves knowing something which we have learnt by means of words without being able to remember a single one of the words which conveyed it to us." Jean-Paul Sartre, *What is Literature?* p. 14 [but I have used the superior translation found in Anthony Manser, *Sartre, A Philosophic Study,* New York, 1966, p. 106]. And: ". . . the important thing about a train of thought is its conclusion. That is the meaning, or, as we say, the topic of the thought. That is what abides when all its other members have faded from memory. Usually this conclusion is a word or phrase. . . . The parts of the stream that precede these substantive conclusions are but the means of the latter's attainment. . . . The relative unimportance of the means appears from the fact that when the conclusion is there, we have always forgotten most of the steps preceding its attainment. When we have uttered a proposition, we are rarely able a moment afterwards to recall our exact words, though we can express it in different words easily enough. The practical upshot of a book we read remains with us, though we may not recall one of its sentences." William James, *The Principles of Psychology,* New York, 1950, I, 260. Just as "the absence of a sign is a sign" on the morphological level (see Merleau-Ponty, "La conscience . . . ," p. 253), so too with words: the absence of a word can be felt as a meaningful gap in our thought. "Suppose we try to recall a forgotten name. The state of our consciousness is peculiar. There is a gap therein; but no mere gap. It is a gap that is intensely active. . . . If wrong names are proposed to us, this singularly definite gap acts immediately so as to negate them. . . . And the gap of one word does not feel like the gap of another . . . the feeling of an absence is *toto caelo* other than the absence of a feeling. . . . The rhythm of a lost word may be there without a sound to clothe it. . . ." William James, *ibid.,* pp. 251–252.

26. Jean-Paul Sartre, *Being and Nothingness,* trans. Hazel Barnes, New York, 1956, pp. 514–517.

27. Merleau-Ponty, *Signs,* p. 91.

28. The most important single contribution is the article by Paul Ricoeur cited above. This whole study is indebted to Ricoeur and I am happy to express my appreciation for being allowed to attend his seminar and lectures on this subject at Nanterre in the spring of 1967. Also see Mikel Dufrenne, *Pour L'Homme,* Paris, 1968, which is a spirited and subtle diatribe directed against the structuralists.

29. Ricoeur skillfully uses the structural analysis of personal pronouns by Emile Benvéniste to make this point. The important thing about the pronoun *I* is not that its reference each time it is used is unique but that language is so organized that it permits each speaker to appropriate it as a whole by designating himself as "I" when he speaks. The whole impersonal

mass becomes his personal thought. By speaking in the first person I incorporate the whole system for my own purposes and make it say something from my point of view. Ricoeur, "La structure," pp. 19–20.

30. Noam Chomsky, *Current Issues in Linguistic Theory,* The Hague, 1967, pp. 7–8.

31. As we should expect, since structural linguistics considers syntax a rather trivial matter, it made very little contribution to the study of syntactical structures. Cf. Noam Chomsky, *Language and Mind,* p. 17.

32. To end with having distinguished these three levels of meaning is not to ignore the possibility of qualitative changes in other orders of meaning as we move from the sentence to such things as a "text" as a whole (which hermeneutics treats as requiring other principles of interpretation than those which suffice on the level of the individual sentence), or myths, institutions, etc. Cf. Paul Ricoeur, "La structure . . . ," p. 11: ". . . il y a peut-être d'autres niveaux stratégiques comme le texte, dont l'enchainement interne appelle une autre sorte d'intelligibilité que la phrase et que le mot en position de phrase. C'est avec ces grandes unités de l'ordre du texte qu'une ontologie du *logos* ou du dire trouverait place; si le langage a quelque part prise sur l'être, c'est à un niveau de manifestation ou d'efficience dont les lois sont originales par rapport aux niveaux antérieurs."

33. Cf. Noam Chomsky, *Aspects of the Theory of Syntax,* Cambridge, Mass., 1965, p. 163, where, at the end of the section on "The Boundaries of Syntax and Semantics," he concludes: "To conclude this highly inconclusive discussion, I shall simply point out that the syntactic and semantic structure of natural languages evidently offers many mysteries, both of fact and of principle, and that any attempt to delimit the boundaries of these domains must certainly be quite tentative."

34. Husserl discusses this primarily in the *Fourth Investigation* and in *Formale und transzendentale Logik,* section 13, and throughout. Cf. also Marvin Farber, *The Foundation of Phenomenology,* 2nd ed., New York, 1962, pp. 311 ff., and Suzanne Bachelard, *A Study of Husserl's Logic,* trans. Lester Embree, Evanston, Ill., 1968, pp. 3 ff. and 131 ff. The best introduction to Husserl's thought on this (and many other) subjects for the uninitiated is: Aron Gurwitsch, *The Field of Consciousness,* Pittsburgh, 1964, pp. 195 ff., 331 ff. Several of these examples are from Gurwitsch.

35. It is for this reason that grammar and the rules of syntax are utterly unaffected by what we use them to say; grammar is essentially untouched by our actual use of words. We can invent new words and give old words new meanings, we can create meanings, without altering our syntax in the least. The number of new sentences we are capable of formulating is practically infinite, but the rules of grammar remain finite and invariant through long periods of historical time (cf. Chomsky, *Language and Mind,* p. 69). Since the move from the grammatical to the semantic is a *metabasis eis allo genos,* "transformational generative grammar" can provide an explanation of the conditions of necessity for the emergence of sense but no more than structural linguistics can it give a complete account of the experience of meaning.

36. This distinction, then, enables us to understand better than hitherto how certain words, like syncategorematic words, can have *only* syntactical meaning and remain unaffected by roles of context that material terms require when they are put within the formal grammatical structure provided by syntactical forms. At least as a hypothesis we could say that syncategorematic words are related in their meanings to categorematic words

as syntax is related to semantics; they have meaning only within the formal system and not by pointing beyond it to meanings transcendent to the system or to things. At the same time there is no doubt that they do have one level of *meaning,* limited to a function within the linguistic system, and that there is such a thing as a "concept" of *and,* of *but,* of *if,* of *etc.,* etc.

37. William P. Alston, *Philosophy of Language,* Englewood Cliffs, N. J., 1964, p. 33 n.

38. I have in mind, in particular, the extremely insightful and synthetic discussion of what the "linguistic turn" may mean for the future of philosophy in Richard Rorty's "Introduction" to *The Linguistic Turn,* Chicago, 1967. "One hears," he writes, "less and less in the current literature about 'dissolving problems' or 'giving analyses.' Instead, one finds claims to have discovered necessary truths about various sorts of entities (intentions, actions, sensation, thoughts, etc.), without any suggestion that these truths are deduced from analyses of statements about such entities . . ." (p. 30). But even when the analysis is devoted primarily to "statements about such entities," linguistic philosophy proceeds, like phenomenology, by the way of *example* rather than demonstration or deduction. It relies on observations that we say such and such but we do not say such and such, we ask whether . . . but we do not ask whether.........................., we usually say . . . but it would be odd to say.........................., and then proceeds to explicate the necessary implications of meaning behind the given use of words. This method, when one thinks of it, is not clearly different from the method of "free variation in imagination" proposed by Husserl in *Erfahrung und Urteil,* and employed less explicitly from the *Logical Investigations* onward, a method which he called the *Wesenschau* ("intuition of the essential"). Some authors seem to feel that one of the differences beween analytical techniques and those of phenomenology is that the former *argues* but the latter, relying on intuition, only *shows.* But, when one examines the structure of "argument" in linguistic philosophy, one finds that it consists of varying a given expression in imagination, by looking for a limited number of well-chosen paradigm cases, which, when enumerated, show a logical or necessary truth about the given use of words. There is no *exhaustive* enumeration or *complete* demonstration. That would be otiose and unnecessary, precisely because one is looking for an "essential" truth about a given usage; when it is seen, through a finite number of examples—and, as in the verification of a scientific hypothesis, *one instance* is sometimes sufficient to establish the case—that the meaning of such and such is what it is and cannot be otherwise, the further multiplication of instances becomes redundant. Certainly the essential truth seen on the basis of the paradigms chosen does not become "more true" the more exhaustive the enumeration of instances; there comes a point when it is simply "seen" by any normal user of the language that this is what such and such an expression *means,* and that it cannot mean otherwise, that no appeal to future experience will affect it, and that, if one does not see this, he simply does not know the meaning of the phrase yet. The method of "free variation" used by Husserl to determine, for instance, the *essence* of a physical object in the phenomenology of perception is not different, except that, in this case, it is directed toward an object of experience rather than to a category of meaning. (Cf. Rorty, p. 21, with reference to Stanley Cavell's "Must We Mean What We Say?")

39. "Ich nenne alle Erkenntnis *transzendental,* die sich nicht sowohl mit Gegenständen, sondern mit unserer Erkenntnisart von Gegenständen, sofern

diese a priori möglich sein soll, überhaupt beschäftigt. . . ." Kant, *Kritik der reinen Vernunft,* 2nd ed., p. 25. Cf. Husserl's first chapter of *Ideas,* "Fact and Essence," trans. W. R. B. Gibson, New York, 1931, pp. 51 ff., and Aron Gurwitsch, *The Field of Consciousness,* pp. 196–197. It is, no doubt, unnecessary to remark that in this paper we are using the term "object" in its Husserlian sense, namely, as "object of consciousness" which refers to a possible *Gegenstand* but which has a "meaning-structure" or "essence" independent of any actual experience. As we turn correlatively from "fact" to "essence" the word "object" can signify an *object-as-experienced* or its *meaning.* It is within the experience of "objects," phenomenologically elucidated, that we find the basis for the distinction between meaning and reference.

40. I am indebted to Paul Ricoeur for this suggestion. His analysis of Kant's theory of "use" given in his lectures at Nanterre in the spring of 1967 is, so far as I know, unpublished.

41. "Although many philosophers influenced by Wittgenstein have made use of this idea in discussing the meaning of particular expressions, virtually nothing has been done by way of going beyond Wittgenstein's cryptic remarks to an explicit analysis of semantic concepts." William P. Alston, *Philosophy of Language,* p. 33.

42. I want to leave in suspense here the question of whether language is essentially a question of communication. Certainly, we use language for other purposes, as in philosophical writing for instance, to clarify and bring to consciousness the articulations of experience. Merleau-Ponty argues (in "La conscience . . .") that, although communication is an essential possibility of language, language as such is not primarily "to communicate." The least we can say is that, if communication is essential to language, this is a "formal" condition of its essence, i.e., language essentially involves the possibility of its being understood by others and is thus intersubjective and "public" by its (logical) nature.

43. Alston, *Philosophy of Language,* p. 39. For the present, I am using this notion uncritically. There is a difficulty with the notion of an "illocutionary act" in that it does not involve a clear distinction between the psychological act (*noesis*) itself and its content (*noema*). It is not clear that Alston would accept such a distinction.

44. *Ibid.,* p. 36.

45. Husserl treats of this in detail in the *First* and the *Fifth Investigations.* Cf. Marvin Farber, *Foundation of Phenomenology,* pp. 221 ff., 333 ff.

46. Alston, *Philosophy of Language,* p. 36.

47. Since both phenomenology and linguistic philosophy reject both mentalism and the reference theory of meaning, I am dispensing with any argument about this here. Alston gives a good exposition of the inadequacies of these theories in the first chapter of the book to which we are referring. The phenomenological theory of meaning, as expounded by Husserl, is decidedly not a "mentalism" in any Lockean or Cartesian sense. One does not discover the meaning-content of an act by "turning within" but by turning to transcendental consciousness (in its experience of objects and in its use of linguistic expressions). This can also be called a "description of behavior" if one is willing to accept intentional experiences, in their specificity, as "behavior." Such behavior issues in "the having of objects" (i.e., an intentional structure of consciousness).

48. Alston, *Philosophy of Language,* pp. 28–32.

49. In this connection I would like to cite the very illuminating and

important chapter on "La philosophie du langage" in Mikel Dufrenne's recent *Pour L'Homme,* which is centered on the observation that the analysis of the meaning of words, phrases, sentences, etc., cannot take place without reference to the speaker who uses language ("c'est toujours a un locuteur qu'elle se refère," p. 64). It should be noted that the distinction between *la langue* (language) and *la parole* (speaking) which we have invoked several times, following Saussure, Merleau-Ponty, and now Ricoeur and Dufrenne, is not exactly the same as the distinction between "language" and "speech" invoked by Alston (*ibid.,* p. 61). For Alston, "speech comprises the totality of verbal behavior that goes on in a community," whereas "language is the abstract system of identifiable elements and the rules of their combinations which is exemplified in behavior." In our sense, *la parole* refers to the actualization of language in an act of consciousness and the incarnation of an experienced meaning-intention in speech (something that could not, for instance, be accomplished by a phonograph or a machine—except as an extension of a meaning-intention of a conscious subject); our sense of "language" includes both "speech" and "language" in Alston's sense.

50. Alston, *Philosophy of Language,* pp. 40–41. We must limit ourselves to instancing only one of the several interesting examples Alston uses to make his point, but, although we perforce lose the richness of variation and detail of his analysis in such an abridgement, we do not, I think, lose his central point.

51. This latter distinction is much less clear in Alston's examples than the former, perhaps because of the behavioristic framework of his general theory; his theory requires that he "touch" on this distinction but somehow prevents him from making it explicitly. To this extent the analysis falls short of our expectations.

52. We cannot here go into the theories of *hermeneutics* developed by Heidegger, Gadamer, Ricoeur, and others which this observation permits, but it is worthwhile to note that they have an essential place in any completed phenomenology of language and the expression of meaning.

53. In this respect Alston's own account suffers from psychologism and, insofar forth, is unsatisfactory. He wants to account for the necessity of meaning-conditions of this kind in terms of the "responsibility" a person takes for his sentences, in much the same sense, he says, in which "an administrator is responsible for the efficient functioning of the department in his charge" (p. 41). Our interpretation, therefore, imposes a heavier weight on Alston's analysis than his own psychologistic language permits.

54. When Bertrand Russell rendered Meinong's rather harmless German term *bestehen* as "to subsist" rather than, as he could have, as "to be the case," he apparently innoculated a whole generation of British and American philosophers with behavioristic tendencies against all talk of "ideal objectivities" and other "ghosts" and "queer entities." (Cf. Herbert Spiegelberg, *The Phenomenological Movement,* The Hague, 1960, I, 96 ff.) In writers like Alston we see a behavioristic theory of meaning, which puts the speaker at the center of interest and discovers his "acts" of meaning, on the verge of giving a sophisticated behavioristic sense to the kinds of experience with which Meinong and Husserl began.

Language and the Future of Metaphysics

James W. Cornman

In this as well as in my earlier paper I am attempting to assess the relevance of various kinds of philosophical analyses of language and, more generally, the relevance of language itself to metaphysics. In the first paper I drew what may seem to be somewhat pessimistic conclusions about the future fruitfulness of philosophical analysis for ontology. Furthermore, it might seem that if I am to be an analytic philosopher, my domain should be language and not ontology. Nevertheless, I am centrally interested in ontological problems and consider myself in one clear sense both an ontologist and an analytic philosopher. That is, I am an analytic philosopher in the sense that I find it important for doing philosophy to analyze carefully key philosophical concepts, to use the resources of symbolic logic to express theses and arguments, and, wherever possible, to lay out arguments carefully premise by premise. Someone can be an analytic philosopher in this sense, while at the same time rejecting certain kinds of analysis, such as reductive meaning analysis. And he can be both this kind of analytic philosopher and an ontologist while agreeing that analysis is not uniquely relevant to resolving ontological problems.

As a consequence of being this kind of analytic philosopher, I am also a linguistic philosopher in a clear sense. That is, I believe that clear and precise uses of language to state and argue for and against various positions is centrally important for progress in resolving philosophical problems. I do not mean, however, that this clarity and precision is essential at all stages in the discussion of ontological views. Sometimes the free rein of imagination clearly overrides the requirements of clarity.

There is also another and perhaps a more interesting sense in which I would call myself a linguistic philosopher, even though I do not think that philosophical concerns are purely linguistic, or that any purely intralinguistic claims are sufficient to resolve ontological problems. It seems probable to me, based on the events of the recent past, that language has an important and perhaps even a unique role to play in future attempts to resolve ontological problems. The aim of this paper is to pinpoint this view of language more precisely and to defend one view of just how certain sorts of linguistic facts are relevant to ontology.

Before doing this, however, I want to discuss briefly some current philosophical work dealing with language which, although often helpful for approaching ontological and, indeed, many other kinds of problems, is not suited to the task of resolving them. Such work, then, does not exemplify the kind of approach to language in which I am interested here, and I consider it primarily to show this. After this brief examination, I shall turn to contemporary attempts to use language to resolve ontological problems. Hopefully, this will provide clues to the future fruitfulness of linguistic philosophy for ontology.

PHILOSOPHICAL APPROACH TO LANGUAGE RELEVANT BUT NOT PECULIAR TO ONTOLOGY

I wish to mention briefly four different ways in which philosophers are currently concerned with language. All these ways may be philosophically helpful, and many of them have consequences for ontology. For some philosophers some of these approaches to language constitute the whole of philosophy, regardless of their value as a means to other philosophical concerns. One such approach to language is that which attempts to provide explicit definitions of philosophically interesting terms and phrases. Some of the terms which are relevant to ontology and whose definitions would prove valuable are 'materialism', 'physical', psychological', 'theoretical', 'observable', 'free will', 'determinism', 'omnipotence', and 'empirically verifiable'. Certain sentential phrases, which have received and still are receiving much attention, are 'S knows that P', 'It is evident that P', and 'S directly perceives that P'.

A second kind of concern with language is an attempt to provide criteria for the application of terms. Such criteria must be at least sufficient conditions for the correct application of the terms. Examples of this approach to language are found in Chisholm's use of intentionality as a mark of the psychological and his statement of evidence-making characteristics.[1] There have also been attempts to set up criteria for logical category differences as in the work of Ryle,[2] for semantic anomaly as Katz and Fodor have attempted,[3] and for rational acceptance of hypotheses.[4]

A third widespread concern with language is to provide contextual definitions by means of axiom systems, usually of logical and quasi-logical constants. Prime examples are alethic, deontic, epistemic, and doxastic modalities, operators for imperative sentences, and a kind of logical entailment that expresses a relevance between statements that is not captured by logical entailments based on material implication.[5]

A fourth currently influential approach to language by philosophers is the work done as preliminary to a future science of linguistics. Here, Katz and Fodor have attempted to lay out requirements for a semantical theory to be grafted on to a Chomskian grammar.[6] In so doing, they have attempted to set up different criteria for deciding whether or not sentences are analytic or ambiguous or semantically anomalous. If successful, such criteria will have obvious consequences for work done in many areas of philosophy.

As stated above, all four of these approaches to language may have consequences for various attempts to resolve ontological problems, but none seems peculiarly suited to resolving those problems. Nor does any seem more directly relevant to ontology than to any other area within or outside of philosophy.

PHILOSOPHICAL ATTEMPTS TO USE LANGUAGE TO RESOLVE ONTOLOGICAL PROBLEMS

In talking of linguistic approaches to ontological problems, the methods that come most readily to mind are those involving various sorts of philosophical analysis of language. These were the topic of my first paper. I shall therefore very briefly review the four approaches of this kind discussed in that paper. The first two, logical atomism and logical positivism, both essentially involve meaning analysis. Logical atomism attempts to derive ontology from the application of a picture theory of reference to the results of definitions in use of the nonprimitive terms of a *Tractatus*-like ideal language. Ultimately these definitions must be in terms of the primitive terms of the language in atomic sentences. It is these sentences which are said to picture what there is. The second theory, logical positivism, denies the cognitive significance of ontological claims on the basis of the verifiability criterion of meaningfulness. On this theory philosophy is primarily the clarification of language. For some it is clarification by means of an ideal language similar to that language required by logical atomism, but for others the clarification of ordinary language is by definitions in use, using the resources of ordinary language.

One problem common to logical atomism and logical positivism is the lack of success with significant meaning analyses. Many of those who think this problem results from the vagueness of ordinary language turn to reconstruction analyses. This is the linguistic method which in some way reconstructs certain of the rules of a given expression, thereby changing its meaning, in order to achieve some purpose or other. In general, the purpose of reconstruction analysis is to modify those rules governing the expression in question which are defective in some way, while preserving those rules which are not defective. Thus the ideal is to keep the meaning of the analysans as close as possible to the analysandum by reconstructing only those rules of the analysandum which are defective.

The fourth approach to ontology by means of analysis which was discussed in the previous paper is use analysis. This is the view that many so-called enduring ontological problems can be solved or in many cases dissolved by properly classifying the uses of the language in which the problems are expressed. This approach to ontological problems, which stems in large part from the later Wittgenstein, involves pointing out logical similarities or differences between the linguistic expressions in which the problem is expressed and other linguistic expressions, the use of which is clear. On the basis of these results about the logical similarities and differences, conclusions are drawn about whether the expressions in question have a certain use, generally about whether they have a referring or descriptive use. The problem that we saw facing this kind of analytic approach to ontological problems is that anyone using it must justify a premise something like one of the form: "A term is used referentially (descriptively) if and only if it has logical features A, B, C, ..." But this has not been done and some would claim that it cannot be done.

We have seen above that many philosophical investigations of language are neither designed nor seem able to resolve ontological problems. We have reviewed the conclusion in my previous paper that there are objections to those linguistic methods which are designed as approaches to ontology and which rely on philosophical analysis of language. Have we then gathered sufficient evidence to warrant the conclusion that no facts about language are uniquely suited to the resolution of ontological problems? It is, I think, too soon for such a conclusion, for at least two reasons. First, even if we reject all linguistic approaches to ontology that require analysis, there might be some fruitful linguistic approach that does not rely on anything like these standard sorts of analysis. Second, as stated at the end of my previous paper, we have not yet found reason to conclude whether or not the problem for use analysis, reviewed briefly above, is fatal. Although if we follow Wittgenstein it would seem we should draw that conclusion, I have previously claimed that we can avoid such a pessimistic conclusion.[7]

In the rest of this paper I wish to explore more deeply the two preceding reasons for rejecting the claim that there is no particular relevance of language to ontology. Hopefully, such an exploration will help us discover at least one way that facts about language may be fruitful for future work in ontology.

LINGUISTIC APPROACHES TO ONTOLOGY WITHOUT ANALYSIS

Strawson, 'Persons', and Persons

Based upon the problems we have found confronting attempts to use philosophical analysis to provide the linguistic tools needed to resolve ontological problems, it might seem that the best chance to find the relevance of language to ontology is to turn to linguistic approaches that do not require any of the standard kinds of analysis. P. F. Strawson, whose approach has much in common with use analysis, has based some of his ontological arguments on linguistic facts which seem to differ from those uncovered by the kinds of linguistic analysis previously examined. To illustrate this briefly, let us consider his attempt to derive his conclusion that persons are ontologically basic from certain linguistic facts. He begins by defining the concept of a person as "the concept of a type of entity such that *both* predicates ascribing states of consciousness *and* predicates ascribing corporeal characteristics, a physical situation, etc., are applicable to a single individual of that single type." [8] For the materialist, idealist, and Cartesian, persons are ontologically derivative because for each of them, in referring to persons we are always also referring to some entities of another kind, that is, bodies, minds, or embodied minds. But, according to Strawson, persons are not in any way reducible to any more basic kinds of entities. What a person is identical with is, in the last analysis, neither a body, nor a mind, nor an embodied mind. Thus, if Strawson is right, materialists, idealists, and Cartesians are wrong in their claims about the kinds of entities that are ontologically basic.[9]

Strawson's argument to establish his objection can be construed as having two parts. First, he attempts to show that it is correct to ascribe states of consciousness to something in such a way that the relationship between the entity and states of consciousness is not a contingent one of causal dependence, but rather is some kind of "non-transferrable ownership." That is, the entity that has or owns a certain state of consciousness has it in some kind of noncontingent way. Here Strawson tried to destroy what he calls "the no-ownership theory," that is, the theory that the only kind of ownership of states of consciousness or experiences is the contingent ownership expressed by the causal dependence of such states upon certain bodies. Second, having established some kind of necessary ownership of experiences, he tries to prove that the owners are persons by eliminating the only other possible owners: bodies and Cartesian egos, that is, pure subjects of experience. Having established both these points, Strawson can then conclude that it is wrong to claim that either bodies or minds are ontologically more basic than persons because such claims imply that the ownership of experiences is, contrary to what Strawson has shown, transferrable from persons to either bodies or minds.

I think that Strawson has established neither part of his argument. I shall here, however, consider only his argument to establish that, because there are noncontingent owners of experiences, and because bodies have only a contingent relationship to experiences, there must be something that is not a mere body and that therefore materialism is false.[10] Let us state Strawson's argument as follows:

(1) Any body's ownership of experiences is contingent—for example, the relationship is causal.

(2) There are noncontingent owners of experience.

(3) If bodies are merely contingent owners of experiences and there are noncontingent owners, then materialism is false.

Therefore

(4) Materialism is false.

Although it is not clear what a noncontingent or necessary owner of experiences is, I think we can safely concede to Strawson that no body, no physical object, is a necessary owner of experiences. The second premise, however, is more debatable, and we should carefully examine Strawson's attempt to establish it. It is, furthermore, the premise he tries to establish by means of certain facts about language.

Strawson's attempt to prove there is a necessary owner of experiences and thereby to disprove the no-ownership theory goes as follows.[11] The no-ownership theorist, like anyone else, must use noncontingent ownership words in some of his sentences if he wishes to assert true sentences. Such words can neither be omitted nor eliminated by rephrasing the sentences, that is, they are essential to the sentence. In talking of the contingent causal relationship between experiences and bodies, for example, we say something of the form, "All experiences of person P are contingently dependent upon a certain body B." In this sentence, some expression that functions like 'of person P' is necessary, because, if we eliminate it altogether, the sentence is false. Furthermore, the no-ownership theorist cannot claim that 'experiences of person P' can be replaced in the sentence by 'experiences contingently dependent upon B' because the two expressions mean the same thing. They differ in meaning, because with the former the sentence is synthetic, but with the latter it is analytic. Thus P's ownership of experiences is necessary, and cannot be reduced to the contingent ownership by bodies. Therefore there must be a noncontingent kind of ownership, and materialism is false.

Does Strawson's refutation of the no-ownership theory succeed?

I shall use a logical analogy to show that it does not. Strawson's premises about language are:

(1) In the sentence 'All experiences of person P are contingently dependent upon body B,' the phrase 'of person P' cannot be eliminated (is necessary) if the sentence is to be true,

and

(2) 'Experiences of person P' does not mean and cannot be replaced by 'experiences contingently dependent upon body B' if the sentence is to remain contingent.

The ontological conclusion Strawson draws from these premises is:

(3) Person P's ownership of experiences is a different kind from body B's contingent ownership.

As it stands, however, the argument is invalid; it lacks a premise relating linguistic facts to its ontological conclusion, such as:

> If a sentence of the form 'All *x*'s of *y* are causally dependent on *z*' is not true if 'of *y*' is eliminated, and if '*x*'s of *y*' does not mean '*x*'s dependent on *z*', then *y*'s ownership of *x*'s differs from *z*'s ownership.

But this additional premise is false as can be seen by letting $x =$ orbits, $y =$ the Morning Star, and $z =$ Venus. The Morning Star's ownership of its orbit is the same as Venus' ownership.

Strawson seems to have overlooked the possibility that two logically different expressions can be used to refer to the same thing. Thus Strawson's premises are consistent with the theory he thinks he refutes, that is, the theory that person P's ownership of experiences is no different from a body's ownership because 'person P' and 'body B' may be two logically different ways of referring to the same thing, a particular body. He has mistakenly moved from facts about certain linguistic terms in certain sentences to ontological conclusions. His error seems to result from a mistaken view about a relationship between certain linguistic facts and other nonlinguistic facts.

Scientific Realism, Explanation, and Description

Another linguistic approach to ontology that does not rely on analysis is that of certain contemporary scientific realists. One of these men, Wilfrid Sellars, says, "That in the dimension of describing and explaining the world, science is the measure of all things, of what is that it is, and of what is not that it is not." [12]

Although there are several versions of scientific realism, many, including Sellars' own theory, can be said to include the thesis that all physical objects have as constituents and properties only the objects and properties referred to by certain of the pure theoretical scientific terms that are required for the best scientific explanation of the observable consequences of the behavior of the objects. These theoretical terms are to be distinguished from the observation terms which describe the behavior that the theoretical terms are used to explain. Some of the theoretical terms are to be included in the axioms of a postulate system the theorems of which express the theory, some are contingently related to observation terms by means of correspondence rules, and some are construed as primitive terms of the postulate system which are used to define the others.

A more extreme version of scientific realism extends the preceding claim about physical objects to persons. That is, for each physical object and each person, those pure theoretical terms of science that provide the best available explanations of its behavior also provide the best available descriptions of its behavior. That is, not only is each theoretical sentence at least as accurate a means of picturing or describing as any other sentence available for describing the same thing, but all theoretical sentences that explain the behavior of a particular entity, when taken together, provide a true description of what they explain that is more accurate and more comprehensive than any other description (including those containing observation terms) of the same phenomenon.

This thesis is clearly relevant to at least one ontological problem, the mind-body problem. If, for example, as many of these scientific realists believe, the theoretical terms of neurophysiology provide the best available explanation of the behavior that psychological terms are also used to explain, then some set of neurophysiological sentences would provide a true description of someone that is more accurate and comprehensive than any set that includes psychological sentences. Strictly speaking, there would be nothing mental—no sensations, no beliefs. Our claims that there are such phenomena would result from a misapprehension by us of what really occurs, perhaps some brain process with only physicalistic properties.

This approach to ontology through the language of science does not require any kind of linguistic analysis. It does, however, assume a theory of a relationship betwen language and reality, because it claims that certain terms of science give us the best picture or description of what there is. It does not seem, however, that in stating this assumption it is required to say anything like what Wittgenstein claimed is meaningless. Of course the problem of justifying the assumption remains. It may be, however, that, like scientific theories, some kind of indirect justification of this assumption can be provided. An important part of the justification of scientific theories is based on the extent of their predictive and explanatory power. An important part of an analogous justification of an ontological thesis would be based on the extent of its power to resolve ontological problems. Consequently, it should enable us to resolve ontological problems. We have just seen how the approach to ontology by means of the theoretical language of science has consequences relevant to the mind-body problem. Roughly, if sensation-terms are required for scientific explanations of human behavior, then there are sensations; if they are not required, then there are no sensations. The question before us is whether this approach by means of the language of science is relevant to other ontological problems, such as the problem of the external world, the problem of free will and determinism, the problem of human agency, the problem of the existence of God, the problem of universals, and the problems of whether existence, goodness, and beauty are properties of things.

Many of the expressions most relevant to these ontological problems such as 'sense-data', 'free will', 'omnipotence', 'exemplification', 'good' seem quite unnecessary for the explanatory vocabulary of science. How should we deal with such terms? If we assume that a term being required for theoretical scientific explanations of things is merely a sufficient condition for the term being part of the most accurate and comprehensive description of what there is, then the method would provide no way to decide about terms such as those mentioned above, and there would be no way for this approach via the language of science to resolve the ontological problems involving them. The approach, then, would lack something essential to being justified in this indirect way. If we assume, as would many scientific realists, that being such a scientific theoretical term is both a sufficient and necessary condition of being part of the best description of what there is, then we are committed to what seems to be a most dubious assumption. That is, the assumption that all of the preceding expressions and all other terms that are not theoretical terms are not included in the most accurate and complete description of the world.

But why should there be such a correspondence between scientific explanation and description? Perhaps, although theoretical terms are best for explanation, observation terms are best for description. Furthermore, the phrase 'best explanation' is elliptical. A set of statements best explains something for some purpose, and what explains best for one purpose does not always explain best for another. Describing human behavior in terms of events and giving physiological explanations of these events is not the kind of procedure best suited to ascribing legal and moral responsibility to persons. Such ascriptions require actions rather than events, and, although each action has an event component, no one has shown how to reduce actions to events. Nor has anyone shown how to relate actions by "correspondence rules" to the events explained by physiology in order to make physiological explanations of event-behavior relevant to action-behavior. Neither is there any reason to think that physiological descriptions and explanations are best for the kind of communication required to conduct everyday affairs. Why should we not consider one of these different kinds of explanation, which are best for purposes different from those of scientific explanation, to provide the best, or at least an equally good, description of what there is? I know of no way for the scientific realist to answer this question and justify his initially dubious claim about a relationship between language and reality, without some additional assumptions also requiring justification. Consequently, this approach to ontological problems is not justified. Either it is incapable of resolving many ontological problems, or it involves a dubious assumption.

AN ATTEMPT TO JUSTIFY USE ANALYSIS AS AN APPROACH TO ONTOLOGICAL PROBLEMS

Thus far our search for ways to avoid the conclusion that no facts about language are uniquely suited for resolving ontological problems has failed. Meaning analysis and reconstruction analysis have been rejected. We also have found reason to doubt the only two linguistic approaches that I have found which do not involve philosophical analysis. Of the linguistic approaches to ontology we have considered, only use analysis remains to be examined. As previously mentioned, although the crucial claims of use analysis have not been justified, I have claimed that there may be a way to justify them. In the rest of this paper I shall summarize my claim and then defend it from two objections.

In my earlier paper (p. 32) we saw that to justify employing use analysis in resolving ontological problems, a person should justify, first, that there are certain logical features that an expression has if and only if it is a referring (descriptive) expression, and, second, which logical features these are. But we found that no one has yet accomplished these two tasks. Furthermore, following Wittgenstein, there is reason to doubt that these are the kinds of facts about language that can be discovered by an investigation of language. The best that we will be able to do, then, is to make certain assumptions and hope that there is some way to justify them as assumptions. The assumptions we should make, I suggest, are just those which are required for completion of the two preceding tasks. We are to assume, in effect, that an expression is used referentially (descriptively) if and only if it has the characteristics A, B, C, ...[13] This, then, would be to make explicit an assumption about logical features of language which is much like those that men such as Nowell-Smith, Hart, Ryle, and others have implicitly assumed to be the criteriological features of referring expressions when they employ use analysis to solve or dissolve ontological problems.

How might we justify the assumption that certain logical features are the criteriological or symptomatic characteristics of referring expressions? The answer is that it can be justified pragmatically by considering how fruitful the method utilizing the criterion is when applied to a certain class of problems, that is, ontological problems. Thus to justify this criterion we must have such a class of problems available. There clearly is such a class, as examples I have mentioned previously indicate. In essence, I am suggesting that such an assumption can be indirectly justified in a way modeled on the indirect justification of scientific theories, that is, in terms of its consequences for the problems that the method using it is designed to resolve. It is, then, the same kind of justification previously considered for the approach to ontology by means of the language of science. In that case, however, we found either that it could not be applied to many ontological problems or that it ruled out arbitrarily and unjustifiably many terms as not suitable for accurate descriptions of what there is. I would claim that this is not true of the kind of assumption I have proposed for use analysis. There is no reason to think that it is not applicable to all terms involved in any ontological problem, or that it arbitrarily and unjustifiably limits the class of accurate referential and descriptive terms.

Objections to Indirect Justification of Use Analysis

There are, however, two other objections I wish to consider which might be raised to this kind of justification of the method of use analysis as a uniquely fruitful way to resolve ontological problems. The first objection is that an assumption of a criterion for referring cannot be justified in the way that scientific theories are justified. It has been claimed that this is

> because of the dissimilarities of the confirmatory procedures. The scientific hypothesis is, and can only be, confirmed by independent testing of deduced consequences. The assumed criteria for referring cannot, however, be similarly confirmed, since their deductive consequences (logically) cannot be independently tested. Their consequences (e.g. that certain terms are or are not referring terms) are confirmable only through prior confirmation of the criteria. Consequently, Cornman's proposal that the criteria for referring be justified "pragmatically" by the ability of consequences deduced from them to solve [ontological] problems, appears impossible of fulfillment, without begging the question. Lacking independent evidence that the conclusion is a solution to a[n ontological] problem, it cannot be claimed that it is a solution, and therefore it cannot be claimed that the conclusion is justified, or that it serves to pragmatically justify the assumption from which it was derived.[14]

One point is clearly correct in this criticism. There is an important disanalogy between scientific theories and the kind of assumptions needed to supplement use analyses. When the statements of a theory are conjoined with certain premises expressing certain facts about observable initial conditions, conclusions expressing observable facts can be derived. Thus the theory can be given an indirect justification through empirical testing of its empirical consequences, and this testing can be done independently of assuming the theory. This, of course, is not the case for the ontological assumptions. What we would derive about whether or not a term is referential or descriptive from such assumptions combined with a premise about the "observable" logical features of the term is not testable by observations made independently of assuming the theory. This seems to rule out, among other desirable features, the possibility of crucial experiments to help decide among competing assumptions.

The question, however, is whether this disanalogy suffices to show that such assumptions cannot be justified in this way. For one thing there can be something like crucial experiments, at least for eliminating many assumptions. There are certain terms which are paradigm examples of referring or descriptive terms, for example, general nouns such as 'rock', and predicates such as 'red', and other terms which are clear examples of nonreferring and nondescriptive words, for example, logical constants. If, all else being equal regarding the extent of power to resolve ontological problems, one of the competing assumptions allows us to derive that certain color words are not referring terms or that certain logical constants are, then there are sufficient grounds to reject that assumption. But, of course, these two tests may not suffice to single out one reference-assumption as *the* justified one. There are, however, other tests which can further narrow the choice considerably. Some examples of plausible additional tests are that, all else being equal, it is more reasonable to choose that assumption which assumes the least untestable assertions and the fewest entities, which is simplest to apply, and which accords most closely with our preanalytic beliefs about which terms are referring terms.

These tests are much like those applied to scientific hypotheses and, I would also claim, hypotheses of quite different kinds, such as ethical and political standards. Consequently, if an approach to ontological problems by means of an assumption about which logical features are the criteriological features of referring terms resolves those problems and, in addition, passes all these tests, and perhaps some others, then, although there is no observable independent test to settle the issue, it certainly seems that the assumption and the resolutions of the problems are justified.

Given that the preceding answer to the previous objection provides reason to think that we can justify some assumption about a criterion of reference indirectly through its fruitfulness in resolving ontological problems, an objection may be raised that this is also a reason for concluding that there is no need for any linguistic approach to ontological problems. Just as competing reference assumptions are to be indirectly weighed in this way, we can also evaluate different resolutions of ontological problems without the need to justify claims about language and reference. That is, according to this objection, we can evaluate a particular ontological claim in terms of its ability to avoid objections to competing claims and to escape objections uniquely its own. It may be that no claim completely avoids objections but it might well be that for any particular ontological problem one particular resolution of the problem is confronted with fewer or less serious objections than any of its alternatives.

There are, I find, at least three reasons to reject the preceding objection to taking a linguistic approach to ontological problems. Many of the competing positions, for example, in the mind-body problem, are stated using claims about language. For example, the analytic behaviorist's position cannot be stated, and thus neither justified nor refuted, without making some statement about the analysis of psychological sentences. One species of what I have called "eliminative materialism" is stated in such a way that it includes a thesis about the referents of sensation-terms. Furthermore, because it must be stated in such a way as to distinguish it from the theory that sensations are identical with brain processes, it is not clear how to restate it without the reference claim.[15]

A second reason for not limiting oneself to a nonlinguistic approach to ontology is that this would fail to include what is perhaps the most unique contribution of linguistic philosophy to ontology. This is the attempt to dissolve ontological problems by showing that there seem to be problems only because certain terms are mistakenly thought to be referential or descriptive.

The third reason is based upon inductive evidence from past nonlinguistic approaches to ontological problems. Although an indirect weighing of alternative ontological theses may eliminate some alternatives, so many of roughly equal plausibility remain that some additional way to eliminate competing views is needed. This is clearly true for the mind-body problem, and for the problem of the external world where few of the competing alternatives have yet been eliminated. Consequently, although I certainly think that as many alternatives as possible should be eliminated in this nonlinguistic way, it would be a mistake not to allow oneself the additional tools that are made available through a linguistic approach to ontology by means of use analysis.

CONCLUSION: LANGUAGE, ANALYSIS, AND THE FUTURE OF ONTOLOGY

I have above sketched one way language and one kind of philosophical linguistic analysis seem to be uniquely relevant to ontological problems. I have suggested what seems to be the sort of assumptions it requires and the sense in which they can be justified. I am not claiming that these are the only assumptions possible or even that they are the only plausible assumptions. They are, however, the only ones I have, thus far at least, found reason to think are plausible. Perhaps we shall find that no set of such reference-assumptions meets even this rather weak standard of justification, but, until it has been shown that this is the case—and there seems to be no a priori reason to think that it is—I can find no reason not to pursue ontological problems in a way such as the one I have suggested. For this reason, I conclude that there is a role in the future, not only for language, but also for linguistic analysis, in what may turn out to be a uniquely fruitful approach to ontological problems.

NOTES

1. See R. Chisholm, *Perceiving,* Ithaca, N. Y., 1957, chap 11 and chap. 6, respectively.
2. See G. Ryle, "Categories," in *Logic and Language,* Second Series, ed. Flew, Oxford, 1955; and J. Cornman, "Types, Categories and Nonsense," *American Philosophical Quarterly Monograph Series,* no. 2, 1968.
3. See J. Katz and J. Fodor, "The Structure of a Semantic Theory," *Language,* 1963, XXXIX, 170–210; and J. Cornman, "Categories, Grammar, and Semantics," *Inquiry* (forthcoming).
4. See I. Levi, *Gambling with Truth,* New York, 1967. For an excellent and comprehensive bibliography, see *Induction, Acceptance, and Rational Belief,* ed. M. Swain, Dordrecht, Holland, 1970.
5. See G. von Wright, "Deontic Logic," *Mind,* 1951, LX, 1–15; and A. Anderson and N. Belnap, "The Pure Calculus of Entailment," *Journal of Symbolic Logic,* 1962, XXVII, 19–52.
6. See Katz and Fodor, "The Structure of a Semantic Theory."
7. See J. Cornman, *Metaphysics, Reference, and Language,* New Haven, 1966, esp. "Summary and Concluding Remarks."
8. P. Strawson, *Individuals,* London, 1959, pp. 101–102.
9. See *ibid.,* chap. III.

10. For a discussion of Strawson's argument against Cartesian egos, see J. Cornman, "Strawson's 'Person'," *Theoria,* 1964, XXX, 145–156.

11. Strawson, *Individuals,* pp. 94 f.

12. W. Sellars, *Science, Perception and Reality,* London, 1963, p. 173. For more details about Sellars' scientific realism, see J. Cornman, "Sellars, Scientific Realism, and Sensa," *Review of Metaphysics,* 1970, XXIII, 417–451.

13. For ease in this discussion, I have used 'refer' broadly to include describing, as I have done in *Metaphysics, Reference, and Language.* See esp. pp. 83–85 and pp. 142–145.

14. R. Finkelstein, "On Answering External Questions," *Philosophical Forum,* 1969, I, 359–363.

15. I have examined this view in "On the Elimination of 'Sensations' and Sensations," *Review of Metaphysics,* 1968, XXII, 15–35.

Philosophic Logic, Linguistic Form, and Analytic Metaphysics

R. M. Martin

In 1914, in *Our Knowledge of the External World,*[1] Russell wrote, it will be recalled, that the problems he was discussing "all reduce themselves, in so far as they are genuinely philosophical, to problems of logic. This is not due to any accident," he continues, "but to the fact that every philosophical problem, when it is subjected to the necessary analysis and purification, is found either to be not really philosophical at all, or else to be, in the sense in which we are using the word, logical." [2] Russell goes on to explain that by 'logic' he does not refer to that of the scholastic tradition, nor to the inductive methods of Bacon, Galileo, and Stuart Mill, nor to the idealist logic of Hegel and Bradley. He refers rather to logistic or mathematical logic, mentioning in particular the work of Leibniz, Boole, and Frege. But "mathematical logic, even in its most modern form (that of 1914)," Russell goes on, "is not *directly* of philosophical importance except in its beginnings. After its beginnings, it belongs rather to mathematics than philosophy. . . . [I]ts beginnings . . . are the only part . . . that can properly be called *philosophical* logic. . . ." [3]

Later Russell notes that logic consists of two parts. "The first part investigates what propositions [i.e., sentences] are and what forms they may have; this part enumerates the different kinds of atomic propositions, of molecular propositions, of general propositions, and so on. The second part consists of certain supremely general propositions, which assert the truth of all propositions of certain forms. The second part merges into pure mathematics, whose propositions all turn out, on analysis, to be such general formal truths. The first part, which merely enumerates forms, is the more difficult, and philosophically the more important; and it is the recent progress in this first part, more than anything else, that has rendered a truly scientific discussion of many philosophical problems possible." [4]

In a more modern terminology, we would say that this second part of logic in turn consists of two branches. The first comprises the elementary theories of the truth-functional connectives, of the quantifiers, and of identity. The second branch consists of the theory of classes and of relations as based on the simplified theory of types. (Russell's "propositional functions" may for the present be disregarded.) The first branch we now call 'first-order logic', the second 'higher-order logic'. Since 1914 there has been of course an enormous development in what is essentially this second branch, extended now to include such topics as set-theory, model-theory, proof-theory, the theory of recursive functions, and various special topics in metamathematics. But these belong properly to mathematics, as Russell in effect pointed out, and most of the really serious and significant contributions to them since 1914 have been made by professional mathematicians.

Let us concern ourselves with philosophic logic only, which, according to Russell, investigates what sentences are and what forms they may have. Furthermore, it provides an enumeration of such forms. Strictly, of course, Russell made no contribution to the analysis of what sentences are, that is, sentences of a natural language. Russell scarcely concerned himself with this problem at all. Nor did he provide a full enumeration of logical forms. He presented a logistic system containing various forms, to be sure, but this is a very different matter. To construct a logistic system is one kind of enterprise; to show it applicable in some way to a natural language, is quite another. In doing the one Russell no doubt thought he was doing the other. But these are quite different enterprises, so it will be contended, and more will be said about them and their interrelation in a moment.

Although he contributed little to it, Russell's characterization of philosophic logic was apt. Also it was good to emphasize the very central role that logic plays in the more analytic parts of philosophy. Russell's actual claim that logic provides the "essence" of philosophy, most of us would think, is excessive; he claimed too much on too narrow a basis. Even so, logic justifiably "meddles with all subjects," in Peirce's phrase, in the sense that it seeks to provide linguistic forms for the sentences in which those subjects may be discussed. For the construction of many forms the elementary logical words or phrases 'and', 'or', 'if—then', 'if and only if', and 'not' are needed. Likewise the quantifiers 'for all *x*' and 'there exists at least one *x* such that' and identity. Thus philosophic logic should include presumably the elementary or first-order theory mentioned above. For Russell, this elementary theory seems to belong to the second part of logic, however, because within it are enunciated certain "supremely general" sentences that assert the truth of all sentences of certain forms. But there is not much point in relegating, as Russell does, forms containing certain logical notions to one domain of logic and the principles governing them to another. In any event, it seems almost universally agreed upon nowadays that philosophic logic should include elementary or first-order logic, and the point need not be further argued.

The truth-functions, quantifiers, and identity had been well studied by 1914, when Russell wrote *Our Knowledge of the External World*, and little of philosophic significance has been added to what was known then. The developments of philosophic interest since 1914 have been more in *metalogic,* that is, in logical *syntax* and *semantics*. Syntax is the theory of expressions or symbols as such and of their interrelations one to another. Semantics, roughly, is the study of how symbols relate to whatever it is that is symbolized. The most important relations here, it seems, are those of referring or designating or denoting. And out of the theory of these relations, if properly developed, emerges the semantical truth-concept. Truth and reference are so intimately interrelated that without one we lack the other. No truth, no reference; no reference, no truth.[5] For the exact connection here, we must, of course, consult the technical development itself. And note that this development need *not* involve the second branch of Russell's second part of logic or its modern prototype, set- or class-theory.

Just as logic divides into first-order (or elementary) and higher-order logic, so syntax divides into first-order (or elementary) syntax as distinguished from higher-order (or theoretical) syntax. First-order syntax is formulated in such a way as to presuppose only a first-order logic.[6] Often it is thought that the resources of higher-order logic are needed fundamentally, but this is not the case. By suitable technical maneuvers, first-order syntax may be made to suffice for many purposes, in fact, for most. In any case, it is only first-order syntax that is of any direct philosophic interest. It is natural then to extend philosophic logic in Russell's sense to include not only first-order logic but first-order syntax as well.

A similar distinction may be made in semantics, which is often formulated on the basis of a higher logic or set-theory. On the other hand, a semantics suitably developed on the basis of only a first-order logic may be made surprisingly powerful.[7] Here too it is only first-order semantics that is of direct philosophical interest, and the field of philosophic logic should surely be extended further to embrace it. Another extension is to be made, into pragmatics, in which the user of language is brought explicitly into account.[8] But, of this, more in a moment.

Thus far, then, philosophic logic may be thought to consist of first-order logic, together with a first-order syntax, semantics, and pragmatics. On such a basis a reasonably broad and inclusive "inventory of logical forms" can be given. And only as conceived in this quite broad sense can philosophic logic reasonably be claimed to provide the "essence" of analytic philosophy.

In first-order logic the objects over which our variables range are *individuals,* and quantifiers over such variables are admitted. In higher-order logic, in addition to variables over individuals, variables over properties or classes of, and relations between or among, individuals are admitted, as well as variables of still higher logical type. And quantifiers are admitted upon all these kinds of variables. In syntax, our variables range only over the *expressions* of a language-system. In first-order syntax no further kinds of variables are admitted. In first-order semantics and pragmatics the matter is somewhat more complicated, as we shall see, because of the admission of variables for individuals of various sorts, persons, times, and so on.

A rough and ready inventory of some useful logical or linguistic forms may be given as follows. Let us begin with some simple forms suggested by Russell and then go on to others to be given within metalogic, including pragmatics. Many of these are familiar, some of them less so. Nothing especially new will be said about them, but it is perhaps not without interest to bring them all together under a single head.

Consider the sentences 'Socrates is mortal', 'Jones is angry', 'The sun is hot'. "What is common here is the *form* of the propositions, not an actual constituent," Russell notes. The form is namely

'*x is an F or Fx*'.

In place of '*x*' here we are allowed to put in a proper name in English of an individual and in place of '*F*' a predicate of English applicable to individuals. The form contains only variables and the special letter '*F*', but an English sentence results from the form by appropriate substitution or replacement.

Consider next the sentences 'Peter is older than Paul', 'Jones is more courteous than Smith', 'The sun is bigger than the moon.' Here the form is

'*x* bears *R* to *y*' or '*xRy*',

where in place of '*x*' and '*y*' we are allowed to put in proper names of individuals and in place of '*R*' a two-place relation-predicate. Consider next 'Alys is jealous of Bertrand's affection for Dora'. Here we have the form

'*x* bears *S* to *y* and *z*' or '*Sxyz*'.

Similarly for forms involving four-place relation-predicates, and so on.

We then go on to forms involving 'not', 'and', 'or', 'if—then' and 'if and only if' in familiar fashion. Here a few typical forms are

'*x* is not an *F*',
'*x* does not bear *R* to *y*',
'*x* is an *F* and *x* does not bear *R* to *y*',
'*x* is an *F* or *x* does not bear *R* to *y*',
'If *x* is an *F* then *x* does not bear *R* to *y*',

and so on.

Having included identity as a notion of first-order logic, we have also the form

'$x = y$'.

Consider an instance wherein '*x*' and '*y*' are both replaced by proper names. The instance is true (or false) depending upon whether the two names designate (or do not) precisely the same object.

In familiar fashion we go on to forms involving the quantifiers:

'Every *F* is a *G*',

'There is at least one *F* that bears *R* to at least one *G*.'

'If every *F* is a *G*, then every individual that bears *R* to some *F* bears *R* also to some *G*'.

Here all manner of molecular forms involving quantifiers and identity are admitted.

Note that, up to this point, we have merely been enumerating some forms for English sentences. We have been using certain English words as logical constants but we might equally well have used special symbols as is customary. The custom of blurring these two is not especially to be recommended, however. It is almost universally assumed, and usually without comment, that the English word 'and' is somehow closely connected with the logical symbol '·' (or 'v' or '&') for conjunction, and similarly the English 'not' with the '$\sim$' for negation. And similarly for other English words or phrases and other standard logical signs. The *exact nature* of the connection is obscure, however, and surely needs looking at "from close to." How *precisely* are the two sorts of expressions, one sort from a natural language, the other from an artificially constructed logical system, connected? How is this connection established? And why? The connection seems rather more remote than is usually thought. In any event, the two sorts of terms are *very different,* so we should contend, and it will not do to correlate or connect them, or whatever, without good reason and without being pretty sure of exactly what it is that we are doing.

That the English 'and' does not always correlate or go over into the symbolic '·' is shown by the following example (from Copi): [9]

'All mathematicians and philosophers are invited'

becomes

'For every *x*, if (*x* is a mathematician v *x* is a philosopher) then *x* is invited'.

rather than

'For every x, if (x is a mathematician . x is a philosopher) then x is invited'.

This latter would say that all mathematicians who are also philosophers are invited. Similarly, the English 'any' is highly ambiguous, in some cases going over into a universal quantifier and in others into an existential one. For example,

'If any gold goblet is missing, some one will call the police'

goes over into

'For all x, if x is a gold goblet and missing then John will find x'.

Examples of these kinds can be multiplied of course *ad nauseam*.

What is needed now is an exhaustive classification of *all* uses of English words such as 'and,' 'or', and so on. We would then formulate *rules of correlation* as between contexts containing them and purely symbolic contexts containing the logical symbols. Nothing short of an exhaustive study of this kind could justify our correlating the English 'and' in many contexts with the symbolic '.'. And exceptions here might help to reveal some interesting aspects of the English 'and'.

With nonlogical proper names and predicates, the situation is easier. The proper name 'Jasper Johns' is correlated by fiat with 'j', say, just as 'is wealthy' is correlated by fiat with, say, 'W'. Then 'Jasper Johns is wealthy' becomes by fiat 'Wj'. We merely pay the symbols 'W' and 'j' here overtime and make them behave as we wish.

As is well known, in terms of the truth-functions, quantifiers, and identity, contexts containing Russellian descriptions, phrases of the form 'the one individual having such and such a property', can be defined in full glory. We have then further forms such as

'The one and only individual having F has G',

where one-place predicates are inserted in place of 'F' and 'G' The usefulness of descriptions is well known and proper names may often be introduced as abbreviations for them.

It is not clear that descriptions have been exploited to the full, however, by students of natural language. Egocentric words such as 'I' or 'here' or 'now' can perhaps be handled in terms of them;

likewise the demonstratives 'this' and 'that' as well as tensed verbs. Sentences containing such words or phrases are ambiguous until something more is specified. This something more can often, perhaps always, be given by replacing the ambiguous word or phrase by an unambiguous description. In any case, the addition of contexts containing descriptions to our inventory of linguistic forms is surely welcome.

Let us turn now to some syntactical forms. In syntax we are interested only in linguistic expressions; nothing more, nothing less. To indicate our interest in 'Jasper Johns' or 'j' rather than the person so named, let us use single quotes as is customary. The variables of syntax—let them be '*a*', '*b*', and so on—will then range over just linguistic expressions and sequences of them. Some of these sequences will be words or phrases of special kinds. For simplicity, and to make our ideas clear, let the expressions be those of some first-order logical system *L*. Typical forms are then as follows:

> '*a* is a variable of *L*',
> '*a* is a two-place predicate of *L*',
> '*a* is an atomic sentential function of *L*',
> '*a* is a molecular sentential function of *L*',
> '*a* is an occurrence of a variable *b* in a formula *c* of *L*',
> '*a* is a sentence of *L*',
> '*a* is a logical consequence in *L* of *b*',
> '*a* is a theorem of *L*',

and so on.

The various notions in the syntax of *L*, such as *variable, sentential function, sentence,* and *theorem,* are introduced by fiat. *L* is constructed in such a way that these definitions define what we wish them to. In a natural language the matter is more complicated. We do not define 'noun', 'verb', 'adjective', and so on, by fiat. How do we define them? Where do these notions come from? Are they really useful notions or merely a carryover from traditional grammar? These are difficult questions, about which at the moment one cannot speak with assurance. The suspicion, however, is that these traditional words embody very obscure and worn-out notions in need of a complete overhauling.

A primary aim of the syntax of a natural language *NL* is to gain an adequate definition of '*a* is a sentence of *NL*'.

The methods used by logicians in defining

'*a* is a sentence of *L*',

for *L* a symbolic system, have helped contemporary linguists to make progress in defining

'*a* is a sentence of *NL*'.

Nonetheless, we are as yet far from a complete definition of this notion, even for any one *NL* of sufficient richness or expressive power.

Syntax by itself is perhaps not of much philosophic interest. It becomes so primarily as a prelude to semantics, the study of how words are related to objects. Insofar as semantics makes mention of words and their interrelations, a syntax is presupposed. Syntax without semantics is a quite respectable discipline, but a semantics without a syntax is unthinkable.

Well, how are words related to objects? Or, rather, specifically what relations are there that words bear to objects? Here, again, let us merely list certain forms. Because we are dealing with both words and objects, it is appropriate to allow two sorts of variables, syntactical variables over expressions of the language and object-variables over individuals. Let '*a*', '*b*', and so on, be the first, and '*x*', '*y*', and so on, the second, as above.

Typical forms are then as follows:

'*a* designates *x*',
'*a* denotes *x*',
'For all *x*, *a* denotes *x* if and only if—*x*—' (where '—*x*—' is some sentential form containing '*x*' as a free variable),
'*a* is true' and '*a* is false',
'*a* is L-true', '*a* is L-false',
'*a* is F-true', '*a* is F-false',
'*a* L-implies *b*',
'*a* is L-equivalent with *b*',
'*a* analytically entails *b*',

and so on. Here *a* and *b* are in some cases proper names, in others predicates, and in others sentences. We can go on to other form involving various kinds of *intensions* or "meanings." The theory becomes progressively more elaborate as it is developed. Starting out with merely the theories of designation or denotation, we go on to the theory of truth, to the theory of L-truth and analytic truth, and thence to the theory of various kinds of intension.[10] Under intensions are included such "objects," if they may be so called, as *facts* and *propositions* or *states of affairs*. It is usually assumed that we all know well enough what these latter are—the kind of knowledge we all have except when asked to give an account of it. To give an account of facts and propositions is by no means easy and "takes us out on deep waters in philosophy," in the phrase of von Wright. They are highly obscure "objects," and it will not do to use them without analysis, in the manner of modal logicians and many of our Oxford friends.

The various semantical forms listed are of interest in two ways. They give us suitable linguistic forms for English sentences containing such words as 'designates', 'denotes', 'true', 'false', 'entails', and so on. Without these forms, English sentences containing these words just have to be disregarded. In fact, many of them were disregarded by Russell, whose inventory could not include them. Of course we must distinguish, as Russell did not always, between the use and mention of expressions. All of these semantical forms rest upon interrelating the use of an expression with the mention of an expression, not necessarily the same one, of course. In fact, it is not oversimplifying too much to say that semantics *is* the science of correct use and mention. Syntax is not. In syntax, we merely mention the expressions of some language; we do not use them. In semantics we both use and mention them, and the semantical laws or rules tell us to some extent precisely how.

Semantics is also of philosophical interest for another reason, namely, that it provides a well-knit *theory* concerning these forms and their interrelations. Linguistic forms do not come in solitary splendor, they come in bundles, and the members of a bundle exhibit structural and other relations to each other. Semantics provides a theory as to how 'designates', 'true', 'analytically entails', and so on, are interrelated—much more intimately, be it said, than is usually supposed. That such a theory is philosophically desirable goes without saying, and it is provided by no other discipline. Thus, if one wishes a well-knit theory of these various notions, there is no known alternative. Just as, if one wishes a well-knit theory of numbers and of their interrelations, there is no known alternative to arithmetic. Of course, there are alternative formulations, but no alternative kind of theory.

The semantical theory of a given symbolic language is explicitly characterized by laying down certain syntactical and semantical *laws* or *rules* in the form of axioms or rules of inference. The choice of these is to some extent arbitrary but not wholly so. The symbolic language is to some extent always under the conscious control of the logician. He is free to make the symbols behave as he wishes. His wishes are not mere whims, however, for he is ever seeking a symbolic language of wide expressive power with this double aim, as we have noted: on the one hand, to provide linguistic forms for more and more sentences of natural language, and, on the other, to provide a well-knit theory concerning these forms. The theory should be not only formally correct, that is, well constructed in accord with modern technical standards, but also materially adequate in the sense of satisfying certain broad, general requirements thought to be desirable. Suitable syntactical and semantical rules can be formulated, providing a theory in accord with both of these requirements, for suitable object-languages.

Strictly, however, we have no semantics of the kind mentioned for the full natural language. What is to be done, then, to provide such? Well, we can go about it piecemeal, by taking up notion by notion *ad hoc,* as it were, trying to make them fit the full natural language and paying no attention at all to the syntax and semantics mentioned above. In other words, to go about it as though Frege, Russell, Carnap, Tarski, Ajdukiewicz, and a host of others had never written. But this method is failing and is bound to fail, it would seem, in linguistics as elsewhere. Carnap predicted this years ago. "The method of (logical) syntax [and semantics]," he wrote in 1937, "will not only prove useful in the logical analysis of scientific theories—it will also help in the logical analysis of the word languages. . . . The direct analysis of these, which has been prevalent, *must inevitably fail* [italics added], just as a physicist would be frustrated [and in fact would fail in his main task] were he from the outset to attempt to relate his laws to natural things—trees, stones, and so on. In the beginning, the physicist relates his laws to the simplest of constructed forms; to a thin straight lever, to a simple pendulum, to punctiform masses, etc. Then, with the help of the laws relating to these constructed forms, he is later in a position to analyze into suitable elements the complicated behavior of real bodies, and thus to control them. One more comparison: the complicated configurations of mountain chains, rivers, frontiers, and the like, are most easily represented and investigated by the help of geographical coordinates—or, in other words, by constructed lines not given in nature. In the same way, the syntactical [and semantical] properties of a particular word-language, such as English, . . . are best represented and investigated by comparison with a constructed language which serves as a system of reference." [11]

Chomsky has criticized this famous passage, but without, it would seem, understanding fully the aims and methods of metalogic, as Carnap himself has pointed out. Fully to substantiate Carnap's contention here would be a long, hard business, of course. The point is not so much that Carnap is correct—for he may have overstated his case—as that linguistics can profitably learn from the methods to which he has drawn attention, as the late Uriel Weinreich was wont to observe. Meanwhile, the precise role that these methods should play in linguistics remains controversial.

Let us not tarry further with the problem of formulating a semantics for the full natural language. Meanwhile logical syntax and semantics provide sharp theoretical notions which, like those of mathematics, are useful for those who know how to use them. The analogy seems apt. If one has not studied mathematics, one will not know how to use its methods in natural science. If one has not mastered logical syntax and semantics, one will not know how to go about using them in linguistics. In both cases, *musica non habet inimicum nisi ignorantem.*

Two other areas of theory, which philosophic logic naturally embraces, are the so-called *calculus of individuals* and *tense-logic.* The former is concerned with such relations between individuals as *discreteness, overlapping, part-to-whole,* and so on. The origins of the calculus of individuals go back to Leśniewski's *O padstawach matematyki* of 1927–31.[12] The significance of the subject for philosophy was well emphasized by Leonard and Goodman in 1936, and for biology, more particularly, for the theories of cell fusion and division, by Woodger in 1937.[13] Then in 1951, the subject came to the fore again in the constructional system of

Goodman's *The Structure of Appearance*.[14] Despite these significant uses of the calculus of individuals, most philosophers continue to ignore the subject and thereby to deprive themselves of a most useful area of theory. To be sure, there are difficulties in interpreting the subject, which its proponents have perhaps not quite faced up to, in connection with space and time. Let individuals for the moment be physical objects. To say that the physical object x is a part of the physical object y is to say that x is a part of y with respect somehow to space and time. The calculus of individuals, however, is concerned only with those properties of the part-to-whole relation, of overlapping, and so on, which hold no matter what spatiotemporal framework is adopted. Although we cannot really be clear about the part-whole relation as between physical objects without being clear as to the spatiotemporal structure involved, the converse also holds. We cannot be really clear about spatiotemporal structure without being clear concerning the relation of part-to-whole. In any event, the use of the calculus of individuals is no doubt indispensable in any serious attempt to delineate that structure.

Tense-logic has been under development recently in such faraway places as Oxford and the University of California at Los Angeles. The leading idea is to accommodate differences of tense by means of suitable linguistic forms. In some methods extension is made at the metalinguistic level by admitting such forms as:

'p is true today but was false yesterday'.

Other methods allow additional forms, but in the object-language, such as:

'x is green at time t but is blue at time t' for t' later than t',

This is not the occasion to criticize details in either the Oxford or California approach, neither of which seems acceptable. The Oxford approach makes fundamental use of unanalyzed propositions, regarded as entities *sui generis* and suspect at best, confuses use and mention, and neglects most of the niceties of syntax and semantics. The California approach, on the other hand, incorporates the subject within mathematical model-theory, and hence within the second branch of Russell's second part of logic. But this seems too much. To involve essentially the whole of mathematics for the simple purpose of analyzing tense differences is to involve too much and anyhow is unnecessary. And model-theory itself is not above suspicion, as constructivist mathematicians themselves have urged. If we see through a glass only model-theoretically, as in California, much that may otherwise be seen clearly face to face will be seen only darkly.

An alternative to, and enrichment of, tense-logic has been proposed elsewhere in what has been called *'an event-logic.'*[15] Here such forms as:

> 'Event e_1 is before event e_2',
> 'Event e_1 is simultaneous with event e_2',
> 'e is a Brutus-stabbing-Caesar event',
> 'e is an event consisting of all events that happen to physical object x',
> 'Event e is a part of the life history of physical object x',
> 'Physical object x was F relative to event e',
> 'Physical object x will bear R to physical object y relative to event e',

and so on. In event-logic, many useful locutions are admitted, including some which may be used as basis for a theory of tenses. Event-logic quickly overflows into the theories of space and time, however, and is thus not easy, but its main features can be sketched independently of the details of those theories. In other words, event-logic may be thought of as providing just those characteristics of events that are neutral as to alternative physical or cosmological theories of space and time. Event-logic is similar in this respect to the calculus of individuals.

Let us turn now to pragmatics, in which the human user of language is explicitly brought in. Let 'X', 'Y', and so on, be variables taking users as their values. Let 'a', 'b', and so on, as above, be the variables over the expressions of L, 'f', 'g', and so on, for action-kinds, 't', 't'', 't_1', and so on, for times. Some typical forms for pragmatics are then:

> 'Person X apprehends the sentence a at time t',
> 'Person X accepts the sentence a at t',
> 'X utters the sentence a at t',
> 'X asserts a at t',
> 'X rejects a at t',
> 'Person X is cognitively indifferent to a at t',

'X cognitively prefers a to b at t in the sense that he is more willing to accept a than b at t',
'X performs an action f upon the object x at t',
'X intends at t to perform an action for f on x at t'',
'Person X performs an f on x at t in order to perform g on y at t'',
'X asserts a to Y at time t',
'X asks a of Y at time t',
'X commands a of Y at t',
'X performs an action f at t upon the basis of his accepting sentences $a_1, \ldots a_n$ at t',
'X believes of objects x and y that such and such holds of them',
'X is obliged to perform f at t on the basis of the moral code C',

and so on and on.

Of course, the mere listing of these forms is not very informative. With each a theory trails along, and these theories quickly spill over into psychology, psycholinguistics, sociolinguistics, and the like. Nonetheless, significant properties of these forms can be given before becoming embroiled in the details of these special sciences. Just as with event-logic, we are concerned here with matters that can be settled, to some extent at least, before turning to empirical science. At the same time, it is welcome that pragmatics, and applied logic generally, should spill over into these sciences, being concerned fundamentally with their basic linguistic forms.

Pragmatics branches off easily into what might be called '*praxiology*' on the one hand and '*epistemics*' on the other. Praxiology is the theory of action and is based upon forms concerning performance and intending. In epistemics, the relations of believing and knowing play fundamental roles. To be sure, there is much that is controversial here. The point is merely that the best way of approaching these subjects seems to be by means of the conscious use of logic. Ramsey was perhaps the first to note this explicitly in 1927 when, in discussing belief, he presupposed that "the thinker with whom we are concerned uses a systematic language without irregularities and with an exact notation like that of *Principia Mathematica.*" Of course, such a supposition involves some oversimplification, just as those of the physicist or theoretical biologist or psychologist do.

It is interesting to note parenthetically that Frege, in his very late paper "Der Gedanke" (1918–19), seems to have been the first to call attention to some of these pragmatical forms, in germ at least, especially those concerned with apprehension, acceptance, and assertion. Carnap also has discussed some of these forms, but has in addition suggested other intensional ones that seem dubious and objectionable and anyhow are not needed.[16] It is interesting also that H. P. Grice, in a very recent paper, has called attention to the form:

> 'Person *X* utters sentence *a* (at *t*) in order to assert (or mean) such and such',

a form presumably definable on the basis of the foregoing.[17] This form is useful in discussing the "utterer's meaning" in contrast to "word-meaning" and "sentence-meaning," and as a basis for what have been elsewhere called 'subjective intensions'.

There has been scarcely any mention above of modal logic and its train deontic logic, erotetic logic, imperatival logic, and so on. The reason is that these subjects were all conceived in sin. Modal logic rests upon several fundamental errors which, like diseases, are then bequeathed to her offspring. Many of these have been pointed out by Quine, and I have added to the list in my paper "Does Modal Logic Rest upon a Mistake?" [18] Nonetheless, what modal logic aims to do can be done correctly and efficiently in semantics, it would seem, the modal predicate 'is necessary' being handled in terms of the notion of logical or analytic truth. Likewise, it seems very likely that deontic logic, erotetic logic, and so on, can all be accommodated within pragmatics in terms of suitable linguistic forms.

There has been no mention of *inductive* logic in the foregoing, and some will think this a grievous omission. No one seems to be quite sure, however, as to just what inductive logic is—probably a mixture of a little semantics and real number theory, plus perhaps some general methodological principles concerning acceptance. If so, inductive logic then takes its legitimate place in the foregoing, by our combining some of the forms admitted and then adding a few more.

It might be thought that, in the emphasis here, so-called "informal logic," that is, the "logical geography of concepts" and the "context of discovery," is left out of account. But surely this is not the case. In the analysis of any term, even of those of philosophic logic itself, there are always difficult informal decisions and choices to be made, and there are always alternatives. Furthermore, one man's logic is another's mythology, and it is difficult if not impossible to say whose is the correct or most acceptable one. In the formulation of any system of ideas there is, moreover, much informal thinking and discovery that must take place before systematization is achieved. This kind of thinking is of course an essential part of what the philosophic logician does. In mathematics we can distinguish between proving a theorem, say, and discovering the proof. The discovery is informal, by trial and error, by hit or miss, or by thinking out how, on the basis of the antecedent—where we are assuming the theorem is of hypothetical form—the consequent might reasonably follow upon the basis of axioms, the previous theorems, the definitions, and the rules of inference. It is analogous in informal geography where, however, we do not seek to "prove" anything but only to discover linguistic forms and conceptual interconnections. Once a discovery is made, which we think reasonable or acceptable, we state the results as precisely and carefully as we can. We then move on to the "context of justification" and systematization. In all this, of course, informal and heuristic methods play an integral role.

In this paper we have covered the vast terrain of philosophic logic in bold strokes. For details concerning the various linguistic forms that have been suggested, especially those that are new, one may consult the more technical papers in which they are introduced. And of course there are always alternative forms to consider. No one form is necessarily final. Should a better one come along, by all means let us adopt it. But a clear-cut form, even one not quite up to snuff, is better than no form at all, if it can be improved upon or emended in this way or that. Also there should be no hint of completeness in the list of kinds of forms, or among the forms of any one kind. Our inquiry is open-ended and we are free at any point to adopt new forms should the need for them arise.

There has been a good deal of recent talk by structural linguists and others about so-called *depth grammar,* but no one seems to have given a very clear delineation of just what it is. Herbert

Bohnert's suggestion that the "deep structure (of a sentence) be represented by an actual paraphrase in the notation of logic" is a valuable one.[19] But the notation of logic must be suitably augmented, perhaps by the admission of some of the forms above, in order to make this suggestion work. In any case, these logical forms should surely be studied by the linguist and should help to reveal significant grammatical and other features of natural language.

This is not the occasion to discuss fully the teaching of logic, and our miserable failure to give it an adequate place in our curricula. We have relegated the subject to Russell's second branch, and have for the most part neglected the first. The teaching of the first we have put into the hands of those whose only genuine interest is in the second. This of course had led to a situation as unfortunate as one could wish, in which amateur mathematics passes as professional philosophy. Other relevant areas of philosophy, including history, we continue to teach, I am afraid, as though no progress had been made in the study of logical form since the days of Port Royal. Yet, clearly, logic in the sense of *philosophic* logic should occupy a fundamental place in the curriculum, being applicable to all subjects, being (in the great words of Petrus Hispanus) both an *ars artium et scientia scientiarum, ad omnium aliarum scientiarum methodorum principia viam habens.* And it should be taught in a helpful, positive, and liberal way and not as an arid branch of set-theory or metamathematics. Too much emphasis is put on the sciences and not enough on the logic of the humanities. This latter subject, it seems, is one that we have scarcely even begun to explore on a firm modern footing.

Well, now, once philosophic logic including pragmatics has done its work, what remains? Metaphysics, some will answer. Once the foregoing linguistic forms are distinguished, the various sorts of variables needed for them enumerated, and the basic predicates admitted analyzed, it is not clear that much *of a purely philosophic and wholly general kind* remains. Of course there remains the application of all this material to special disciplines, including the *philosophy of* this or that or the other. In the philosophy-of disciplines special predicates are introduced germane to the subject matter at hand. It is not clear that new sorts of variables need be admitted, however, over and above those in the survey. If new sorts do seem needed for some special discipline, it may well be that they should have been admitted somewhere along the line. Thus it may reasonably be claimed that philosophic logic, in the sense of the survey, gives us the heart of metaphysics—or at least of a part of metaphysics, 'analytic metaphysics' let us call it—in the sense of the most general ontology and theory about it.

In particular, analytic metaphysics consists of a doctrine as to the various sorts of entities needed within philosophic logic and metalogic and as to how these entities are interrelated. As a first, rough list, the following sorts have been suggested: physical objects, linguistic expressions, times, events, human persons, action-kinds, and real numbers. Not all of these need be taken as fundamental, for some are reducible to others and in alternative ways. Thus, for example, times may be reduced to events by regarding a time as a class (or virtual class) of simultaneous events. But, equally well, events may be regarded for some purposes as complex constructs given specificity in part by reference to a time. Similarly, a physical object can be regarded as a sum of fusion of a virtual class of genidentical events—where 'genidentical' is taken essentially as in relativity theory. Equally well, an event can be regarded as a construct, part of whose specificity arises from reference to human persons, physical objects, and so on. For example, the event of Brutus' stabbing Caesar with a dagger on the Ides of March, 44 B.C., involves reference to two persons, a physical object (the dagger), and a time, as well as to the triadic relation of stabbing-so-and-so-with . . . If one reduces far enough, one gets back ultimately to the fundamental particles, wavicles, or whatever, of physical theory.

The rough enumeration of sorts of entities is of course only preliminary. But suppose a full list were available, and were complete in the sense that no further sorts, nor variables upon them, were needed for the articulation of logical forms for all the declarative sentences of a natural language of considerable richness, such as English. This is of course a tall supposition, but it is the hope of philosophic logic to be able to supply such a list. Even if a list were not fully complete in this sense, it might still contain enough to be of some interest and to get us started.

Given the list of sorts of entities, analytic metaphysics seeks to interrelate them as closely as possible within a well-knit theory. Part of this interrelating may consist in reducing one sort of entity to another, until we end up with one or more sorts as fundamental. Suitable relations are then to be invoked and characterized as between or among entities of the various sorts. By 'characterized' here one means that suitable principles are laid down, some of them axiomatically, governing the relations in question.

A conception of analytic metaphysics not very different from this was suggested by the late Henry Leonard in his important, but neglected, essay "Logical Positivism and Speculative Philosophy."[20] Leonard contended there that "scientific method is the only genuine method of increasing knowledge," that the procedures of "speculation" are "a part of the technique of the scientific method," that "all philosophic speculation is theoretically reducible to the presentation of a constructionalist system," that logical positivism is itself "a type of speculative philosophy" and that its method is "the sound technique in philosophy." Leonard's "speculative philosophy" seems very close to analytic metaphysics as conceived here.

Logical positivism was based, roughly, on two tenets: that all knowledge is in some sense reducible to knowledge gained in sense perception, plus total reliance upon and use of the techniques of modern logic. It is interesting that, of these two, Leonard emphasizes only the second, so that by 'logical positivism' he means in effect the formulation of a "constructionalist system" somewhat in the manner of Carnap's *Der Logische Aufbau der Welt* or of a philosophic logic as mentioned above. There are alternative "bases" upon which such a system may be built. There is no indication that these must be such that all knowledge is somehow to be traced back to sense perception.

One need not cavil with Leonard's rather loose account of scientific method. It is surely broad enough, however, to condone all the procedures needed in philosophic logic, and hence in analytic metaphysics. To make these features precise is not easy and Leonard does not do so, and we need not step in here where he failed to tread.

Leonard contends that "all philosophic speculation is theoretically reducible to the presentation of a constructionalist system." And in a much-quoted passage, Whitehead stated that "[s]peculative philosophy is the endeavor to frame a coherent, logical, necessary system of general ideas in terms of which every element of our experience can be interpreted." [21] The system is to be "coherent" in the sense that "no entity can be conceived in complete abstraction from the system of the universe. . . . The term 'logical' has its ordinary meaning, including . . . consistency, or lack of contradiction, the definition of constructs in logical terms, the exemplification of general logical notions in specific instances, and the principles of inference." Whitehead goes on to state, however, that "[p]hilosophers can never hope finally to formulate . . . metaphysical first principles. Weakness of insight and deficiencies of language stand in the way inexorably. Words and phrases must be stretched towards a generalization foreign to their ordinary usages; and however such elements of language be stabilized as technicalities, they remain metaphors mutely appealing for an imaginative leap."

Speculative philosophy for Whitehead transcends what may be gained by "the scientific method"; for Leonard, not. Speculative philosophy for Whitehead embraces a cosmology, a physics, a mathematics, an ethics, an aesthetics, a sociology, a theology; for Leonard, not, or at least not explicitly so. If Leonard's view had been developed more fully, it might well have spilled over into these several domains. The spirit animating Whitehead's view is genuinely speculative, however; that animating Leonard's is primarily analytic.

Can we draw a real distinction here between analytic and speculative metaphysics? This would seem doubtful. The difference is more one of emphasis, of degree, or of interest. And, even though "weakness of insight" and "deficiencies of language" stand in the way and "metaphors mutely appealing for an imaginative leap" must be invoked, there is always room in principle for improvement and advance in clarification on the basis of an expanded logic.

In 1936, John Dewey asked Whitehead, on a famous occasion, to choose between the "genetic functional" and "mathematical formal" approaches to philosophy, a choice Whitehead declined to make.[22] The real point, it would seem, is that mathematic-formal methods—that is, the methods of philosophic logic—are needed for the study of genetic-functional material. No matter how evanescent or irregular the waves of the sea or the winds of the sky, no methods are more suitable for the study of their motion, direction, velocity, and so on, than those based on the mathematical theory of real numbers. For philosophic purposes, however, mathematical methods are often a luxury and often inappropriate. But those of philosophic logic are always applicable, legitimately "meddling," like a Socratic gadfly, with all areas of philosophic discourse in which inferences, either deductive or inductive, are made in a systematic way. Try as one may and no matter how hard, logic is the one branch of philosophy one can never escape from. Now that it itself has developed so tremendously, this is a situation we ought all to learn to welcome. Furthermore, there promises to be no future diminution of its philosophic relevance.

"When in the distant future," Whitehead concluded prophetically, symbolic logic "has expanded, so as to examine patterns depending on connections other than those of space, quantity, and number—when this expansion has occurred, I suggest that Symbolic Logic, that is to say, the symbolic examination of pattern with the use of . . . variables, will become the foundation of aesthetics. From that stage it will proceed to conquer ethics and theology." Well, that stage has not yet been reached, but we have come a long way.

NOTES

1. *Our Knowledge of the External World,* 2nd ed., New York, 1929, pp. 35–63.
2. *Ibid.,* p. 35.
3. *Ibid.,* p. 44.
4. *Ibid.,* p. 61.
5. An exception is of course *nontranslational* semantics. See my *Truth and Denotation,* Chicago, 1958, chaps. VIII and IX. See also H. Hiż, "The Aletheic Semantic Theory," *Transformations and Discourse Analysis Papers,* 1968; University of Pennsylvania, No. 77.
6. See especially *Truth and Denotation,* chap. III.
7. See *Truth and Denotation,* chaps. IV and V.
8. See especially my *Toward a Systematic Pragmatics, Studies in Logic and the Foundations of Mathematics,* Amsterdam, 1956; *Intension and Decision,* Englewood Cliffs, N. J., 1963; and *Belief, Existence, and Meaning,* New York, 1969. For quite different conceptions, see R. Carnap, *Meaning and Necessity,* 2nd ed., Chicago, 1956, pp. 248–250; and R. Montague, "Pragmatics," in *La Philosophie Contemporaine,* ed. R. Klibansky, Florence, 1968, I, 102–122.
9. See I. Copi, *Symbolic Logic,* 2nd ed., New York, 1965, chap. 4.
10. See *Belief, Existence, and Meaning,* chaps. VII, VIII, and IX. See also the author's "On Abstract Entities in Semantic Analysis," *Nous II,* 1968, 373–389 and "On Leonardian Intensions of Class-Terms," in *The*

Logical Way of Doing Things, the *Festschrift* for Henry Leonard, ed. K. Lambert, New Haven, 1969.

11. R. Carnap, *The Logical Syntax of Language,* New York, 1937, p. 8. See also *The Philosophy of Rudolph Carnap* in *The Library of Living Philosophers,* LaSalle, Illinois, 1963, pp. 940 ff.

12. In *Przeglad filozoficzny* 30–34, 1927–31.

13. H. S. Leonard and N. Goodman, "The Calculus of Individuals and Its Uses," *Journal of Symbolic Logic,* 1940, V, 45–55, and J. H. Woodger, *The Axiomatic Method in Biology,* Cambridge, 1937, including Appendix E by A. Tarski.

14. Cambridge, Mass., 1951.

15. See the author's "On Events and the Calculus of Individuals," *Akten des XIV. Internationalen Kongresses für Philosophie,* Vienna, 1969, III, 202–208.

16. See Carnap, *Meaning and Necessity.* The reference to Frege is "The Thought: A Logical Inquiry," *Mind,* 1956, LXV, 289–311; that to Ramsey is *The Foundations of Mathematics,* London, 1931, pp. 138 ff.

17. H. P. Grice, "Utterers' Meaning, Sentence-Meaning, and Word-Meaning," *Foundations of Language,* 1968, IV, 225–242.

18. See chap. III in *Belief, Existence, and Meaning.*

19. See H. G. Bohnert and P. O. Backer, *Automatic English-to-Logic Translation in a Simplified Model: A Study in the Logic of Grammar,* IBM Research, 1967.

20. In *Philosophical Essays for Alfred North Whitehead,* London and Toronto, 1936, pp. 125–152.

21. *Process and Reality,* New York, 1929, pp. 4–6.

22. A. N. Whitehead, *Essays in Science and Philosophy,* London, 1948, pp. 93–99.

Science and Metaphysics: Method and Explanation in Metaphysics*

Errol E. Harris

Positivism in its heyday in the 1930's and 1940's restricted the methods of attaining knowledge and of expressing the results of research to those of the natural sciences. By "knowledge," here, is meant all that is of primary importance, that is, knowledge about the world. The positivists allowed a secondary and derivative kind of knowledge, about the symbolism and language used for the expression of the primary sort, which they made the province of philosophy, confining it to semiotic—syntatics, semantics, and the like. But for metaphysics no place was found, no subject matter, no legitimate or significant mode of expression, no method of procedure.

In the last two decades positivism has steadily declined. The verification principle, on which the rejection of metaphysics rested, was found wanting and succumbed to criticism, both from within the empiricist camp and from without. But its influence is still powerful and its implications are still accepted, if only tacitly, by an influential body of contemporary writers. Although metaphysics has again been permitted some place among theoretical disciplines and has been readmitted to the realm of sensible discourse, it is still with doubt and hesitancy that it is mentioned, and the general run of professional philosophers acknowledge no great desire to pursue it. Although it is no longer castigated as disreputable, much

* Reprinted with permission from the *Proceedings of the American Catholic Philosophical Association*. Washington, D.C.: 1967, pp. 125–131.

question is raised, and little agreement is reached, as to its proper method and actual province. P. F. Strawson has made concessions to it by distinguishing what he has called descriptive from revisionary metaphysics, conferring upon the former a safe respectability by assimilating it, in large measure, to linguistic analysis (particularly to ordinary-language philosophy). But the "revisionary" variety is treated with more caution or is avoided altogether. In spite of Strawson's venture, many still associate metaphysics with vagueness and mystification; and others regard it at best (though with obvious inconsistency) as the fabrication of hypotheses for which no empirical evidence is obtainable, which, by systematic reinterpretation of primitive terms and prescription of theoretical concepts, makes empirical refutation of these hypotheses impossible, yet which is valuable as a foil and a source of alternatives to current scientific theories (like quantum theory) which present special philosophical difficulties.[1]

But as the verification princple has collapsed in well-nigh all its recognizable forms, the ban against metaphysics should be altogether void and we should be able to proceed as was done before it was pronounced. One of its most lasting effects, however, has been to discredit the methods and theories of older philosophies and to raise a generation of students partly ignorant of the older tradition and partly biased by ready-made criticisms so that what was done before is both unfamiliar and suspect. If we are to rediscover an appropriate method for metaphysics, therefore, we should not be ill-advised to glance once again at the historical record.

By this I do not mean, so much, that we should remind ourselves what Plato, or Aristotle, or Spinoza said was the correct method of speculation, but rather what was the practice of these and other great philosophers and its relation to other sciences. We are all aware that the very earliest Greek philosophers were both metaphysicians and natural scientists at once; not that they all pursued both disciplines as separate branches of study, but that for them no distinction was drawn between science and philosophy and none is imputed to them by later commentators. This state of affairs persisted until Aristotle subdivided the forms of theoretical knowledge into different sciences, but even he did not regard metaphysics as really divorceable from physics, the connection being so close that, included in the treatise which gives the science its name, is a portion of the Physics itself. Right up to the eighteenth century, the term "philosophy" continued to cover all the exact and the natural sciences, as well as everything that goes by that name today, and even now in Cambridge University and in the older Scottish universities physics is still known as "natural philosophy."

Moreover, many of the great metaphysicians of the modern period, Descartes, Leibniz, Kant, Bergson, and Whitehead, were also scientists, and no considerable philosophical theory has been uninfluenced by scientific discovery or failed in its turn to have some effect on the course of scientific research. In the words of A. E. Taylor, "Every great metaphysical conception has exercised its influence on the general history of science, and, in return, every movement in science has affected the development of metaphysics. . . ."[2] This persistent historical association between science and metaphysics cannot be without significance and is symptomatic of an intimate relation between both their methods and their subject matter.

Curiously enough, the positivistic indictment against metaphysics is that it lacks what is taken to be the hallmark of science—empirical reference—and that its method is one of speculation and a priori deduction, as opposed to induction and verification by empirical evidence. I shall attempt to defend the accused against these charges by showing that they misconceive the methods of science, on the one hand, and misrepresent that of metaphysics, on the other, and that the long historical association between metaphysics and the natural sciences is normal because their methods are in principle the same and their subject matters akin. I shall maintain that, so far from neglecting empirical evidence, metaphysical theory rests upon it just to the extent that it is provided and interpreted by the natural sciences, and that the relation between theory and observation is the same for both.

I shall begin with the latter.

Observation is the deliverance of sense perception, and all the current and most widely canvassed theories of perception today seem to agree in rejecting the notion that the percept is an immediately given atomic and simple datum that can be isolated from all others and from other elements in experience. Ryle's view that it is an achievement has come to be widely accepted among analysts, who point out that all verbs of perceiving, as used in reference to acts of perception, are achievement words. They imply that some piece of information has been attained, presumably as a result of some effort or process of trial. Such verbs are held to have intentionality and imply the presence of an actual (material) object, and a knowledge of its presence. No such knowledge could be given as a simple unmediated datum, for the presence of a physical object is a complex fact, involving its solidity and persistence as well as its causal efficacy and liability to extraneous causal influences. Without these, no material object would actually be presented. The achievement (for instance) of seeing such an object must thus be the end result of a discursive process of some kind, however rapidly accomplished, and could not be the result of any merely immediate intuition of an unprocessed datum.

The old idea of the existence and apprehension by the senses of sense-data has long been scouted, and philosophers today are more apt to regard material objects, in all their complexity of character and mutual relation, as the primary objects of perception. If this is not precisely what they say, it is the direct implication of the views set out at length by P. F. Strawson in *Individuals,* Stewart Hampshire in *Thought and Action,* and D. M. Armstrong in *Perception and the Physical World.* It is also implied in Alan Donagan's critique of Collingwood.[3]

In Armstrong's terms, an act of perception is an act of acquiring knowledge, or belief, about particular facts in the physical world by the use of the senses. But no knowledge of a particular fact in the physical world is a simple matter. Take Armstrong's favorite example—that the cat is on the mat. To know (or believe) this involves knowing what sort of things cats and mats are, and how they are distinguished from other, different, things. It involves an understanding of spatial relations in general and that of "being on," in particular; and it presumes an acquaintance with a particular region of space, with its contents, enabling the percipient to identify the particular cat and mat as belonging to the set of domestic furnishings to which implicit reference is being made (for presumably the statement is not just about any unspecified cat being on any unidentified mat).

In short, the achievement that constitutes an act of perception of this kind is one that presupposes an already, to some extent, developed body of background knowledge, by reference to which what is presented to the senses is recognized and interpreted. Apart from this no perceptual achievement would be possible.

From a somewhat different angle a similar conclusion is reached by Professor R. J. Hirst in his book *The Problems of Perception.*[4] He considers perception to be a relation between a person and other public objects and events, which involves mental activity and so presents an inner and an outer aspect. On the inner side it is the "(awareness or consciousness of) an external object," which must be distinguished as "a whole activity of the person." To the person who is perceptually conscious the content of his consciousness is an external object or scene. In short, perception is essentially an intentional activity. Professor Hirst rejects any theory of sense-data and all suggestion of private objects, although he admits perceptual errors and hallucinations. For him perception is a matter of degree, an activity which may be performed more or less successfully, in which the percipienda are elaborated in various ways and to different extents in order to produce the percepta. In describing this process, he follows the psychologists, who assert that the percipient achieves his percepta by the use of "cues" and correlations which modify the purely sentient elements of his experience, largely in accordance with past learning. I have argued elsewhere [5] that the use of "cues" and correlations (some psychologists even speak of "assumptions" and "hypotheses" in this connection) cannot be reduced to mere physical or physiological processes but is essentially epistemological, implying an activity of reference and interpretation, which again implies a body of more or less developed and organized knowledge to which reference is made and in terms of which presentations are interpreted. It is not necessary, and would, in fact, be misguided, to regard this process as intellectual in the sense that it requires the explicit use of abstract concepts and ratiocination. The suggestion, attributed to Blanshard,[6] that it is a thought process, and the view advanced by Helmholtz and some of the older psychologists that it is "unconscious inference" is commonly criticized (and insistently by Hirst) for this reason. But these writers, Blanshard especially (who should be given credit for drawing attention to this essentially mediate character of perception long before the others whom I have mentioned), by insisting that the process is "implicit" or "unconscious," themselves recognize its nonintellectual character. Unless we are to revert to sense-data (and perhaps even then) the recognition of some such process of mediation is inescapable. Equally inescapable is its logical and epistemological character as reference of a focal object to a context, articulated in some degree, spatiotemporally extended, and significant for the perceiving subject as a body of knowledge, understood in a dispositional sense.

Corroboration of this conclusion comes from another quarter when we turn to the work of Merleau-Ponty, for whom (as for Spinoza) perception is a functioning of the body as a whole, and not just the sense organs. But the organism is sensitive not to separate, atomic, stimuli, but to a whole situation constituted by their constellation. Even below the level of self-awareness and intentionality proper, he points out, it displays behaviors "as if oriented toward the meaning of certain elementary situations." The significant word is "meaning." This orientation is no merely physical or physiological adjustment but involves an apprehension of the structure of the presented situation. Every perception, he says, takes place within a certain "horizon" or setting (*entourage*) and ultimately in "the world"; the perceived object itself being a unified and articulated texture of qualities and relations. If it is a visual spatial object it is given as "an infinite sum of an indefinite series of perspectival views," the interrelation of which is developed in a definite, recognizable order or form, so that the perceived thing is an inexhaustible system (*ensemble*). Consequently, perception is a synthesis performed by a subject able to delimit perspectival aspects and to transcend the immediately given—a reference to a whole which can be grasped only through certain of its parts.

In short, the percept is an object apprehended in a setting as belonging to a world which must therefore be in some way appreciated as a whole, or in general terms, however indefinite; and the logically prior condition of perceiving objects is the possession of some overall idea of the world, however vague, to which they belong and in which they are integrants. Observation, the fruit of perception, is thus embedded in and inseparable from interpretation, even at the level of common sense.

Science grows out of common sense and is continuous with it, in that the commonsense level is simply the progressive development and clarification of the interpretation of percepts through the perceptual and intellectual exploration of the setting which gives them significance, and science carries this process to higher levels by fuller, more explicit, and more precise exercise of the intellectual factor. *Pari passu* the observational aspect is sharpened and refined and becomes more accurate.

For scientific observation, moreover, the dependence on background knowledge is especially indispensable. The untutored savage presented with the instruments of a scientific laboratory in an experimental situation, can make no scientific observation whatsoever. Even the educated layman can understand what is happening with great difficulty and only with the help and explanation of the expert. Before any quantitative measurement can be made the experimental situation as a whole has to be understood: what is being measured? in what connections? for what purposes? No instrument reading has significance unless its place in the experimental situation is known and its relevance to the questions that the experimenter is trying to answer. Only in answer to questions is any observation significant, and the questions arise only out of a theory already entertained and a body of scientific knowledge already achieved.

Moreover, what precisely is being observed in any experiment can be known only to one who is versed in the science concerned. That a particular pointer stands opposite a particular number or mark on a scale is altogether insignificant unless one knows that these things are part of, say, a galvanometer. That the indicated figure gives the measure of resistance to an electrical current cannot be appreciated unless the observer understands the principles on which galvanometers are constructed and to what this one in particular is connected. Clearly, a considerable body of knowledge of physical theory is presupposed in any one reading made with an instrument of this kind.

This is true at any level of scientific development. Observation is observation only if it answers relevant questions, these questions arise only out of prior knowledge—they are the *aporiae* of theories already adopted or at least entertained. Apart from them, even though the objects are present to be observed, the percipient will not notice them—that is, he will *not* observe them; and if he does, what he observes will depend upon the extent to which it is enlightened and interpreted by means of the theories to which the observation is contributing material. In short, theory is always, and always must be, prior to observation, and without it science would have no relevant empirical basis.

In any given situation the observable facts are infinite in number. Even those which are relevant to a particular problem in science may be innumerable. The scientist cannot observe them all and does not observe at random. To do so is strictly impossible, for the reasons already given, for to achieve knowledge of the observable facts one has to bring to bear upon them knowledge already acquired. He must, therefore, select and discriminate, and this he can do only in the light of the theories and hypotheses he has in mind and only so far as he can make his observations significant in reference to them.

This is well known to scientists. L. Bolzmann the founder of modern thermodynamics complained that "the lack of clarity in the principles of mechanics seems to be connected with the fact that one did not at once start with hypothetical pictures framed by our minds, but tried to start from experience." [7] We have also the more recent evidence of Einstein and Eddington. The former writes:

> By and by I despaired of the possibility of discovering the true laws by means of constructive efforts based on known facts. The longer and the more despairingly I tried, the more I came to the conviction that only the discovery of a universal formal principle could lead us to assured results. . . . How then could such a universal principle be found? [There follows the description of a piece of imaginative thinking impossible to test in any experiment which gave him "the germ of the special theory of relatively."] [8]

Eddington is still more positive:

> A scientist commonly professes to base his beliefs on observation, not theories. Theories, it is said, are useful in suggesting new ideas and new lines of investigation for the experimenter; but "hard facts" are the only proper ground for conclusion. I have never come across anyone who carries this profession into practice—certainly not the hard-headed experimentalist, who is more swayed by his theories because he is less accustomed to scrutinize them. Observation is not sufficient. We do not believe our eyes unless we are first convinced that what they appear to tell us is credible. . . . For the reader resolved to eschew theory and admit only definite observational facts, *all* astronomical books are banned. *There are no purely observational facts about the heavenly bodies.*[9]

But lest we should think these physicists prejudiced by their preoccupation with mathematics (though it is clear that this is not what inspires their remarks) let us hear that great biological observer Charles Darwin: "Without hypotheses," he says, "there can be no useful observation." [10]

This is why the method of science is misconceived by those who persist in the view that both for knowledge in general and the natural sciences in particular, sense observation is primary and self-contained, and must somehow be used as an independent check upon the accuracy of theories; and that the hallmark of scientific method in natural science is inductive reasoning from particular matters of fact to general laws, an invalid process of inference which, Karl Popper rightly asserts, is actually never used in science and cannot be validated in logic.

Scientific thinking, or for that matter thinking at any level worthy of the name, is the systematic development of a conceptual (or theoretic) scheme covering a field of investigation in terms of which percepta, or observations, are interpreted. Without such a scheme we cannot even begin, and at every level of scientific development an accepted scheme is already at hand. This does not mean that it has its source in some mysterious a priori independent of experience. It is itself experience as it has been organized and developed up to that point; and experience is primitively sentient, and sentience becomes percipience only through organization. To ask which is temporally prior in this development, sense or thought, is to ask which came first, the hen or the egg.

I shall not attempt to excavate origins but shall try to illustrate how, at a relatively elementary stage of scientific development theory serves as the organizing factor in the construction of a coherent conception of the subject matter. The night sky presents the appearance of a myriad of bright points in a dark background, along with the moon as a superior luminary. The immediate presentation is one of completely random arrangement but more careful attention reveals recognizable patterns of spatial relation, some of which, if the observation is prolonged, remain constant while others vary, so that over a protracted period the stars can be discovered to move across the heavens in various ways, some in circles, some along arcs which are greater or smaller segments of a circle, some in looping, oscillating courses, some faster and some more slowly. At first sight this is a bewildering variety; but these apparent movements (which, let us note, do not appear to the senses, but only to the thinking mind ordering the sensuous appearances), if they are related to the position of the sun at its rising and setting, and if we hypothesize that the heaven is a great globe, at the center of which is the earth in the form of a relatively small sphere, and that the greater celestial sphere rotates about the small one on an axis, one end of which is marked by the polestar, we can in large measure reduce this variety to order and regularity; and by marking out among the stars the path of the sun around the celestial sphere during the twelve months of the year (namely, the ecliptic), we get a coherent conception which will account for the movement of the majority of the heavenly bodies. This conception (sometimes called the two-sphere view) was, roughly, the earliest astronomical theory, and the history of astronomy, since it was adopted, up to the beginning of the nineteenth century was, almost exclusively, that of successive attempts to develop it so as to account for those aberrant motions which this simple theory leaves inexplicable, as contradictions within it—for example, the planetary movements and the intermittent appearance of comets.

Each science is a similar sustained effort to comprehend an area or aspect of human experience in terms of a conceptual system which will reduce the relative chaos of percipient experience to coherent order. Success in this undertaking constitutes explanation. A fact or event is explained when it is seen in systematic context and is interpreted in terms of a systematic set of concepts. Explanation is not just "analysis," in the sense of "taking to pieces" or resolving into elements. Such analysis may be involved in explanation, but by itself it explains nothing, unless the structural principles which originally held together the elements, into which the analysandum has been resolved, can also be demonstrated. Explanation is always synthesis just as much as analysis.

As the sciences progress they react upon one another and the effort becomes general to relate all their conceptual schemes and coordinate them into a single all-embracing theory. To describe the matter thus, however, is misleading, for in the nature of the case and as a matter of historical fact, the overarching conception is there from the beginning, first as a halting, naive, and largely pictorial synthesis, but becoming more conceptual, more systematic, and better articulated as the sciences develop. The discipline that produces this finally comprehensive synoptic conception is metaphysics, which began in the West with Thales and Anaximander, gave birth to the sciences one by one, stimulated their development and profited by it, so that each owed its successive advances to the progress of the other, and the historical association, which I noted earlier, was natural and necessary.

Accordingly, metaphysical explanation is the same in character as, and is only an extension of, scientific explanation, and metaphysical method is in principle a development and continuation of scientific method, as the latter may be said to be a specification, in different fields, of the former. The aim of metaphysics is a comprehensive conceptual scheme in the light of which the whole of experience can be organized and become intelligible. It is for this reason sometimes said (for example, by Whitehead) to be concerned with the most general and pervasive features of the world, and at others (for example, by Plato) to be the most synoptic of the sciences. But, to quote A. E. Taylor again, "Metaphysics does not profess to deal with a certain group of facts lying outside the province of the 'sciences', but to deal with the same facts which form that province from a point of view which is not that of the experimental sciences." [11] The phrase "the sciences" is meant here to refer to all sciences, not just "the natural sciences" if that means only physics, chemistry, and biology. Not only must the social sciences and the sciences of the mind be included, but whatever others may be necessary to deal with any field or aspect of experience; for, as has been said, metaphysics seeks a conceptual scheme comprehensive of the whole of experience.

The differences between scientific and metaphysical method derive only from this difference of scope. The self-limitation of the special sciences permits, and is defined by, initial assumptions, which the lack of such limitation in metaphysics forbids. The sciences do not examine or call these assumptions in question, but metaphysics must do so and may not itself adopt any, except provisionally. So Plato maintained that Dialectic eliminated hypotheses and was ἀνυποθέτος, and Kant declared any hypothesis in metaphysics contraband. Moreover, hypotheses are of two kinds, both in some measure relative to the limitation in scope of a science. There are working hypotheses, which scientists adopt consciously and deliberately, and which direct and canalize their researches; and there are more fundamental presuppositions, often made as a matter of custom or tradition and without explicit reflection: such, for instance, as that every event has a cause or that all causation is efficient. For metaphysics all such hypotheses are contraband and the critical examination of them is consequently part of the metaphysician's business.

Similarly, in the special sciences, theory is more directly related to observation, whereas metaphysical theory is related to the empirical evidence indirectly through the special sciences. This, to the casual observer, may give the impression that metaphysics is purely speculative and "deductive" in its method, "scorning the base degrees by which it did ascend" and producing empirically unverifiable theses. But this impression is false. All science is speculative. If I may quote a scientist once more, Professor le Gros Clark says: "Contrary to views which are sometimes expressed, speculation is by no means to be eschewed in scientific pursuits—indeed it is essential for progress since it is the generator of ideas and ideas stimulate enquiry." [12] In this respect metaphysics does not differ from science, nor does it differ in its manner of verification.

Theory and observation in science are not two separate and independent factors by one of which we may check or test the other. A scientific theory is a more or less organized and coherent interpretation of what is observed, without which the observed facts lose their character and significance. Observation, we have already noted, is saturated with interpretation, of which theory is no more than the development. Theory and observation together form a single whole of knowledge. But this is only "more or less" coherently organized and the endeavor of science is constantly to improve the system so that it becomes more comprehensive and self-consistent. Verification, therefore, always consists in the assembling of mutually corroborative evidence, the interconnections of which make the denial of the theory impossible without the breakdown of the entire conceptual scheme. Falsification consists in the failure of corroboration, which demands either modification of the theory or the discovery of new connections which will reconcile the conflicting evidence. The process, in science, obviously involves observation, for without it theory would have no subject matter. In the case of astronomy, if no stars were observed there would be no science, but the two-sphere view cannot be "verified" by comparison with some independently observed body of facts; it is simply the way in which the observed facts are organized. The Copernican system is another way of organizing them which can explain more satisfactorily planetary and cometary movements, as the earlier theories could not. Verification in science is, therefore, by mutual corroboration of evidence.[13]

Metaphysics is no more and no less than an attempt to organize comprehensively the deliverances of the sciences into a single world view by means of a universal conceptual scheme in which all sciences can be integrated. That this can be adequately or successfully done without clarification and analysis of concepts is hardly to be expected; so part of the metaphysician's task, and part of the explanatory function of metaphysical theory, will be conceptual analysis, which will naturally consider the ways in which terms and concepts are used, and how they function in science. But metaphysics cannot be restricted to such analysis, which is ancillary to its constructive purpose of providing a coherent explanatory scheme in which all possible sciences can themselves find place.

Moreover, the extension of scope involved in metaphysical explanation is bound to require the modification of the use and application of concepts, and what is appropriate in one science may well prove unacceptable in another and still more in a wider context. The term "evolution," for instance, and its connotation are not the same in physics (for example, in "the evolution of the galaxy") as in biology; and, as Collingwood pointed out, when the idea is given philosophical significance it has to be modified still further.[14] Analysis of concepts, therefore, will also involve criticism, and adjustment in the light of such criticism. Consequently, metaphysics is inevitably "revisionary"; and because the use of a concept in each science is not separate and independent of its use in the others, and because the transition from one science to the next can be represented as a continuous development, this revisionary function is essential to the descriptive, which cannot be adequately or accurately carried out without it.

Furthermore, this process of analysis and criticism of concepts and presuppositions is bound to call in question the credentials and assess the claims of the sciences concerned. Metaphysics, therefore, like all philosophy will be what Collingwood called a criteriological science and will have a normative as well as a descriptive character. Moreover, as it seeks what we may now, without mystification, call ultimate explanation, it will be concerned with and will inquire into the ultimate grounds, whatever they be and if there are any (questions metaphysicians must raise), of the existence and nature of the subject matter of all the special sciences that fall under its purview.

The method of verifying a metaphysical theory, therefore, is to seek corroborative evidence among the sciences. It will, naturally, be for the most part theoretical evidence, itself an interpretation of observed fact; but the verificatory process is no different in principle from that of science. To neglect the evidence, as science provides it, would be fatal, and, through the mediation of science, this evidence is as "empirical" as any need be. Metaphysics, then, is an interpretation of interpretations; it is science of the second, or possibly of an even higher, degree. It is, in short, metascience—and what else did the word "metaphysics" ever legitimately mean?

NOTES

1. Cf. P. Feyerabend, "Problems of Empiricism," *Beyond the Edge of Certainty,* ed. R. Colodnoy, Englewood Cliffs, N. J., 1965, pp. 178, 181 ff.
2. A. E. Taylor, *Elements of Metaphysics,* New York, 1916, p. 13.
3. See also A. M. Quinton, "The Problem of Perception," *Mind,* 1955, LXIV, 28–51.
4. R. J. Hirst, *The Problems of Perception,* London, 1959.
5. E. E. Harris, *The Foundations of Metaphysics in Science,* New York, 1965, pp. 407 ff.
6. Brand Blanshard, *The Nature of Thought,* London, 1939, vol. I.
7. I. Bolzman, *Vorlesungen über die Principen der Mechanik,* Leipzig, 1897, p. 2.
8. *Albert Einstein, Philosopher Scientist,* ed. P. A. Schilpp, New York, 1959, pp. 52–53.
9. Sir Arthur S. Eddington, *The Expanding Universe,* Cambridge, 1933, p. 17.
10. Quoted by W. E. le Gros Clark in "Anatomical Perspectives in Neuropsychiatry," *Perspectives in Neurophysiology,* ed. D. Richter, London, 1950.
11. *Elements of Metaphysics.*
12. Le Gros Clark, in *Perspectives in Neurophysiology,* p. 10.
13. Karl Popper has implicitly subscribed to a similar view in a significant footnote in *The Logic of Scientific Discovery,* New York, 1959, p. 87, "If I assert that there is a family of white ravens in the New York zoo, then I assert something which can be tested *in principle.* If somebody wishes to test it, and is informed, upon arrival, that the family has died, or has never been heard of, it is left to him to accept or reject my falsifying . . . statement. As a rule, he will have means of forming an opinion by examining witnesses, documents, etc.; that is to say by appealing to other intersubjectively testable and reproducible facts."
14. R. G. Collingwood, *An Essay on Philosophical Method,* London, 1933, p. 34.

Value and Metaphysics

Joseph Owens

It is no secret that philosophy of value has resulted in a state of discussion that is both confused and confusing.[1] There has been notable lack of clarity in establishing a field for the study, both regarding the way a value is contradistinguished from a fact and the way the various instances are to be brought under the common notion of value. Although the good is generally accepted as a value, it gives rise to questions whether the moral good is the supreme value or whether other types of good predominate over it,[2] and what its nature has to be to allow it to function as a value. The true and the beautiful are quite commonly accepted as values, yet there have been strong protests against their recognition as values *qua* true and *qua* beautiful. Some indirect way of bringing them under the notion of value seems required. Numerous other characteristics are ranged under the conception of value, such as the sublime, the heroic, the holy, the nice, the amusing, and so on. The difficulties in working out a general philosophy that will deal satisfactorily with all these problems seem commonly acknowledged today. There is a lessening of the verve to elaborate overall explanations of value, and marked recession of interest in the topic. The *Proceedings of the Seventh Inter-American Congress of Philosophy* (Quebec, 1967–1968) gives the subject no special emphasis, and the Fourteenth International Congress of Philosophy at Vienna in 1968 placed the study not in its plenary sessions or colloquia, but in an afternoon section under the combined heading "Ethics and the Philosophy of Values," in which the majority of the titles were from the ethical rather than from the value approach.

In spite of the confusion it has engendered, however, and in spite of impatience in some quarters with the whole notion of the philosophy of value,[3] the discussion has focused attention upon a crucial and truly basic issue for philosophical procedure. The issue is the distinction between two types of objects that confront philosophical scrutiny. One is the type of things that exist and have their structural determinations apart from any intervention of the human will. The other is the type of things that depend upon human will or choice or decision.

Even prima facie this distinction seems to parallel the fundamental Aristotelian contrast of speculative knowledge with practical and productive cognition. The contrast was not brought out too clearly in later Aristotelian tradition, but it is better appreciated today. It seems to offer a background against which the current problems of philosophy of value may be profitably assessed. It invites exploration in this setting. The distinction between judgments of fact, on the one hand, and judgments of value, on the other, has become part of ordinary language and seems here to stay. If it can be explained satisfactorily by the tenets of traditional philosophy, it has in the present state of confusion the best of reasons for submitting itself to careful examination in their light.

A glance over Western philosophical literature before the nineteenth century encounters no explicit interest in developing a branch of knowledge under the caption of a philosophy of value. Its themes, however, were dealt with extensively. Even the notion "value" occurs rather frequently in Plato and Aristotle.[4] The basic meaning of the word was taken from the economic order, in accord with the etymology of the Greek *axia* that implies weighing on a scale. The grading of objects that could be metaphorically weighed is nicely illustrated in Aristotle's brief discussion about things prized and things praised, in the *Nicomachean Ethics* (I 12,1101b10–35). In the Middle Ages the themes involved in these considerations were developed under the notion of the transcendent properties of being, including the good, the true, and the beautiful.[5] After Kant, nineteenth-century German philosophers, taking the notion of value from its use in economic writers, began to exploit it successfully on the psychological and philosophical levels. In the last decade of the nineteenth century a thoroughgoing philosophy of value began to emerge. On the Continent and in America, and to a somewhat lesser extent in England, it became widespread as it matured in the first part of the present century. It became the commonly accepted approach to the good, and, with qualifications, to the true and to the beautiful.[6]

The question, accordingly, is whether the traditional notion of the transcendental properties of being, with the fundamental distinction between practical and speculative knowledge, can provide an adequate framework for examining the important problems that have sparked the philosophy of value. In this paper I shall attempt to undertake this investigation. I shall try to see how the traditional conception of the transcendentals meets the current issues of values, and to inquire whether there are any reasons why the wisdom that is centuries old should not be allowed to offer enlightenment for the modern problem.

What, then, is the current conception of a value in the philosophical sense? Perhaps the best starting point is a definition of the term in its widest accepted sense, as given by Frankena in Paul Edwards' *Dictionary of Philosophy* (s.v. Value and Valuation): "the generic noun for all kinds of critical or pro and con predicates, as opposed to descriptive ones," and which "is contrasted with existence or fact." This seems wide enough to cover the contemporary uses of the word in philosophical writing, and to account for the sharp contrast in current parlance between judgments of fact or existence, on the one hand, and value judgments, on the other.

A close scrutiny of the definition, however, occasions some misgivings. The definition would embrace all kinds of critical predicates. Through being critical these are meant to stand in contrast to descriptive predicates. But is this an acceptable contrast? Every predication is made in a judgment, and is thereby critical insofar as it exemplifies the basic meaning of the word "critical," which is "discerning."[7] The discerning of one shade of color from another, of the taste of one wine from another, or of pitch and tones in music is critical in one ordinary understanding of the term. All scientific judgments are critical, no matter what their subject matter is. In that way they are distinguished from commonsense beliefs. Even this may be a matter of degree. One may claim that every judgment, in applying one predicate and excluding the contradictory, is thereby critical. In any case, the word "critical" has nonevaluative uses. An obvious instance is the way it designates textual criticism. A critical edition of an ancient work hardly implies any value judgment about the work itself or about the worth of the editing. "Critical" is undoubtedly applied in obvious cases to descriptive judgments.

One may suggest that scientific judgments, in being termed scientific, are valuated as of a higher caliber than commonsense beliefs. Applying the term "scientific" would thereby give a value, even in purely theoretical topics. This viewpoint may be acceptable. If anything, it emphasizes the basic difficulty. "Scientific" is also descriptive of a method and procedure. If the same judgment can be both critical and descriptive, how can these two notions be the characteristics that distinguish value judgments from judgments of fact?

Rather, these considerations show that the same judgment that is critical and descriptive of a value is also descriptive and critical of a fact. In most cases it does not go beyond the ordinary understanding of "descriptive" to say that a taste may be *described* as pleasant, a sunset described as beautiful, a life of fulfillment described as good. The notion of values as "tertiary qualities" and, accordingly, as subject to description seems well enough established to merit attention. At least it cannot be dismissed as patently absurd. Each "value-phenomenon" seems to cry out against the separation of value from fact.[8] Nor can one maintain that a critical predicate relates by definition to a standard, while a descriptive predicate does not. Is not the very relation something that may be described? And does not the notion of standard for being as well as for truth go back as far as Aristotle?[9] No matter what the angle from which one regards the problem, the distinction seems based upon different phases of the same object rather than upon separate objects or upon different types of predication. Is not existence itself a value? Is it not a goal for which all things strive?[10] And is it not a *fact* that something is good, or true, or beautiful? Does a value have to be something that is nonexistent, or that ceases to be a value once it becomes a fact?

The reason for one phase of the confusion in the philosophy of value now becomes apparent. There is difficulty in distinguishing fact and value, and accordingly difficulty in setting up a clear-cut field for a philosophy of value. Values seem to exist, and existence seems to be a value. Yet the distinction between judgments of fact and judgments of value seems to meet a real need both in ordinary language and in philosophical discourse. How then may the two types of judgment be distinguished?

Since no a priori method seems feasible here, a procedure in the manner of ostensive definition is indicated. Instances of commonly acknowledged values should be scrutinized, and the way characteristic judgments about them differ from admittedly nonevaluative judgments should be probed. The model most readily suggested for entering upon the study is the good. The good is in one way or another generally accepted as a value. Restrictions in its scope as a value may be made, for instance, in excluding the right and the obligatory from its new ambit. But these restrictions are rather parochial and seem unimportant for the present purpose, which is to examine an instance of value. Likewise truth is regarded as a value in ordinary living, and is something that is sought in the sciences. There must accordingly be some aspect at least under which it may be regarded as a value. Similarly, the beautiful is commonly looked upon as a value, at least indirectly. An investigation of these outstanding instances, the good, the true, and the beautiful, should therefore establish at least roughly and in outline what a value is and how a valuative judgment is to be distinguished from a nonevaluative one. Of the three, the good is the obvious instance for commencing the study.

II

The good has been a topic of intensive philosophical scrutiny from the times of Plato and Aristotle. Its essentially relational character was emphasized in the Platonic circles,[11] and was developed by Aristotle in the framework of analogy or proportion: "Are goods one, then, by being derived from one good or by all contributing to one good, or are they rather one by analogy? Certainly as sight is in the body, so is reason in the soul, and so on in other cases." [12] In this proportional way the good is always relative to something that wants it or needs it or desires it. It is generalized at the beginning of the *Nicomachean Ethics* as that at which all things aim.[13] In this setting the notion of a solitary and externally unrelated thing would be conceived as good for itself. It could not be regarded as good for nothing. With it the good would add a conceptual and internal relation to the thing itself.

According to this analysis, the good is not something that can be considered apart from its relation to a thing. It has to be gauged in reference to whatever is striving for it or enjoying it or possessing it. Consequently, a thing that is good for one individual may not be good for another. Long before Aristotle, Heraclitus had emphasized that seawater is for fish "drinkable and life giving," while "for men, undrinkable and destructive," and that "donkeys prefer chaff to gold." [14] Seawater has exactly the same chemical formula as it comes into relation with fish or with man, but the characteristic "good" or "bad" accrues to it in respect to the one or the other. So one may accept Aristotle's detailed reasoning about the supreme good as logically flawless—the supreme good for man is the highest human activity in regard to the highest object throughout a complete term of life.[15] Against this background an individual may readily agree that contemplative thinking ranks the highest, and yet say "But not for me—I don't want to spend my life contemplating, I want to do something." What he acknowledges as the highest in point of fact is not the good that he pursues in practice, unless he rationalizes it by maintaining that his own work brings about the prerequisite conditions that permit contemplation to be carried on by others.

Aristotle was well aware of this in allowing a goodness of its own, although in a secondary degree, to a life of moral in contradistinction to contemplative virtue: "But in a secondary degree the life in accordance with the other kind of virtue is happy; for activities in accordance with this befit our human estate" (*EN* X 8,1178a9–10; Oxford tr.). The human relation is required to make the life good. What is good is always determined in reference to particular individuals or classes, even in the monstrous tenet that for some men the condition of slavery is better than that of freedom: ". . . the lower sort are by nature slaves, and it is better for them as for all inferiors that they should be under the rule of a master." [16] Consistently, then, the notion of goodness for Aristotle is dependent not so much on the nature of a thing just in itself, as on the relation to whatever desires or needs the thing.

The medieval development consisted in explaining this relation through its two terms. These were appetite and being. Appetite included will, and by Aquinas being was given its most pointed explanation in this setting as the thing's existential actuality.[17] Whatever existed could be the object of some appetite and could accordingly be characterized as good. The goodness added no real characteristic to the existent, but merely a conceptual relation to will or appetite. In this setting it became known in sixteenth-century vocabulary as a transcendental, in the sense of a transcendent property of being.[18] No matter how objectivistic one wishes the good to be, it will always imply a conceptual relation to will or desire or need.[19]

What characteristics of value can be garnered from the way it is exemplified in goodness? The most obvious is that nothing real but only a further intellectual conception is added to that of the thing's existence. One can say that a thing exists, and one can grade it in a scale of existence, without introducing anything about its goodness. But, in speaking of it as good, one has in mind an appetite or need or aim that it can satisfy. Its goodness is gauged in relation to the appetite or need or aim. Goodness accordingly adds a new notion to that of existence, a notion that is not that of an absolute quality but rather a relation to some kind of appetite.

Goodness therefore presupposes existence and involves existence, since it is brought about by a conceptual relation added to and implying existence. There cannot be any goodness in separation from fact or existence. This conclusion may be accepted without difficulty for the realm of nature, where food is good for animals, sunlight for plants, and moisture for soil. If the food, sunlight, or moisture did not exist, it could not exercise this function of goodness. But what of the realm of freedom, the order set up by human choice? Does goodness in it depend upon something that already exists, or rather upon something that does not yet exist but which is to be achieved by human effort? It is undoubtedly in this realm that the notion of value plays its most outstanding role.

For Aristotle the practical order has its starting point in choice, in sharp contrast to the theoretical order which starts from what exists and has its determinations independently of human decision.[20] For Aquinas the practical is similarly an order that human reason sets up through its own considering, in contrast to the natural order that human reason finds already set up.[21] For both these thinkers man lives freely in the world in which he exists, with the result that the good dependent upon human choice is also something that is meant to exist or to come into existence.[22] It is in no way divorced from existence, though its origin lies in the human will. But it does mean a new beginning. It is something not determined by the natures of things but by human choice. It does bring a new order into existence, an order that is the object of a distinct type of judgments. These may well be called value judgments in modern terminology. They are readily distinguishable from judgments about facts that are determined independently of man's will. The difference does not lie in any severance of value from fact, but in the intervention of the human will to set up a further factual order within the existent world. This is amply sufficient to mark off an altogether special field for a philosophy of value, even though this new field is not seen outside the scope of fact or existence.

The background of transcendental goodness, with its necessary presupposition of existence for every instance of the good, seems accordingly to dispel the confusion in locating a field for philosophy of value. It likewise clears up the confusion regarding the different types that may lay claim to the label of value, and the order in which they may do so. The transcendental good is not a genus with different species. It is rather an aspect that is found in different ways in different things, without generic sameness. The morally good will be an instance of transcendental goodness, by the very fact that it exists. But it exists in a characteristically special way, a way that means an utterly new beginning in the universe because of the lack of preceding determination. In the way in which it is morally good it is an instance of transcendental goodness, since unlike a genus a transcendental does not admit specific differentiae. Rather, the characteristic that differentiates moral goodness is the characteristic that assimilates it to other kinds of goodness. Accordingly, the setting in transcendental goodness can explain why values should be located first and foremost in a thoroughly human context, and yet may be found extended by some to the animal kingdom, for instance, that the cat values cream. The reason lies in the common notion of goodness. It may be extended, if a person so wishes, in lessening degrees to the vegetative and even the nonliving realms.

Transcendental goodness, of course, is not geared to explaining values. Its own primary instance is other than the human moral good. But it is wide enough to allow the human moral good to function as the primary instance of value, and to explain all other claimants to the title "value" as analogous to human values. It dissipates the confusion not only in regard to a proper field for values when confronted with the notion of fact or existence, but also the confusion in respect to the different types of goods that are to be considered as values, and the order in which they come under the notion. The practical good in the Aristotelian sense, whether it be called the human good or the good for man or the morally good, will be the standard of value. Analogously to it everything that exists can be a value, insofar as everything that exists can be the object of will or need or aim.

Does this involvement of existence in the good hold for other philosophies than those in the Aristotelian tradition? In Plato all Ideas share in being,[23] even though the good may have the highest place.[24] Whether or not the Platonic good is to be looked upon as an existent in itself, it is at least something to be worked into other existents.[25] Wherever it is found it seems to involve existence. Likewise where goodness is located absolutely or essentially or primarily in a will,[26] it is obviously dependent upon the existence of the will. But, where the good is considered as an ideal that can never be realized in actual existence, where the "ought" is severed completely from the "is," or where progress is always tending toward something further and will never reach an ultimate existent goal, the situation becomes quite different.[27] The need for a conception of goodness not based upon existence arises, and the stage is set for the appearance of a special philosophy of value as a new approach. It was against this conception of an explanation of values divorced from existence that Tillich and Gilson reacted so strongly. Ultimately, an explanation of this type opens the way for noncognitive theories of value, since it does not provide an adequate ground in values for knowledge of truth or falsity. For that reason the noncognitive approach has drawn sharp rebuttal even from empiricist quarters.[28]

The explanation of value in terms of a transcendental property of existence seems accordingly to meet adequately the major initial confusions. It provides a distinct field for philosophy of value, and a comprehensive means for gradating values. But does it not do this work perhaps a little too well? Does it not make goodness so complete an explanation of value that no room is left for any other kinds of value? How then does it allow scope for the other commonly accepted values? The list of values today does not begin and end with the good. What are these other values, and how are they related to existence and to the good?

III

One such recognized value is truth. Truth is striven for in ordinary life, in fact-finding for business dealings, in social, juridical, and political matters. It is something people want to know. Likewise the sciences and philosophy want their conclusions to be true.

What, then, is truth? As a value it is quite obviously something that pertains to what one knows, or at least to what one strives to attain in one's beliefs.[29] Accordingly it does not as a value characterize perceptions or concepts or words, but judgments and statements.[30] It consists in having one's judgments conform to a standard that seems to be spontaneously recognized by all, for everyone distinguishes true from false statements. Yet the standard is difficult to explain philosophically. The difficulty has given rise to different explanations of truth in the tradition of Western thought, and to various "theories of truth" in the present century. These explanations and theories, however, do not seem to be reciprocally exclusive of one another. Rather, they each emphasize one or the other of the elements that go to make up the notion of truth.[31]

What is the standard that emerges from a study of these views? It seems clearly enough to be existence. Whether a judgment's truth consists in conformity to what exists, or in coherence with what exists, or is explained as the existence itself, or as a metalinguistic assertion of existence, or as an emphasis on existence, the standard to which a true judgment conforms is the actual existence it purports to represent. Existence, consequently, should be the measure and norm of truth. Even in value statements truth is an assertion's conformity to approved choices and in that sense to existent values; for example, "it is true that stealing is bad and temperance is good" expresses the conformity of the latter assertion to an already approved moral estimate of the conduct.

How, though, can a judgment be measured against the existence it claims to represent? First of all, and basically, judgment is an intellectual activity. It is an activity that engenders a side product, also known by the same name, a judgment. In the latter sense the synthesis of notions in "The cat is black" is a judgment that in a logical context is called a proposition. It is clearly articulated in the distinct elements of subject, copula, and predicate, each expressed by a different word. In the really existent cat there is no such spreading out in the three different elements. Each of them may be given separate cognitional existence, but they do not have each in itself separate real existence. The intellectual activity by which the real existence is grasped has to represent subject and predicate separately and as synthesized by the existence. The representation is the judgment in the second sense just noted. It can be reflected upon and studied as a static object already present in the mind,[32] like a single slide in Bergson's cinematographic simile. The cat and its color may cease to exist in the real world, but the judgment can still be held intact before the mind's gaze for logical analysis. The real existence and its intellectual representation are accordingly the objects of two different cognitive acts. The two objects can be held before the mind together, and the one can be compared with and measured against the other. If the representation is in agreement with the existence, it is spontaneously seen to be true. Through direct judgment one is aware that the cat is black, through simple reflection on the form of that cognitive activity one sees the intellectual construct "The cat is black," and on comparing the two one recognizes their agreement and knows that the judgment is true.[33]

The multiplicity of elements in the representation and their thoroughgoing unity in the real thing may be better illustrated by judgments in which subject and predicate are in the same category, for instance, "The cat is an animal." For anyone who has the concept of "cat" and the concept of "animal," the existential synthesis of the first with the second is seen at once. The words designating the concepts may change, but the concepts themselves remain the same.[34] It is not hard to show that today one can have the same concepts of shuttle, chariot, sword, and so on, that were in the minds of Plato and Xenophon as they wrote. Hence one can read their works with understanding. The truth conveyed by them is accordingly stable and unchanging. It is measured against a fixed standard, the existential synthesis of the one concept with the other. Similarly, the principles and conclusions of Euclid are just as true today as ever for the type of surface to which they apply. Even the factual truths, frozen as judgments, retain their agreement with the existence they represent. "Caesar crossed the Rubicon" is as true today as it was in the first century B.C., and in exactly the same way.

These considerations show that there is such a thing as truth, and that it is something permanent and attainable and able to be striven for. The philosophical arena is no exception.[35] Demonstrations worked out by Aristotle and Aquinas hold today as much as ever, and principles isolated by them, such as the first principle of demonstration or the actualization of things by existence, retain the same force now as then. The truth of judgments, whether principles or conclusions, consists in their relation of agreement with the existence they purport to represent. In the practical order the existence is that of a conformity in the moral object to correct desire—the judgment is true because the conformity is there.

But if truth in the sense under discussion is essentially a relation of agreement, how can it be regarded as a value? The agreement seems something to be recognized rather than something to be willed or achieved. It is something there in its own determination independently of human will. Accordingly, there is compelling ground for the strongly asserted position that truth *qua* truth cannot be a value.[36] But undoubtedly it is good to know the truth.[37] Since the aspect of transcendental goodness extends to everything existent, it is exemplified in formal truth as a good in relation to the human intellect. *Qua* good, formal truth is a value. "Formal truth" is the name given traditionally to the truth that people strive to attain in their thinking, the notion of truth found in the modern discussions about values. In this context truth is located formally as a property of judgments. Transcendental truth, in contrast, is far wider, and in its primary instance differs profoundly from a conceptual relation existent in the human mind. Transcendental truth is the conformity everything has with the intellectual plan according to which it was designed. This is not an ordinary-language use of the word "truth," although it includes in its scope the perfection given the intellect by formal truth. It is also exemplified in a secondary way in the assertion that the lines of a building are true because they conform to the required design, or that friends or soldiers are true because they live up to what is expected of them. As with the good, the transcendental conception of truth was not excogitated to meet the problems of the philosophy of value, yet it provides a background in depth in which the issues can be intelligently thought out and the confusions removed. In its framework the crisp modern denials that truth *qua* truth can be a value are upheld, while the more common acceptance of truth as an important value is consistently vindicated. In it likewise truth is firmly grounded upon existence and seen thereby with the character of stability and permanence that marks it as a value in contrast to a fleeting and ever-changing phantom.

IV

Another regularly listed value, or at least a topic commonly treated of in the context of value, is the beautiful. Yet in its regard one may ask the same questions as in the case of truth. Is it a value in the characteristic way in which it is beautiful? Or is it a value precisely because it happens to be good for the people who seek it? And exactly what is its relation to existence? [38]

In point of fact, the beautiful has proved an exceptionally difficult notion for philosophers to explain. It is described as the object of an intuition, sensible as well as intellectual, and is enjoyed through contemplation. From this viewpoint it is essentially or at least radically the object of cognitive activity. It seems to consist in a capability that the forms of things possess for charming and satisfying the intellect's gaze, when the capability is made manifest in actual existence.[39] It extends throughout all orders. The morally good, for instance, was called by the same name as the beautiful by the Greeks, *to kalon*. Mathematical symmetry is not without a beauty of its own.[40] In varying degrees and with other names this object of intellectual intuition is spread through the realms of the heroic, the sublime, the humorous, and other aspects too numerous to list.

The detailed study of truth provides a framework for locating beauty as a value. As something intuited, the beautiful is not evaluated. It is just contemplated. But the contemplation and its object are desirable and good. As a good, therefore, the beautiful is a value, but not in its role as a transcendental property of being. Yet, because it is a transcendental property, it will always presuppose existence. It will thereby imply goodness, and be a value *qua* good. As with goodness and truth, the transcendental conception of beauty was not meant to deal with the modern problems of value, but it does serve as an apt framework in which they can be studied.

There is another transcendental that appears in the traditional lists, unity.[41] Is it to be regarded as a value? It does not enter notably into the current discussions under this aspect. It seems demanded in the beautiful, for without unity the required effulgence of form would not be possible. As a good involved in the beautiful it could well rank as a value. In various ways one may strive to bring unity into one's life and conduct. But here again it is a particular good that one is pursuing. Finally, one may recall how Plotinus placed the One above being and all other predicates, and made it the goal of all human striving. From this standpoint it would appear as the highest value. Yet, to apply the predicate "value" to it, one has to go outside Plotinian philosophy and regard it as the object of free human endeavor and human will. But that is to regard it as a good.

Another characteristic that sometimes enters into modern discussions about value is the "holy." [42] It seems difficult if not impossible to bring this characteristic under philosophical focus. It seems rather an object of theological consideration, to be explained in terms of grace. Like beauty and truth and unity, however, it may be regarded as a good, and in this way come under the philosophical notion of a value. But its investigation will belong to theology.

Numerous other objects may be listed under the general notion of a value.[43] In fact, where value is understood as the object of interest or desire or want, it extends to everything that can be the object of appetition. In this way it becomes fully as broad in scope as the Scholastic transcendental called "the good." The true, the beautiful, and all other instances become particular types of value, just as they were instances or phases of the good in the Scholastic setting.

V

A metaphysical scrutiny of the leading instances of values seems to show, accordingly, that the most widely accepted notion of value may be subsumed under the traditional notion of the good. Values in their basically human sense are the goods of the intellectual appetite. This means that they will be freely chosen.[44] They cannot be determined or decided by metaphysics the way degrees and modes of being are assessed. They are not already there for a theoretical science to study independently of human choice. They have to be first set up by acts of a human will. The choice is always individual, but is conditioned by a common culture and preceded by rational deliberation. The common culture and the commonly shared objects upon which rational deliberation takes place assure for the values a public setting and a public status.[45] By the role it plays in the common culture and by the conclusions it offers for the deliberation, metaphysics is able to make its contribution, minimal perhaps but yet important in its steadying influence, to the formation and maintenance of values. Hegelian dialectic may have exercised little motive force in engendering Communist choices, yet who can doubt the profound contribution it has made to them? Similarly, the metaphysics of intellect and will, substance and attribute, the temporal and the eternal, did not form the Christian attitude toward God. But how easily recognizable is the stamp it has placed upon Christian thinking, and how deeply it has penetrated Christian attitudes through the long centuries! The recent appeal for the de-Hellenization of Christian notions is an eloquent though hostile witness to the part metaphysics has played in the Christian outlook.

But, although it influences the determination of values only through its formative role in a culture and through the conclusions it provides for the deliberation that precedes choice, metaphysics can in its own right undertake a theoretical study of the values already determined. It can on its own level probe their nature and their genesis. It can show that in an Aristotelian or a Scholastic setting no special philosophy of values is necessary. Sufficient theoretical study of them is provided by the scrutiny of the transcendental properties of being. The study of the good, and specifically the moral good, furnishes the explanation of the nature and genesis of what is now called value. The study of the other transcendentals fills in the details in regard to truth and beauty, and the investigation of the various aspects of the morally good, such as virtue and obligation, seems sufficient to cover the remaining instances of value.

Where the good cannot function authentically as an end, however, the situation becomes different. The Aristotelian conception, carried through the Scholastic tradition, was based upon the real existence of an ultimate end. If this end did not exist, no other good could exercise its function as good.[46] What will happen, then, in an Idealism in which the good may be approached in varying degrees but never fully realized? The end attained will never be genuinely final; it will never be authentically an end. The explanation in terms of the transcendentals will no longer function. A special philosophy will be required. The philosophy of value will be born.[47] Similarly, a process philosophy that envisages unceasing progress will have no room for anything that is absolutely final and in this way authentically an end. It too will require a special philosophy of value, which will allow purposes and goals without an ultimate end.[48]

The role of metaphysics in regard to values, then, is hardly a primary one. Triumphalism is much more out of date in philosophy than in theology. Greek and Christian cultures had their values long before they had their metaphysics. The values are determined basically by the culture itself, as operative through free choice.[49] When and where a metaphysics is able to play a part in the deliberations that precede the choosing, it can exercise an active role in the actual determining of values. For the most part this role will be small compared to the influence of other factors. But it can be of great importance, for example in the philosophy used to promote Communism and the Italian and German versions of fascism, or in the guidance and inspiration given to American education by pragmatic and process philosophies, or in the mentality stamped on Christian tradition by Greek and Scholastic metaphysics. In this respect metaphysics, although by no means a primary force in the selection of values, has no need to retire into any perverted self-abasement. It has full rights to a generous share in grants meant to promote culture. It has played an important role in the past, and it still has an important role to play in the future in providing the overall steadying vision that penetrates to the depths of the realities in which the culture grows and that allows them to spread their radiance to the everyday details of its life. Not without deep meaning did Hegel compare the strange spectacle of an educated people without metaphysics to an elaborately decorated temple lacking any object of cult.[50]

The other function of metaphysics with regard to values is also important, but in a different way. It is the "meta" function, the task of explaining epistemologically what values are. In this "meta" field, metaphysics is supreme. There is no higher philosophical court of appeal. Metaphysics can show how values are located in what has been traditionally known as the good, which is something to be achieved and maintained both practically and productively. Because the good is a transcendental property of existence, its ground, namely, existence, is also the ground of the true and the beautiful. These transcendental properties, because they are properties that necessarily follow upon existence, always accompany one another in varying relations. They spread the aspect of value everywhere, wherever there is existence. In this way both ends and means are values, as are also virtues and morality, the fine arts, the crafts and trades, commerce, social and political and religious life, recreation, travel, the sciences, philosophy, theology, and culture in general. The metaphysical explanation of the good, the true and beautiful as transcendental properties of being, shows why value consists basically in the good alone, yet embraces the true and the beautiful as properties that because they are transcendental always share the aspect of goodness. It gives the reason why the true and the beautiful are always values, and at the same time why those thinkers are right who maintain that *qua* true and *qua* beautiful nothing can be a value.[51] Similarly it makes clear why a value always has to presuppose existence,[52] even though this be future existence. As a transcendental property, goodness is something that of its very nature follows upon existence and cannot be present unless there is existence to ground it.

The metaphysics of the transcendentals, accordingly, seems fully equipped to act as a theoretical philosophy of value. In its own setting it is able to dissipate the confusions that have plagued the modern efforts to work out a satisfactory explanation of a most important theme. For some today it may perhaps lack all advertising appeal. It may be expected to meet with disapproval from the contemporary thinkers who are dyslogistically—to use the trade term—inclined toward traditional metaphysics. All sorts of thinkers are required to make a philosophical world. But can any other view, among the many contemporary explanations, offer as satisfactory an account of the topics that are discussed today under the caption of values? [53] If there are any compelling reasons why the topic of values should not be assessed in the light of the traditional transcendentals, these reasons should be brought out clearly and cogently.[54] Traditional philosophy is eager to listen and learn. But the whole project should hardly be dismissed with the glib assertion that the transcendentals are already fixed and static in the universe and are not something to be achieved or otherwise open to the notion of value. Rather, the transcendental good is essentially an object of will, and opens out readily into the whole field of value in all its various gradations.

NOTES

1. Cf.: "For the existing state of discussion shows not only that there is great difference of opinion about the proper theoretical interpretation to be put upon the facts . . . but also that there is great disagreement as to what the facts are to which the theory applies, and indeed whether there are any facts to which a theory of value can apply." John Dewey, *Theory of Valuation,* Chicago, 1939, p. 1. Ten years later, Dewey was even more pointed in his assessment of the situation: "For the confused controversial state of the subject seems to arise from the fact that there is no agreement about the *field* in which events having value-qualifications are located." Dewey, "The Field of Value," in *Value,* ed. Ray Lepley, New York, 1949, p. 64. This volume was a cooperative inquiry, which, as Lepley notes in his preface (p. v), "has not produced unanimity among the various participants—even with regard to proper methods of approach or the most elementary and basic concepts." In fact, one contributor placed the only bond of unity in the word itself: "Whatever it is that philosophers and economists have been talking about under the heading of value in the last fifty years or more, that is the area of our study." Stephen C. Pepper, "Observations on Value from an Analysis of a Simple Appetition," in *Value,* p. 245. Recent appraisal shows no notable change: "The terms 'value' and 'valuation' and their cognates and compounds are used in a confused and confusing but widespread way in our contemporary culture." W. Frankena, in Paul Edwards' *Encyclopedia of Philosophy,* VIII, 229a (s.v. Value and Valuation).

2. E.g., L. M. Loring, *Two Kinds of Values,* London, 1966. Miss Loring sees "ethical values in general" (p. 187) as themselves evaluated in terms of the good or harm they do.

3. E.g., Paul Tillich, in "Is a Science of Human Values Possible?," in *New Knowledge in Human Values,* ed. Abraham H. Maslow, New York,

1959, tells how he "passionately rejected the philosophy of values" (p. 190) because it deliberately sought to explain values without the foundation of being (pp. 189–191). Cf.: "Modern idealism begins by turning the transcendentals into 'values' "—Etienne Gilson, *Painting and Reality,* New York, 1957, p. 191, n. 22.

4. Ast, *Lexicon Platonicum,* I, 199–204, lists numerous instances in Plato, as does Bonitz, *Index Aristotelicum,* 69b33–70a60, for Aristotle. *Timê* may be seen used with *axia* in Aristotle, *Rh.,* II 16, 1391al–2.

5. See H. Pouillon, "Le Premier Traité des Propriétés Transcendantales," *Revue Néoscolastique de Philosophie,* 1939, XLII, 40–77; "La Beauté, Propriété Transcendantale chez les Scolastiques (1220–1270)," *Archives d'Histoire Doctrinale et Littéraire du Moyen Age,* 1946, XXI, 263–314. In relation to the present context the Scholastic conception of the transcendentals is well summed up by Robert S. Hartman, "Problems and Perplexities," *Review of Metaphysics,* 1962, XVI, 149: "Transcendentals . . . are determinations of Being which necessarily follow from its essence; they are . . . properties or attributes of Being, transcending, as does Being itself, all specific and generic modes of Being, . . . co-existent and co-extensive with Being, aspects under which we apprehend it." Hartman rejects this conception on the ground that "it makes no sense logically" (p. 150). But his objections arise from conceiving a transcendental as a *summum genus* (*ibid.*), in spite of his description of the transcendental as transcending all generic modes. The *summa genera* for the Scholastics are not the transcendentals but the categories. No transcendental is a genus or *summum genus.* It cannot be dealt with as a generic or specific "type" as long as it is regarded as transcendental. This sixteenth-century word meant "climbing across" the categories, a notion expressed in the Middle Ages by the form "transcendent." The latter is a term that was also used at the time for transcending the sensible world. In its meaning of "climbing across" the categories it left no possibility of generic restriction and accordingly no possibility of any "higher type" (Hartman, p. 150) by which it might be defined.

6. Titles dealing with value as a philosophical topic begin to appear in the last decade of the nineteenth century, and multiply in the early decades of the twentieth century. Ralph Barton Perry, *General Theory of Value,* New York, 1926, p. 5, n. 2, recalls how in 1885 Hermann Lotze mentioned that the investigation of value "may be conceived" but "has hitherto never been carried out." The notion had become current in economics. The economic background may be seen in Adam Smith's *Wealth of Nations,* I, 4–6, and John Stuart Mill's *Principles of Political Economy,* III, 1–6, 15–16; IV, 2. There is also a background in psychology as well as in metaphysics for the German interest in values. Against this multiple background the interest developed in thinkers like Lotze, Nietzsche, Meinong, Ehrenfels, Scheler, and Nicolai Hartmann. For an early survey of the emerging discipline, see J. S. Mackenzie, "Notes on the Theory of Values," *Mind,* 1895, N.S. IV, 425–439. On the arousal of interest in America through Hugo Münsterberg, see Ralph Barton Perry, *Realms of Value,* Cambridge, Mass., 1954, p. 4.

7. The Greek *krinô,* from which "critical" comes, may be used in a philosophical context for distinguishing light from darkness by sight (Aristotle, *De An.,* III 2, 425b21) or for "decision as to the truth" (*talêthes krinein, Cael.,* I 10, 279b12; Oxford trans.). Without exception every judgment is a decision whether or not a predicate goes with a subject, even though in immediate judgments the decision is spontaneous and without

preceding deliberation. There is of course no objection to investing "critical" with a technical meaning in this application and by definition restricting it to the field of values. A critical judgment will then be coextensive with a judgment about value, for a value judgment will be defined as one that is critical rather than descriptive. The circularity in the explanation should be noted, and other grounds for the distinction probed.

8. See Perry, *General Theory of Value,* pp. 29–32; Paul Weiss, *Man's Freedom,* Carbondale, Ill., 1950, p. 185. Cf. "Value is a natural phenomenon. Excellence of any kind, beauty, power, purity, comprehensiveness, and their negates are facts as hard as smell and shape, number and size." Weiss, p. 105. For Aristotle the virtues or excellences were qualities, along with the sciences, in the first division of the category of quality (*Cat.,* 8, 8b26–29). But in the moral sphere the quality was determined by human choice of good or evil (*E N,* III 2, 1112a2), not by nature. The qualities called primary and secondary from Locke's time on would belong to the third and fourth Aristotelian divisions. But, regardless of the name, "each value-phenomenon as it comes before us, does so as a standing refutation of the Humean diremption of fact and value, or of any contemporary diremption of descriptive and evaluative meaning, . . ." J. N. Findlay, *The Transcendence of the Cave,* New York, 1967, p. 60.

9. *Metaph.,* α 1, 993b24–31. On the extension of this notion to all spheres, in the sense that the highest in each is the measure (*mensura*) of all else within the sphere, see Aquinas, *In I Sent.,* d. 8, q. 4, a. 2, ad 3m; ed. Mandonnet, I, 223. Degrees of being are outlined in Aristotle *Metaph.,* Γ 2, 1003b5–10.

10. Cf. Aristotle, *De An.,* II 4, 415a26–b7; Aquinas, *ST,* I, 5, lc. "Omnia autem quae iam esse habent, illud esse suum naturaliter amant, et ipsum tota virtute conservant." Aquinas, *De Ver.,* XXI, 2c.

11. See Aristotle, *EN,* I 1, 1094a2–3; X 2, 1172b9–15. Cf. Plato, *Plt.,* 284AB; *Phlb.,* 64E–67B.

12. *EN,* I 6, 1096b27–29; Oxford trans.

13. "Quod autem dicit '*Quod omnia appetunt*', non est intelligendum solum de habentibus cognitionem, quae apprehendunt bonum, sed etiam de rebus carentibus cognitione, quae naturali appetitu tendunt in bonum. . . ." Aquinas, *In I Eth. Nic..* lect. 1, Pirotta no. 11.

14. *Frs.* 61 and 9 (DK 22B); trans. K. Freeman. Cf. Aristotle, *EN* X 5, 1176a7–8. Cf. Heraclitus, *Fr.* 111, and Aristotle, *EN,* I 4, 1095a22–25. Modern examples may be seen in R. B. Perry's comparison of the dictionary description of England, the eulogy in Shakespeare's *Richard II,* and the dyslogistic attack in Lissauer's "Song of Hate"—*General Theory of Value,* pp. 1–2; and in Robert S. Hartman's example of the same news as good for a person in one state and bad for a person in another—*The Structure of Value,* Carbondale, Ill., 1967, p. 161. The relative character is quite regularly noted in modern contexts, e.g., Baldwin, *Dictionary of Philosophy and Psychology,* s.v. Worth. Perry's explanation (pp. 115–116; 124) in terms of interest brings out this feature.

15. *EN,* X 7, 1177a12–b26. Cf. I 7, 1097b24–1098a20. As Aristotle's approach is from Plato's viewpoint of a thing's "virtue" or excellence (Plato, *Rep.,* I, 353AC), his formulation is "activity in accordance with . . . the highest virtue" (1177a12–13; Oxford trans.).

16. *Pol.,* I 5, 1254b19–20; Oxford trans. The same type of reasoning had just shown (1254b10–13) that domestication is better than a wild life for animals.

17. "The goodness of a thing consists in its being desirable. . . . Now

clearly desirability is consequent upon perfection, for things always desire their perfection. And the perfection of a thing depends on how far it has achieved actuality. It is clear then that a thing is good inasmuch as it exists, for as we saw above it is by existing that everything achieves actuality." Aquinas, *ST,* I, 5, 1c; Blackfriars trans. The word translated by "desirability" and "desirable" is *appetibile,* and by "desire" *appetunt.*

18. See Louis-Marie Régis, *L'Odyssée de la Métaphysique,* Montreal and Paris, 1949, p. 39, n. 47. Cf. *supra,* n. 4.

19. See *supra,* n. 14. On the meaning of "objective" in an ethical context, see Alfred Cyril Ewing, *The Definition of Good,* New York, 1947, pp. 1–3. On the difficulty in making any pertinent distinction between "value" and "worth" in this setting, see D. W. Prall, "In Defense of a *Worthless* Theory of Value," *Journal of Philosophy,* 1923, XX, 128–136.

20. *Metaph.,* E 1, 1025b18–24. Cf. *EN,* VI 2, 1139a31. The difference in starting points causes a radical distinction between theoretical and practical science, and prevents the subalternation of one type to the other.

21. "*Tertius* autem est *ordo* quem ratio considerando facit in operationibus voluntatis." *In I Eth. Nic.,* lectio 1, no. 1.

22. Aristotle, *EN,* I 6, 1096a23–29; Aquinas, *ST,* I, 5, 1c.

23. *Sph.,* 254B–256E.

24. *Rep.,* VI, 509B.

25. *Rep.,* VII, 540AB. Cf. VI, 501B.

26. On this topic, see A. E. Teale, *Kantian Ethics,* London, 1951, pp. 4–6; 94–95.

27. See *infra,* n. 48.

28. E.g., "But this is one of the strangest aberrations ever to visit the mind of man. The denial to value-apprehensions in general of the character of truth or falsity and of knowledge, would imply both moral and practical cynicism." C. I. Lewis, *An Analysis of Knowledge and Valuation,* La Salle, Ill., 1946, p. 366. For a critique of noncognitivism against the Aristotelian background of goodness as transcendental, see Henry Veatch, "Non-Cognitivism in Ethics," *Ethics,* 1966, LXXVI, 102–116. For a sketch of the development of the emotive view through linguistic approaches, see Stephen Coburn Pepper, *The Sources of Value,* Berkeley, 1958, pp. 18–30. Cf.: "Values are thus as much open to description as any other objects or events in the natural world." *Ibid.,* p. 688.

29. "True belief" is a common enough expression in philosophical literature, even though there may be some doubt about its use in ordinary language. "True" would seem to elevate the tenet to a higher level, and make it knowledge and consequently no longer belief. "Belief," however, has a variety of meanings in philosophical contexts. In regard to Greek philosophy it is used for doxastic tenets in contrast to knowledge, in Christian tradition for faith, and in modern philosophy for tenets assented to. The two latter contexts would allow the expression "true belief."

30. See Aquinas, *In I Sent.,* d. 19, q. 5, a. 1, ad 7m; ed. Mandonnet, I, 489–490. *De Ver.,* I, 3. Cf.: "In fact, truth and falsehood are properties of beliefs and statements." Bertrand Russell, *The Problems of Philosophy,* London, 1929, p. 189.

31. This method by which the various definitions are explained by Aquinas, *In I Sent.,* d. 19, q. 5, a. 1, Solut. (ed. Mandonnet, I, 486–487) seems applicable to the modern theories of truth. Each truth theory does seem to have some truth in it. True judgments will correspond with what exists, coherence may be "a most important *test* of truth" (Russell, *Prob-*

lems of Philosophy, p. 193), pragmatically truth may be expected to succeed in the long run rather than error, semantically truth bears upon a judgment in the sense of a representation, and redundantly and performatively it emphasizes the existence originally known. The basic issue is that truth does all these things through being a property of a judgment (representation), a property that consists in a relation to the existent the judgment purports to represent. In the truth of practical judgments, the existent or fact (cf. *supra,* nn. 8, 22, and 28) is the value status already set up by human choice. "Conformity with correct desire" (Aristotle, *E N* VI 2, 1139a26–31) is seen to exist in a moral object, and the judgment asserting the conformity is on comparison seen to be true. The value itself is set up by human choice, thereby becoming a fact (see *supra,* n. 8).

32. As static it is not the object of an act of judgment but of an act of reflexive simple apprehension. On this topic, see my discussion in *An Elementary Christian Metaphysics,* Milwaukee, 1963, pp. 249–257, and *An Interpretation of Existence,* Milwaukee, 1968, pp. 22–24.

33. "And on this account truth is defined through the conformity of intellect and thing. Hence to know this conformity is to know the truth." Aquinas, *ST,* I, 16, 2c. The truth judgment is accordingly a judgment about a judgment, and in this way is genuinely a "meta" judgment.

34. One can understand easily enough how meanings attached to words can change with the course of human history, since a word can have many meanings. But at least some ecumenical theologians, seeking to smooth out differences in beliefs, propose something deeper, e.g., "What is here in question is no mere change of words. The formula must be changed because in the mental and social structures of the contemporary world there is no longer any room for an exclusivist concept of the Church"—Avery Dulles, "Dogma as an Ecumenical Problem," *Theological Studies,* 1968, XXIX, 407. So: "In order to bring out the deeper and divinely intended meaning, which alone is inseparable from faith, it may be necessary to discard the human concepts as well as the words of those who first framed the dogma." *Ibid.* The issue in regard to truth, however, is whether the existence predicated of those concepts agrees or disagrees with what does exist. In that perspective there can be no change in the truth. If the new concepts represent something different, what is asserted in their regard will have to be judged true or false independently on the basis of what actually exists.

35. "Believing that philosophy must face the facts of life and nature, taking them as both the point of departure and the touchstone of truth. . . ." Perry, *General Theory of Value,* p. vii. The Greek Skeptics, who claimed to be always looking for truth and never finding it (Diogenes Laertius, IX, 70), set themselves up against the rest of the philosophers who definitely assert "dogmas" (*ibid.,* IX, 74). This tacit acknowledgement that philosophers by and large consider themselves engaged in the pursuit of truth seems repeated in contemporary pessimistic remarks like "the philosophical pursuit of a 'truth' that forever escapes until, in the end, 'the philosopher knows nothing of everything.'" Hartman, *The Structure of Value,* p. 303. The modern context, however, envisages a "climb from moral philosophy up to moral science." *Ibid.* Cf. Russell, *The Problems of Philosophy,* p. 243.

36. "Truth in itself is not a value. . . . There is, however, an interest *in* truth: ranging from primitive curiosity to the acquired and advanced pursuits of science." Ralph Barton Perry, *Realms of Value,* Cambridge, Mass., 1954, p. 102. "The true, and its somewhat poor substitute, the likely or

seemingly true, are not, however, in any sense 'values' for the believing mind: they are not things in whose *existence* it has, *qua* believing, an interest, which it seeks to produce, preserve or multiply. . . ." Findlay, *Values and Intentions,* p. 255. On the other hand, the assertion that truth and falsity "are definitely values" may be seen upheld in Pepper, *The Sources of Value,* p. 692.

37. Truth may accordingly be called a particular good: "Sed verum est quoddam particulare bonum, est enim bonum intellectus, ut dicit Philosophus in VI *Ethic.*" Aquinas, *De Ver.,* XXI, 3, arg. 4. Cf. ". . . of the intellect which is contemplative, not practical nor productive, the good and bad state are truth and falsity respectively . . . while of the part which is practical and intellectual the good state is truth in agreement with right desire." Aristotle, *EN,* VI 2, 1139a27–31; Oxford trans. In this sense truth is something to be preferred to friends, I 6, 1096a16–17.

38. Cf.: "Beauty, or excellence for contemplation, or whatever else we may care to call it, is not therefore a case of value, though it is intimately connected with value." Findlay, *Values and Intentions,* p. 244. "Quamvis autem pulchrum et bonum sint idem subiecto, quia tam claritas quam consonantia sub ratione boni continentur, tamen ratione differunt: nam pulchrum addit supra bonum, ordinem ad vim cognoscitivam illud esse huiusmodi." Aquinas, *De Div. Nom.,* c. IV, lect. 5, Para no. 356.

39. "Omnis autem forma, per quam res habet esse, est participatio quaedam divinae claritatis; et hoc est quod subdit, quod *singula* sunt *pulchra secundum propriam rationem,* idest secundum propriam formam." Aquinas, *ibid.,* no. 349.

40. "Any field of inquiry may present an aspect of beauty. It is a well-known fact that scientific theories are valued for their orderly form as well as for their truth." Perry, *Realms of Value,* p. 103. Findlay's assertion (*Values and Intentions,* p. 244) that a mathematical relationship "is not one of which existence could be predicated," restricts existence to existence in the real world. On the topic, see Aristotle, *Metaph.,* M 3, 1078a31–b5.

41. The topic of transcendental unity in Aquinas is covered by Ludger Oeing-Hanhoff, *Ens et Unum Convertuntur,* Münster, 1953. From the angle of value: "Weil ein Seiendes eher als unum denn als bonum erkannt wird, erschliesst dieser Weg in einem ursprünglichen Zugang die gestufte Werthaftigkeit der Dinge, von denen 'ein jedes um so vortrefflicher und wertvoller ist, je mehr es ein unum ist'." *Ibid.,* pp. 182–183. On the statements of Aquinas that unity follows upon the substance or essence of a thing, though the other transcendental properties follow only upon the thing's existence, see my discussion in "Unity and Essence in St. Thomas Aquinas," *Mediaeval Studies,* 1961, XXIII, 240–259.

42. E.g., "Das Heilige ist zunächst eine Bewertungskategorie, die *so nur* auf religiösem Gebiete vorkommt, auf anderes, z. B. die Ethik, zwar übergreift, selber aber nicht aus anderem entspringt, . . ." Rudolf Otto, *Das Heilige,* Breslau, 1917, p. 5. Cf. pp. 120–123. For Kant, *KPV,* I, 2, 4, holiness is the perfect conformity of the will with the moral law. The topic is not listed in Paul Edwards' *Encyclopedia of Philosophy.*

43. "No one would be disposed to deny that there is a common something in truth, goodness, legality, wealth, beauty and piety that distinguishes them from gravitation and chemical affinity." Perry, *General Theory of Value,* pp. 4–5. Cf.: ". . . miscellaneous and homeless values, expressed in such terms as 'nice,' 'terrifying,' 'sublime,' 'ridiculous,' 'amusing,' . . . and a thousand others." *Ibid.,* p. 10. On the division into submoral values, un-

moral values, and "super-moral values, such as blessedness or holiness," see *ibid.*, pp. 5–6. On their specifically human character, see Brand Blanshard, *Reason and Goodness,* London, 1961, pp. 291–293. For a list of values, see Kelvin Van Nuys, *Is Reality Meaningful?* New York, 1966, p. 30; and on their basic relation to human decision, Pepper, *The Sources of Value,* pp. 690–691.

44. See *supra,* n. 20. Choice is the starting point of any practical knowledge.

45. On the universality involved in culture, see Melville J. Herskovits, *Cultural Dynamics,* New York, 1964, pp. 4, 25.

46. Aristotle, *EN,* I 2, 1094a20–21.

47. "In such a context there was no call and no place for any *separate* problem of valuation and values, since what are now termed values were taken to be integrally incorporated into the very structure of the world." Dewey, *Theory of Valuation,* pp. 2–3. "But when teleological considerations were eliminated . . . the problem of value arose as a separate problem." *Ibid.*, p. 3.

48. "Not perfection as a final goal, but the ever-enduring process of perfecting, maturing, refining is the aim in living. . . . Growth itself is the only moral 'end'." Dewey, *Reconstruction in Philosophy,* New York, 1920, p. 177. Cf. "The belief in fixed values has bred a division of ends into intrinsic and instrumental, . . . Dialectically, the distinction is interesting and seems harmless. But carried into practice it has an import that is tragic." *Ibid.*, p. 170.

49. Cf. ". . . the man who has been well brought up has or can easily get the starting-points." Aristotle, *EN,* I 4, 1095b7–8; Oxford trans. "It is to be sought in the general 'spirit' or attitude of mind lying behind our varying value-determinations." Findlay, *Values and Intentions,* p. 24.

50. Hegel, *Logik*, preface to first edition (1812).

51. *Supra,* n. 38. Cf.: "For even if it be held that beauty might exist in a mindless universe, there is no reason for regarding the beautiful things in such a universe as having any value in themselves." W. D. Ross, *The Right and the Good,* Oxford, 1930, p. 130.

52. E.g.: ". . . a straightforward case of *valuation,* since it is concerned with the *existence* of its object." Findlay, *Values and Intentions*, p. 244. In Meinong "while value pertains to what exists, and cannot well be said to pertain to anything else, desire is never of what certainly does exist, nor even, on Meinong's view, of what certainly does *not* exist, but only of what does not certainly fall in either category." J. N. Findlay, *Meinong's Theory of Objects and Values,* 2nd ed., Oxford, 1963, p. 267.

In the metaphysics of the transcendentals, a thing's goodness rests upon the being that its nature immediately calls for. Yet the gradation in being and in goodness is not exactly the same. A thing is absolutely a being through its substantial existence, but is absolutely good only when it has its required accidental perfections; see Aquinas, *CG,* III, 20, Manifestum. On the problematic of the gap between being and value in the modern setting, see Wilbur M. Urban, "Value and Existence," *Journal of Philosophy,* 1916, XIII, 449–465, and Paul Tillich, "Is a Science of Human Values Possible?," in *New Knowledge in Human Values,* ed. Abraham H. Maslow, New York, 1959, pp. 189–196.

53. Admittedly, these topics do not extend as far as does the transcendental good, since the objects of nonvital tendency seem excluded from the modern notion of value: ". . . the case of bodies acted on by physical

forces, where no one would dream of applying the notion of good or value." Ross, *The Right and the Good,* p. 80. The notion may be found extended to the animal kingdom. Perry, *General Theory of Value,* p. 117, quotes with approval Prall's assertion: "For the cat the cream has value, or better and more simply, the cat values the cream." Yet in the same context the model seems to remain "our human bias," as quoted *ibid.,* p. 116, from Santayana. The confusion in the notion is apparent. However, the factor of human choice may be found stated explicitly: "Values, then, are a concomitant of freedom." Walter A. Weisskopf, "Existence and Values," in Maslow's *New Knowledge in Human Values,* p. 109. At least some human reference seems required for the notion: "Now recent thought has emphasized strongly, in my opinion rightly, that all statements of value should be regarded as expressing emotion in ourselves." J. N. Findlay, *Language, Mind and Value,* London, 1963, pp. 106–107. Cf. *supra,* n. 43, for further samplings. The instances of values noted there may be extended almost indefinitely in continued shadings, for instance, the way the holy is extended to include whatever can occasion a celebration, e.g., a wedding or a birth, by John E. Smith, "The Experience of the Holy and the Idea of God," in *Phenomenology in America,* ed. James M. Edie, Chicago, 1967, pp. 295–306.

54. The objections against retaining the traditional term "goodness" are sketched succinctly by Perry, *General Theory of Value,* p. 21. On the differing perspective, cf.: "Theory of value in the modern sense is in effect a sort of democratic revolution against a hereditary aristocracy. Though it may arrive at a new constitutional hierarchy, it begins with a promiscuous acknowledgment of the rights of every value, however lowly or disreputable." *Ibid.,* p. 10.

Metaphysics and Values

Joseph J. Kockelmans

INTRODUCTION

The title of this essay suggests that we examine the relationship between what is called 'metaphysics' and what is meant by the term 'value'. It is clear at once that one can make a great number of statements about the relation between metaphysics and values, in that the expressions 'metaphysics' and 'values' can be, and as a matter of fact are, used in many senses. But in whatever sense one takes these two expressions one will not find a combination whose meaning is not ambiguous and, to a certain extent at least, questionable, except if one were permitted to say that in this title the term 'metaphysics' stands for philosophy and the word 'value' refers to the totality of all possible meaning. For in that case one could perhaps make the straightforward assertion that 'values' constitute the subject matter of philosophy. Although in a certain sense this is, indeed, the thesis which I intend to defend in this paper, I feel that I cannot do so immediately, because if I were to do so I would not have an opportunity to indicate why I think that any other interpretation of the title of this essay would lead to a philosophically unacceptable position. Before presenting my own point of view let me, therefore, first try to establish what might have been meant by the title of this essay, by briefly reflecting on the various meanings which great philosophers have attached to the two words which constitute the title.

What is metaphysics? Everyone knows that this is not an easy question. Throughout the twenty centuries of its history metaphysics has undergone a long process of development during which various conceptions of metaphysics have been proposed by leading philosophers and philosophical schools. Although it would be very illuminating and also quite important to follow the history of metaphysics in greater detail, I shall limit myself here to a few remarks which are of some importance for the thesis I intend to establish.

The term 'metaphysics' was first introduced by Andronicus Rhodus for an untitled group of manuscripts by Aristotle. Aristotle himself sometimes refers to a part of these manuscripts by the alternative titles 'first philosophy', 'theology', or also 'wisdom'.[1] He defines this science as that speculative knowledge which tries to bring to light the first principles and causes of all things.[2] On another occasion he says: "And thus, as was in the past, is now too, and will be ever more, that toward which first philosophy is underway and to which it time and again does not find access, is the question: what is Being?" [3] First philosophy searches for what beings are insofar as they are; it searches for the 'being-ness' (*ousia*) of beings. It focuses attention upon the question of what a being is insofar as it is and from what ground it might receive its ultimate explanation.[4]

Influenced by late medieval sources, Descartes propagated the view that metaphysics is the scientific study of the existence and the principal attributes of God, the immortality of the soul, and all the clear and distinct notions which are in us in regard to the world.[5] Descartes was also the first person to defend the thesis that these insights concerning God, soul, and world can never be 'the principles of our knowledge' as a whole if they are not founded in epistemological reflections which guarantee that (1) no scientific assertions will be made unless they are understood with that kind of clarity and distinctness which are characteristic of mathematical insights, and (2) their truth is apodictically evident on the basis of an immediate intuition, such as is found in the *cogito*.

This view was accepted by all dogmatic rationalists, whereas all empiricist skeptics doubted whether such a metaphysics is possible. Kant tried to overcome critically this dogmatism and skepticism. In the beginning of the *Critique of Pure Reason* he takes the term 'metaphysics' in the sense of Descartes; it is the philosophical discipline concerned with the existence of God, the immortality of the soul, and the origin of the world.[6] When the *Critique of Pure Reason* ended negatively in regard to the possibility of such a metaphysics, Kant used the term 'metaphysics' to refer to all a priori speculation on questions that cannot be answered by scientific observation and experiment. As he formulates it: metaphysics "is the system of pure reason, that is, the science which exhibits in systematic connection the whole body (true as well as illusory) of philosophical knowledge arising out of pure reason." Taken in a broader sense (so as to include the critique of reason), metaphysics comprehends "the investigations of all that can ever be known a priori as well as the exposition of that which constitutes a system of the pure philosophical modes of knowledge of this type. . . ." Metaphysics is either metaphysics of nature or metaphysics of morals. "The former contains all the principles of pure reason that are derived from mere concepts . . . and employed in the *theoretical* knowledge of all things; the latter, the principles which in a priori fashion determine and make necessary all our actions." [7]

In modern philosophy since the time of Kant the term 'metaphysics' is used in a great variety of meanings. Generally speaking, however, the term is used here to refer to that realm of philosophy which deals with questions concerning the various regions of beings and their properties. In dealing with these questions it uses such basic concepts as 'existence', 'thing', 'property', 'event', and so on; it introduces distinctions such as those between particulars and universals, individuals and classes; it studies relations such as those between change and causation; and finally it tries to establish the nature of mind, matter, space, and time.

In contemporary philosophy the term is used in pragmatism, neopositivism, scientific realism, ordinary-language philosophy, and philosophical analysis. Pragmatism claims that metaphysics is an *observational* science whose task it is to study the most general features of reality. It is an attempt to describe how reality must seem to a man imbued with science; reality is what will eventually be agreed upon by the community of scientists. This view has been defended by Peirce and Dewey, and is today still accepted by scientific realism, albeit on different grounds.

Logical positivism, ordinary-language philosophy, and analytic philosophy take the term in the sense given to it in post-Kantian philosophy. They argue, however, each along quite different lines, that traditional metaphysical statements do have a point, but a point which the traditional formulation of the question obscures. The claim is that these questions are to be reformulated, but in so doing these schools follow different procedures and employ different criteria and methods.[8]

Although Husserl himself sometimes uses the term 'metaphysics' and then manifests the fact that he still thinks within the general perspective of post-Kantian philosophy, most phenomenologists and all existentialists avoid the term except to refer to any one of the classical conceptions of metaphysics.

It is now time to turn to our second question: *What are values?*[9] The word 'value,' in opposition to many other philosophical terms, is a word in our ordinary language. It received a technical meaning first in mathematics, and then in economics and aesthetics. The term as used in 'political economy' seems to be at the root of all philosophical usages of the term. In economics the term was used mainly for the economic worth of a thing. Even when the term was not used in that sense, it still pointed to a worth of some kind, and certainly not to what philosophers call 'truth', 'beauty', 'virtue', 'rightness', and so on. As a philosophically technical term the word was first used by Lotze who defined its meaning as follows: a value is something which man emotionally recognizes as something which transcends him and to which he can relate himself by means of intuition, appreciation, veneration, or aspiration. In the latter half of the nineteenth century the term was used in a great variety of meanings, but mostly as a substitute for what Greek philosophers called 'the good', taken either as *Idea* or as *Telos*. Nietzsche has contributed much to the propagation of the term 'value' taken in this sense.

In contemporary philosophy the word 'value' is also used in many ways. Most of these usages, however, seem to be further specifications of one of the following two usages which are also found in our ordinary language: (1) value is a principle, an entity, or a quality which is intrinsically desirable, worthwhile, or good; and (2) value is the relative worth, utility, or importance of something in regard to something else.

The term 'value' is sometimes used as an abstract noun. Then the word is taken either in a narrow sense, so as to cover only that which is called 'desirable', 'worthwhile', or 'good', the latter terms taken in their strict meanings; or it is used in a wider sense, including everything to which such words as 'beauty', 'truth', 'holiness', 'rightness', 'virtue', and so on, are properly applied.

Philosophers who use the term in a wider sense make a distinction between various realms of values. Rickert, for example, speaks about theoretical, aesthetic, mystic, erotic, and religious values. Scheler distinguishes between values of the pleasant and unpleasant, values of vitality, values of the spirit, and values of the holy and unholy. Perry and Taylor mention the following realms of values: economics, science, custom, law, politics, morality, art, and religion. Hartmann's investigation in this direction has perhaps led to the most articulated list of value realms.

Those who use the term in a narrower sense also distinguish between various meanings of the term, but in this case these meanings correspond to the different senses of the word 'good'. Lewis, for instance, distinguishes the following forms of goodness: utilitarian value (the usefulness of something for some purpose); instrumental value (for something which is good as a means toward an end); inherent value (such as the aesthetic value of a statue); intrinsic value (for the goodness of a thing which is desired as an end); contributory value (such as the goodness of a part in regard to a whole of which it is a part). Other philosophers have suggested other distinctions in this connection.

If one takes the word 'value' as a concrete noun, then it is of importance to make a clear distinction between the subjective and the objective usage of the term. The subjective usage of the word 'value' points to a characteristic which is attributed to a thing merely because of the fact that this thing is more or less estimated, desired, or protected by one, more, or all human beings; the term then points to what *is regarded* as good. The objective usage of the term, on the other hand, indicates the characteristic which a thing has and because of which it deserves more or less esteem or respect; the term then means that which *has* value, what *is* good.

This list of meanings which have been attached to the term 'value' indicates already that there is little or no agreement among the many philosophers who have written on value theory. A more careful study of the available literature will even strengthen this impression, as we shall see in what follows.

AXIOLOGY [10]

From the time of Plato and Aristotle philosophers have dealt with many different problems connected with what is generally called 'good', 'right', 'true', 'beautiful', 'holy', and so on. In the post-Kantian philosophy several philosophers were of the opinion that all these problems somehow belong together and that they all are concerned with 'value', with 'what-ought-to-be' in opposition to 'what-is', the 'facts'. All such questions, these philosophers argued, may not only be brought together under the general heading 'value' and 'valuation', but also one can perhaps better deal with these questions and find a systematic solution for them if they are conceived of as elements of a general theory of values called *axiology*.

In such a general theory originally two major domains of investigation were clearly distinguished: an epistemological domain, mainly concerned with the question of our 'knowledge' of values; and an ontological domain whose main task it was to explain the ontological status of values. In their attempts to answer the pertinent epistemological and ontological questions these philosophers came to quite different conclusions. But all these differences notwithstanding, all the philosophers who have explicitly dealt with values have defended the view that the realm of values is to be distinguished from the realm of 'facts', from the realm of 'what is'. Whereas metaphysics deals with 'what-is', axiology is concerned with 'what-ought-to-be'. Most philosophers have felt that such a general theory of values should lay the foundations for ethics, whereas others have defended the view that axiology is identical with ethics, or even with a part of it, depending upon the meanings they attached to the terms 'ethics' and 'value'.

In this connection the following names should be mentioned: Friedrich Beneke, Hermann Lotze, Friedrich Nietzsche, Franz Brentano, Alexius Meinong, Christian von Ehrenfels, Wilhelm Windelband, Hugo Munsterberg, and Heinrich Rickert. Later analogous views have been developed by people such as Max Scheler, Nicolai Hartmann, Georges Gusdorf, Raymond Polin, and Dietrich von Hildebrandt. From the United States, England, and Canada the philosophers who have written on value theory are: John Dewey, C. I. Lewis, Ralph Perry, Wilbur M. Urban,

D. H. Parker, J. N. Findlay, Richard Hare, Patrick H. Nowell-Smith, George H. von Wright, William Werkmeister, and Paul W. Taylor.

Many contemporary English-speaking philosophers make a clear distinction between a normative and a metanormative axiology. Axiology as a *normative* science tries to establish norms by determining in regard to things and activities whether they are good or bad, when and under what conditions they have value; in other words, as a normative science axiology tries to formulate value judgments. Metanormative theories, on the other hand, are concerned with the epistemological and ontological status of values. Instead of making value judgments, a metanormative theory tries to define what value is and under what conditions values can be known by man. Most of the continental European philosophers do not make an explicit distinction between normative and metanormative theories; most of them deal mainly with metanormative problems.

In addition to these two approaches to values, there is obviously the possibility of a merely descriptive approach to values. In such a case an author tries to formulate descriptive generalizations about what is regarded as valuable in a certain culture or a group of cultures. Such a description is sometimes combined with an attempt to explain why certain things are so valued in a given culture. Most authors, however, are of the opinion that descriptive and explanatory theories of values do not belong to the realm of philosophy proper.

Of the two philosophical approaches to the realm of values the metanormative approach is more important for our purpose. Consequently, I shall devote myself here to that approach. In metanormative theories people try to answer one of the following questions: What are values? What is their ontological status? What is the relationship betwen moral and nonmoral values? What is the precise meaning of a value judgment? How can a value judgment be justified with certainty? How can a value judgment be shown to have any objective validity?

In trying to answer the question concerning the ontological status of values a great number of people have come to the conclusion that value statements are meaningless, in that they cannot be verified by sense experience. Value words must be reduced to pseudo-concepts and all value judgments to mere expressive utterances (Ayer). Others have claimed that although value statements are not verifiable and, therefore, do not have a theoretical meaning, they none the less have the meaning of an imperative, or the expression of a wish (Carnap). Stevenson defends the view that value statements have meaning, because they can persuade people and achieve agreement. Most philosophers, however, feel that value statements, indeed, have meaning and that their meaning consists in the fact that they refer to the desirability of things for man. Although it is true that value statements cannot be verified by means of sense experience, they certainly can be verified by experience if the term 'experience' is taken in a broader sense so as to include practical, emotional, aesthetic, and religious experiences.

In their attempts to clarify what precisely is meant by the expression 'the desirability of things for man', some people such as Lotze, von Ehrenfels, Perry, and Parker have argued that this desirability is not an intrinsic property of things, but that we find it in things because man has projected it there. "We find values in things, we discover that the value is not there except in relation to the satisfaction of a need, or desire. . . . The value which things appear to have is therefore, not their own, they do not possess it of their own right, but borrow it from the satisfactions of desire which they provide." [11] Meinong thought that values are not projected into things, but are rather found in them on the basis of objective properties which things have. Scheler distinguishes between objects of desire (goods) and values. Value is that which makes something which is good, good; value is the good-making characteristic of what is good. As such it is a real characteristic of a thing. Although in *Wesensschau* its 'whatness' or essence can be intuited, there is no need for adopting a realm of ideal values analogous to the Platonic Ideas, from which the things ultimately derive their goodness by means of participation. Hartmann, on the other hand, explicitly defends such an ideal realm of values: ". . . there is a realm of values which subsists in itself . . . and which exists as much beyond reality as beyond consciousness—an ideal realm, which is not constructed, not invented or dreamed up, but is actually existing and capable of being apprehended in the phenomenon of value-feeling." [12]

As far as the epistemological status of values is concerned, most philosophers have focused their attention on one or more of the following problems: Are we able to know values objectively? Do we know them a priori or on the basis of some experience? Do we intuit values? Do we know them because of a divine revelation? Do we know them as such merely from the facts which they produce after they have been established? In answering these questions most philosophers have simply applied to the realm of values criteria which they had already accepted in their respective epistemological theories on grounds already independent of the value question.

It is not my intention to continue this enumeration or even to elaborate any of the views indicated. There is, however, one thing I would like to focus attention upon: the idea of developing an axiology in terms of the contrast between the realm of values and the realm of facts is relatively young; all axiological theories have their origin in the problematic characteristic of post-Kantian philosophy. Many historians have pointed to the fact that the historical origin of axiology in the nineteenth century is to be found in a number of factors which are closely connected with one another: the rise of the empirical sciences, particularly the human sciences, which almost inevitably suggest the distinction, if not the opposition, between fact and value, between what-is and what-should-be. Furthermore, there is the downfall of the leading religious views and the inadequacy of all naturalist and humanist attempts to find an acceptable justification for moral laws or standards. Then we must mention the positive criticism of religion on the basis of psychological and sociological considerations by people such as Feuerbach, Marx, and Freud. Finally, there is the negative outcome of Kant's *Critique of Pure Reason* in regard to classical metaphysics and, on the other hand, his claim that a metaphysics of morals is none the less possible, without any appeal to the *metaphysical postulates* of practical reason.[13] The growing complexity of the modern world with its science, technology, and industry confused many people to such an extent that they had to cry out for some clarifying vision of the whole, and particularly for what in this whole is still unquestionably valuable. On the other hand, religion as well as metaphysics seemed to be unable to point to a foundation upon which such a vision could be grounded. It is in the face of this desperate situation that many philosophers have tried to found values without any appeal to religious or metaphysical a priori.

It is obvious to me that neither one of these factors taken in isolation can *explain* the origin of axiological theories as distinct from metaphysical reflection. There is certainly a core of truth in the claim that these and similar factors taken together have created an atmosphere in which special attention to values and the development of axiological theories becomes more understandable. For, if it is true that religion and metaphysics are unable to give a foundation to the values according to which a man must live, and if it is true that science can deal only with facts, then one should, indeed, try to develop a new discipline which is able to concern itself with the epistemological and ontological status of values. The question here obviously is whether all of this indeed *is* true.

It is my conviction that the foregoing consideration rests on a great number of presuppositions which are very seldom explicitly mentioned but which are none the less of vital importance. To mention just a few: [14] Kant's conception of the nature and the 'division' of philosophy, his conception of man, the subject-object separation which is a necessary consequence of that conception, the identification of objectified entities with things as given in immediate experience, which necessarily leads to the distinction between fact and value, and the idea that it is, indeed, the task of philosophy to find and found standards for man's behavior. In other words, what is really at stake here is the question of what philosophy should be. If I were to subscribe to the Kantian conception of philosophy, I would *understand* why an axiology is necessary and why it is different from metaphysics. But it is highly questionable that I will come to the same conclusion the moment I reject Kant's conception of philosophy on the basis of the questionable presuppositions on which it rests. This is the reason why in what follows I wish to approach axiology from the viewpoint of another conception of philosophy in which these presuppositions are no longer found.

WHAT IS PHILOSOPHY? [15]

Like most other contemporary philosophies, existential philosophy adopts a critical attitude in regard to all classical conceptions of philosophy. But in criticizing the classical views its interest is positive in that it firmly believes that in these classical views an ideal shows itself which until now has never been completely materialized. Instead of denying philosophy's history, it wants to make this history into an explicit subject matter of reflection. In eliminating errors made in the past, existential philosophy tries to unfold the genuine meaning of the ideal first seen in Greece by Parmenides and Heraclitus. In this process of 'retrieval' existential philosophy tries to maintain what has been genuinely great in philosophies of the past, notably in the philosophies of Plato, Aristotle, medieval philosophy, Descartes, Kant, and Hegel.

Existential philosophy agrees with Greek philosophers that the subject matter of philosophy is to be found in the 'beingness of beings'. But instead of focusing its main interest on the beings, the *onta,* it turns its attention to the Whole, to Being itself, in and through which the beings can manifest themselves as the beings which they are. With Descartes and Kant, however, existential philosophy is convinced that in the thought of Being man should take his point of departure from human subjectivity. But in opposition to modern philosophy it does not conceive of this subjectivity in terms of a thinking substance, a closed monad, a passively registering knowing device which develops impressions into ideas with the help of determining laws of association, a pure consciousness, or even the place where the Absolute materializes His self-awareness in absolute knowledge. Man experiences himself immediately as a being who finds himself in a world and who (in whatever he does, thinks, or desires) knows that he has a not-yet-articulated knowledge of that world. It is in this 'preontologic' understanding of the world that philosophy must take its starting point in its attempt to answer the question concerning the meaning of Being, that is the meaning of *the* world, of the Whole.

In other words, existential philosophy shares with almost all great philosophies of the past the view that philosophy must be conceived of as a critical reflection on the meaning of the Whole, that is, on the meaning of Being. Unlike Greek philosophy, however, it defends, with almost all modern philosophers, the view that, in dealing with the Whole, philosophy must grant a privileged position to man. But differing from the great majority of modern philosophers it holds that man cannot be conceived of as a closed consciousness, but must be thought of as a subject who in his very essence is to be characterized by his openness, that is, his existential orientation toward the world. Thus, existential philosophy defends the thesis that a genuine 'ontology', which focuses all of its attention upon the question concerning the meaning of the Whole, must take its point of departure in an interpretative analysis of the mode of being characteristic of man. This analysis now shows that the human subjectivity is intentional; man *necessarily* transcends himself in the direction of the world. His mode of being is, therefore, to be characterized as a being in and toward the world. Man ek-sists and as such he is open toward the world. Man is not an ego wrapped up in itself, nor is he a complicated mechanism which is causally interwoven with his environment. From the very beginning and in the deepest core of his being man manifests himself as being-with, being-open-to, being-in-and-toward-the-world. It is through his dialogue with the intramundane things that man lets these things and the world be what they are, uncovers them, and brings their meaning to light.

The moment one realizes that man is nothing but a project of the world and that his existential orientation toward the world can accept many various concrete forms, the question immediately becomes: Which one of these relations with the world is the most primordial one? Whereas Descartes and Kant have felt that our relation with the world is originally and primordially a cognitive relation which is constituted and preserved in theoretical knowledge, here existential philosophy claims with Hegel that theoretical knowledge and science are only special, and actually even derivative, modes of man's fundamental orientation toward the world. Man's orientation toward the world originally takes the form of a concernful preoccupation with intramundane things. Man does not rise to speculation or attain to science except by taking his point of departure in his preoccupation with intramundane things in his concernful activities. Proximally, man's being is a being-already-alongside-the-world and this is at first not just a fixed staring at things which are merely present-at-hand. Originally man's orientation toward the world is concern.

From these reflections very important consequences follow of necessity. First it is clear by now why existential philosophy believes that traditional philosophy since the time of Plato and Aristotle, in questioning itself on the problem of the Whole, that is, the problem of Being, has directed its attention too one-sidedly to intramundane things. It is also clear by now that in modern philosophy the things themselves have been considered too one-sidedly as objects of theoretical knowledge, and specifically as objects such as they appear in empirical science. In this way beings became substituted for by objects, things by objectified entities. Once a thing is understood merely as an object of theoretical, scientific knowledge, it becomes understandable why Being itself, the Whole that is, became understood in terms of reality, that is, as reified. This, in turn, because of the conception of man as closed consciousness, led to the famous epistemological problem as formulated by Descartes as the problem concerning the reality of the world, or by Kant as the problem concerning the relationship between phenomena and noumena. Such questions become unavoidable the moment subject and object are separated. In this context it is also understandable why man attempted to understand himself in terms of objective categories. It finally becomes understandable that people later became concerned about values; for, the moment things are taken merely as objects of scientific knowledge, they obviously do not have any value qualities. But, before returning to this last issue, we must first mention a few other important elements of existential philosophy's conception of philosophy, namely, the essential historicity of philosophy and the idea that philosophy consists in a critical reflection upon man's experience.[16]

Both of these ideas were clearly formulated for the first time by Hegel. It would be extremely interesting at this point to make a careful examination of how Hegel himself understood these ideas and tried to justify them, and why and how existential philosophy has reformulated them. But since I have done so elsewhere I prefer to limit myself here to a brief characterization of the position to which existential philosophy has come in its destructive retrieval of these elements of Hegelian philosophy.

Existential philosophy claims with Hegel that man is essentially temporal and historical and that, if man himself is essentially historical, every human manifestation participates in this historicity as well. This means among other things that man's philosophy is essentially historical, too. In trying to find its own way within the realm opened up by Hegel's view on the historicity of philosophy, existential philosophy argues that this historicity is ultimately rooted, on the one hand, in the essentially historical character of Being itself, the World, the Totality of all meaning which shows and hides itself in various epochs in various ways, and, on the other hand, in man's own historicity. From this it follows at once that there can never be a perfect philosophical synthesis. Each philosopher tries to understand the world in which *he* lives; since this particular world is not *the* world, but merely consists of the peculiar way in which the totality of all meaning shows and hides itself at a particular moment of man's history, and the philosopher himself is essentially co-constituted by that world, it is obvious that his philosophy never can escape the limitations of its own historical condition. In other words, existential phenomenology agrees here with Hegel in that it, too, tries to comprehend the differences in philosophical systems in terms of the progressive development of the truth taken as the process of unconcealment, and, consequently, that naive consciousness is wrong in seeing a contradiction in these differences. The only point on which both Hegel and existential philosophy disagree in this respect is that Hegel sees the various philosophical systems as elements of an organic unity in which the one is as necessary as the other and posits that necessity as constitutive of the life of the Whole, whereas existential philosophy understands later philosophical syntheses as free consequences of earlier forms of thought, and therefore definitely denies that individual philosophies and epochs of philosophy have emerged from one another according to laws based on the necessity of a dialectic process.

In other words, philosophy's history does not bind the philosopher who lives today with the necessity of the unbreakable laws of the Hegelian dialectics, but philosophic tradition, like every other form of tradition, delivers and liberates man. The answer to a philosophical question consists in man's authentic response to what in philosophy's history is already on the way to him. Such an authentic response implies, at the same time, his willingness to listen to what is already said, and the courage to take distance from what he has heard—which makes a certain 'destruction' of the past necessary in philosophy. As we have said already, such a destruction is not a break with the past, nor a repudiation of philosophy's history, but an adoption, in the form of a transformation and adaptation to the requirements of the world we live in, of what has been handed down.

But there is another element in Hegel's conception of philosophy which is of great importance for us here: the idea that philosophy must be considered as a critical reflection of man's experience upon itself. In the *Phenomenology of Mind* Hegel posits that philosophy is the 'science' of the experiences made by consciousness, and, since the totality of all the experiences made by consciousness constitutes what one calls 'history', philosophy is the understanding of man's historical experiences, and history itself the becoming of philosophy. In the *Phenomenology of Mind* it was not Hegel's intention to fit all history into a framework of a preestablished logic. The introduction clearly states that the philosopher should not put himself in the place of the various human experiences; his task is merely to collect and decipher these experiences as history makes them available to him. In revealing this immanent logic of man's experience in all its sectors, the question is no longer limited, as was the case in Kant's *Critique of Pure Reason,* to discovering what conditions make our *scientific* experience possible. Hegel's problem is one of knowing how social, moral, aesthetic, and religious experiences are possible and, therefore, one of deciphering man's fundamental situation in the face of the world and of other men. What Hegel really wanted to do was to understand the social order, economic and legal systems, works of art, science, technology, ethics, and religions as so many ways for man to flee or to confront the *limitations* of his own condition. From this point of view it will be understandable that Hegel defines 'experience' as the dialectical process which consciousness executes upon itself. Experience here no longer simply means our merely theoretical and reflexive contact with the sensible world as it did in Kant; the word here reassumes the 'tragic' resonance which it has in common language, as for example when a man speaks of what he has lived through.

Hegel later interpreted this idea in an idealist way and explicitly defended the view that through thought the philosopher, and the philosopher alone, can get at the truth about all experiences, integrate them, go beyond them, and, from the depth of his wisdom, obtain the revelation of the real meaning of world history to which other men simply submit in faith. Existential philosophy rejects this interpretation and claims that to be a philosopher is just one way to ek-sist, and that it is nonsense to flatter oneself with the idea that one can exhaust man's religious, moral, political, juridical, social, and aesthetic life and all other modes of man's ek-sistence within a purely philosophical ek-sistence.

Philosophy is the explicitation of our prephilosophic life in and with the world. It reveals to us the truth which is still concealed in it in an implicit way. It brings our original understanding of the world and of ourselves over into a philosophic understanding. Philosophy is not, however, only a determinate elaboration of our everyday knowledge concerning the world and our being in it; first and foremost it is a destruction of it. For when we start to think as philosophers and to pose philosophical problems to ourselves, we already have our opinions, conceptions, ideas, and insights, whatever their root and origin may be. As everyone knows from his own experience, it is very difficult to escape from the power of the 'self-evidence' of these preconceptions, because these preconceptions govern our thought without our knowledge. 'Reduction' is a necessary process here, and, as Hegel has already shown, such a process manifests itself first and foremost as a destruction of our natural and naive certainties.

The problem, however, is much more complicated than it seems to be at first sight. This becomes immediately evident when one realizes that his prephilosophic life is not identical with the primary experiences of a child, or the world view of a primitive. In the domain of prephilosophic life characteristic of our natural attitude, our life, which is rooted in the most original experience of our own being-in-the-world itself, is already 'organized' in many ways. In the primordial experience, which is our being-in-the-world itself, all kinds of very fundamental but limited experiences announce themselves. The most important of these articulated and elaborated experiences are known as 'myth', 'religion', 'theology', 'art', 'politics', 'social theory', 'ethics', 'science', 'technology', and in general our 'culture'. It is precisely against this complex of experiences which are already articulated and elaborated in a nonphilosophical way that philosophy must time and again defend its right of existence.

Thus, in addition to the dialectical relation between a certain type of philosophy and the different philosophical currents which preceded it, there is another set of relations (at least as essential as the one just mentioned) between every determinate philosophy and one or more forms of nonphilosophical experience which, generally speaking, belong to the same cultural-historical period as the philosophy in question.

In a certain sense, therefore, one could say that history of philosophy is nothing more than a dialectical movement in which philosophy has tried continuously to defend its own rights of existence against all kinds of reactions which were evoked for the most part precisely by its own development. Philosophy is inseparable from everything which is not philosophy. That is why philosophy must give to the different forms of nonphilosophical experience the possibility of developing independently, and even of explicitly and repeatedly resisting and opposing philosophy itself. On the other hand, however, we must realize that the different kinds of nonphilosophic experiences will never be able to take over the task of philosophy itself, which is concern for the Whole.

In other words, philosophy itself does not have a title to constitute meaning. For this is precisely the task of the different forms of man's experience. Being nonphilosophical, however, these experiences are not able to do so in a totally comprehensive and reflexive way. Experience wants to be reason without knowing this explicitly. The perception of intramundane things, the reflection of man about himself, the comport of society, the constitution of science and technique, and the creation of art—all of this is not yet philosophy, although all are obviously the work of reason. Philosophy, which is essentially oriented toward these different forms of experience and attempts to bring to light their proper meaning within the Whole of meaning, knows that neither at the very beginning nor at the end will it ever have at its disposal all the means with which it can once and for all normatively prescribe what the function of each articulated form of experience within the totality of meaning should be. The only thing philosophy knows is that the constitution of meaning always has already begun, and that, although it has never completely succeeded, it has never completely failed either. Philosophy's task is merely to say in what this process precisely consists and how, in and through it, the Whole manifests and hides itself at the same time.

The sense in which the nonphilosophical experiences are the source of philosophy should now be clear: philosophy must take its starting point in them and must then try to transcend them in the direction of the Whole. This relation between philosophy and original experience, however, is not sufficient to explain the origin and genesis of a new kind of philosophy. The 'horizontal' relation between philosophy and the nonphilosophical forms of experience must be combined with a 'vertical' relation of philosophy in regard to its own history. This means that a philosophy, although it concretely comes into being on the basis of an experience which is new and even alien to it, nevertheless materializes its deepest intention and even its very nature by explicitly situating itself within the horizon of its own, typically philosophical problematic. This, however, it will know only when it critically turns its attention to its own past.

SUMMARY AND CONCLUSION

In the preceding section we have seen that according to this conception philosophy is concerned with the question about the meaning of the Whole and that in its attempt to formulate and examine this question it must reflect critically upon its own history as well as upon the various forms of nonphilosophical experience which, at a certain moment of history, are found in the world. It will be clear that if this is philosophy's main concern, it is no longer necessary to divide it into various disciplines. A philosophical study of values distinct from philosophy's concern for the Whole is superfluous, although philosophy obviously has a bearing on the bases of any ethical view. The importance of philosophy in regard to ethical problems is not found in the fact that, as theoretical, it could guide our actions, because philosophy is neither theoretical nor practical, but occurs before any such differentiation. Nor is its importance to be found in the fact that it would be able to point to concrete laws or norms which man would have to follow in order to reach his destination. The importance of philosophy for any ethical view must be found first and foremost in the fact that it shows that man, ek-sisting in the truth of the Whole, must primarily concern himself with the Whole, and that only insofar as man is concerned with the Whole, can the assigning of all the directions which must become value, law, and norm for man come from the Totality of meaning itself. One could say, also, that this philosophy is inherently 'ethical' in that it urges man to be concerned with two things which are essentially connected with one another: his own authenticity and the unconcealment of the genuine meaning of the Whole in his world.

If we now develop the insights which follow from this conception of philosophy in greater detail, it will be evident at once that the impact of our reflections will not be to state that there are no values, or that philosophy should not be concerned with them. Philosophy should certainly be concerned with the values things have for us, but existential philosophy suggests a completely different approach to the value problem. First of all it tries to convince us that the distinction between value and fact rests upon an abstraction. On the level of our prephilosophical experience we never experience things without values, nor do we ever experience values which are not values of things. Anyone who begins his reflection on values by isolating 'that-which-ought-to-be' from 'what-is' will find himself confronted with a pseudo-problem. From an epistemological point of view this problem is: how do we know values?; and from an ontological perspective: how can values be? On the level of our immediate, prephilosophical experience upon which philosophy must reflect, the fact is undeniable that there are values, that we do know them, and that we know them as the values which things have for us.

But, more importantly, one must also realize that values are never experienced in isolation; we experience them in contexts, in a certain horizon of meaning, and, in the final analysis, within the totality of all possible meaning, as this now manifests and hides itself in our Western civilization. It is from this point of view, thus, that values should be approached in philosophy. If one approaches values from the horizons of meaning within which they manifest themselves, it is easy to avoid another quasi-problem, namely, that of whether values are to be conceived of monistically or pluralistically. For then it is obvious that, regardless of whether or not on the basis of nonphilosophical grounds one subscribes to an ultimate Good or an absolute Value, even these 'Absolutes' can appear meaningfully only within the totality of meaning as this shows and conceals itself in our civilization. But in this totality of meaning many values appeal to man's concern, and why they appear there philosophy cannot decide; it merely tries to understand how they appear.

Within this conception of philosophy, it is obviously possible to consider explicitly the relationship between the world of science, which is a world without values, and the world we live in, which, for the very reason that we live in it, is obviously a world of values. But in this case there is no longer any reason to panic in the face of the questions that arise. For before any one problem that manifests itself here can become dangerous, a solution is already at hand, in principle at least. For the artificial situation which led to the question is not the one we take our starting point in, the moment we try to solve it. When the question comes up on the one level, we already know on another level that values are obviously the values of things and values for men living in historical societies. The main question here is, therefore, not one of whether things have value, but rather of why science must abstract from the value of things in order to master them methodically. In other words, in this conception of philosophy values and ontic things should always be considered together within the perspective of a totality of meaning in which 'that-which-is' and 'that-which-ought-to-be' are still found together. This obviously does not mean that it would be without importance to try explicitly to relate to one another the different realms of meaning constituted and articulated in the different forms of nonphilosophical experience, within the totality of meaning as this now shows and hides itself. If we do so in regard to the world we live in today, it is not unlikely that we will find that values indeed are endangered by the scientific and technological world view which imposes itself upon us and in which values are systematically eliminated in order to make empirical investigation and technical application possible. But by pointing to this situation as a matter of fact and seeing all the dangers which it involves, we are then no longer paralyzed by it. For seeing the danger is to unnerve it the moment one knows the way and has the means to conquer it.

In concluding I would like to say that modern man should, indeed, be very concerned about values—that is, the meaning things have for us, particularly now that science and technology confront us so tenaciously with a schematized and objectified world. But this concern need no longer lead to insoluble philosophical questions, such as whether or not values are, how they are, where they are, or whether we are able to know them the way they are. All these questions are already answered in the affirmative on the level on which our lives are lived, that is, on the level of our prephilosophical experiences. It is not philosophy's task to question the unquestionable, but to try to understand what undeniably manifests itself in these experiences within the perspective of the totality of meaning as this today positively and negatively gives itself. Within this perspective it is important to find the right balance between the different realms of man's articulated experience and to project a new world in which the balance between these realms is better guaranteed than it is in the one in which we live today. Thus it is and remains important to ask the question of how the world of science, for instance, should be related to other realms of man's articulated experience, such as, for instance, religion, art, and our social and political life—and thus how 'facts' are related to 'values'—but the question should not be taken out of the context in which alone it could arise as a genuine question and where all the elements necessary to answer it successfully are found.

One final word. Many contemporary philosophers who ask questions about values somehow suggest that in asking these questions they are going to engage themselves in a kind of a game. Personally, I feel that in asking serious questions the philosopher should be deeply aware of the responsibility he bears in regard to himself as well as in regard to the world in which he lives; for what is at stake here is the authenticity of man and the humanity of our world.

NOTES

1. Aristotle, *Metaphysics,* A2, 982a4 ff.
2. *Ibid.,* A2, 982b2 ff.
3. *Ibid.,* Z1, 1028b2 ff.
4. Martin Heidegger, *What Is Philosophy?* trans. Jean T. Wilde and William Kluback, New Haven, n.d., pp. 51–59.
5. René Descartes, *Philosophical Works,* 2 vols, trans. E. S. Haldane and G. R. T. Ross, New York, 1955, I, 139, 211.
6. Immanuel Kant, *Critique of Pure Reason,* trans. Norman Kemp Smith, New York, 1965, pp. 21–33 (esp. 30–31).
7. *Ibid.,* pp. 659, 653–665.
8. Roger Hancock, "Metaphysics," in *Encyclopedia of Philosophy,* ed. Paul Edwards, New York, 1967, V, 289–300.
9. André Lalande, *Vocabulaire technique et critique de la philosophie,* Paris, 1962, pp. 1182–1186; William K. Frankena, "Value and Valuation," in *Encyclopedia of Philosophy,* VIII, 229–232.
10. R. Frondisi, *What Is Value?,* trans. Solomon Lipp, La Salle, Ill.,

1963; W. H. Werkmeister, *Man and His Values,* Lincoln, Neb., 1967, pp. 59–98; William K. Frankena, "Value and Valuation"; O. Kraus, *Die Werttheorien,* Vienna, 1937; Vernon J. Bourke, *History of Ethics,* New York, 1968, pp. 237–248.

11. Dewitt H. Parker, *Human Values: An Interpretation of Ethics Based on a Study of Values,* Ann Arbor, 1944, p. 19.

12. Nicolai Hartmann, *Ethics,* 2 vols., trans. Stanton Coit, London, 1932, I, 226.

13. Georges Gusdorf, *Traité de l'existence morale,* Paris, 1949, pp. 48–55 (esp. 53–54).

14. Martin Heidegger, *An Introduction to Metaphysics,* trans. Ralph Mannheim, New York, 1961, pp. 164–167.

15. Cf. Joseph J. Kockelmans, *The World in Science and Philosophy,* Milwaukee, 1969, pp. 3–32, and the literature quoted there.

16. A. De Waelhens, *La philosophie et les expériences naturelles.* The Hague, 1961, pp. 1–40; Kockelmans, *The World in Science,* pp. 33–51.

Metaphysics and the Problem of Dissent

Thelma Z. Lavine

Historically there have been three main types of metaphysical theories by which Western societies have sought to understand and to justify themselves. Natural law, organicism, and utilitarianism all survive today in differing states of disrepute, deterioration, and partial reconstruction. Of these three metaphysical theories, only organicism will here be considered, in view of its pervasive influence upon social philosophies and philosophies of man, its widespread adaptation by the social sciences, and present signs of its philosophical revival.

The specific interest in organicism for the present discussion is in its implications for the individual member of society, and especially for the individual as a seat of independent judgment. Although the abstract problem which is hereby raised is of perennial philosophical importance, for our own time it may be claimed that a mark of the responsibility of a metaphysics, a social philosophy, or a social science is its ability to provide a logical ground or principle by reference to which the individual can distantiate himself from, reflect upon, judge, criticize, dissent from, defy, or rebel against the acts of other individuals or groups, including actions of his own nation, other nations, and international organizations. Against the background of modern mass society, with its network of governmental, industrial, military, educational, and professional bureaucracies and its opinion-making communications industries, a crucial question must be asked of all types of theorizing about social reality: does the theory provide any role for the individual except the role of Adolf Eichman—the law-abiding citizen, the trustworthy government official, who was reliable and effective in carrying out directives from bureaucratic superiors in the service of his country, and maintaining good interpersonal relations both in his employment and in his private life?

The nineteenth-century organicist theory which we have inherited is the confluence of two distinct sources. One is the biological concept of organism, the significant characteristics of which are held to be the harmoniously hierarchical interdependence of the parts in their subservience to the maintenance of the life of the whole. The structure and functions of the biological organism served to conceptualize society and its parts for the positivistic sociological systems of both Comte and Spencer. But the organicism that is associated with the flowering of German idealistic speculative philosophy discovered, for its own conceptualization of reality and human life, subjective consciousness in its unity-in-diversity and the uniqueness of the self. The structural unity of consciousness had its counterpart in the structural unity of reality. This concept of selfhood or spiritual unity was applied horizontally to the life of a people (*Volksgeist*) in which interacting parts such as language, custom, economy, religion, art, and law performed vital functions by which the total societal configuration was subserved. Vertically—that is, historically—institutions, societies, and world history are conceived by both Hegel and Marx as moving toward consummatory ends [1] in the form of intellectual closures, or as unities of opposition such as ideal-actual and individual-group, and finally as dynamic functions within the unitary system of total reality. Part-ends and the self-maintaining end of total reality are modeled upon the holism of self or spirit. The organicist philosophy of consciousness and the metaphysics of nineteenth-century German idealism form an important source of the holism according to which twentieth-century social sciences have conceived the interdependence and integration of their data.

Hegel provides the most influential and instructive statement of organicist metaphysics and social philosophy. His own thought gives evidence of responding to various types of influence upon it. In its development his philosophy appears to have been in part responsive to the profound political and cultural turmoil of his time and place. His early commitment to the ideals of the French Revolution gave way, after the Napoleonic invasion of the Germanic territories, to the political urgency of providing a counter-ideology to the French Enlightenment, which had culminated in the anarchic violence of the Terror, followed by the imperialism of Napoleon. Hegel became a philosopher of restoration,[2] taking the problem of social order as central and finding in the concept of an organic society, with appropriate hierarchical subordination of its members, a model for the unification of the Germanic peoples into a nation-state. It has also been argued that Hegel's identification of reality with the systematic totality of rationality expresses the isolation and powerlessness in the realm of political action of the German educated classes, for whom the real was confined to the realm of ideas and for whom freedom was available only in the form of Lutheran inwardness, while in the outside world piety and civic virtue demanded obedience to existing authorities and reconciliation with existing social conditions. Art, religion and philosophy, which form Hegel's triad of Absolute Spirit, are the philosophic counterpart of the cultural idealism [3] which held these to be true reality and thus provided an intellectual refuge for the politically powerless educated groups in Germany. Still another influence upon the thought of Hegel was his violent reaction against Romanticism which he looked upon as a philosophy of radical subjectivism and destructive creativity, leading to social alienation and self-alienation and to that "vertigo of the spirit" which his friend Hölderlin had succumbed to in madness. But, if he rejected the dangerous *Weg nach innern,* neither could he accept the objectivism of external things. By the year 1800 he had found, instead, a third way: an "agreement with the age," a reconciliation with "what is." In the existing social order he discovered the "objective element" upon which to base his philosophy, a fortification against intellectual vertigo. These personal, political, and intellectual circumstances of his life, of all of which he was to a high degree aware, appear to have worked together to move Hegel toward the anti-individualistic, quietistic, and conservative nationalism which appears most sharply in his *Philosophy of Right.*

For the comprehension of Hegel's metaphysics and social philosophy it is all the same whether one begins with his affirmation that Spirit, a structure integrating the totality of rationality, is "alone reality" and then proceeds to its externalization in the human, finite spirit within history and within particular societies; or whether one begins with the spirit of a particular society (*Volksgeist*) and proceeds to locate it as one dialectical stage of the unfolding truth of the Absolute. In the language of the preface to the *Phenomenology of Spirit:*

> The truth is the Whole. The whole, however, is merely the essential nature reaching its completeness through the process of its own development. Of the Absolute it must be said that it is essentially a result, that only at the end is it what it is in very truth; and just in that consists its nature, which is to be actual, subject, or self-becoming, self-development.[4]

Hegel struggles to communicate the theory of reality as being not only "Substance but as Subject as well," as a Self which "is the process of its own becoming, the circle which presupposes its end as its purpose, and has its end for its beginning; it becomes concrete and actual only by being carried out, and by the end it involves." [5] The movement toward the whole truth which is the movement toward self-consciousness of the Absolute self is teleological; it seeks the end of total rationality. In this sense it is perfectly appropriate to say that "reason is purposive activity," by contrast with the inappropriate attribution of purpose to non-human nature, which Hegel notes has "brought the idea of purpose in general into disrepute." "All the same," he hastens to add, "in the sense in which Aristotle, too, characterizes nature as purposive activity, purpose is . . . *the unmoved which is self-moving; as such it is subject.*" [6] In his effort to communicate the holistic and consummatory aspects of human experience, Hegel makes use of biological metaphors and similes throughout his writing:

> Our epoch is a birth-time, and a period of transition. . . . But it is here as in the case of the birth of a child; after a long period of nutrition in silence, the continuity of the gradual growth in size, of quantitative change, is suddenly cut short by the first breath drawn—there is a break in the process, a qualitative change—and the child is born. In like manner the spirit of the time, growing slowly and quietly ripe for the new form it is to assume, disintegrates one fragment after another of the structure of its previous world.[7]

No doubt the most successful of Hegel's biological figures of speech is the one developed in connection with philosophy itself. It is the task of philosophy to discern and to integrate into one dialectically self-completing "System" the entirety of rational structures which form the dimensions of reality. Historical philosophies are themselves one such structural area. The task here is to show that opposing philosophic systems do not falsify each other but form "the progressive evolution of truth":

> The bud disappears when the blossom breaks through, and we might say that the former is refuted by the latter; in the same way when the fruit comes, the blossom may be explained to be a false form of the plant's existence, for the fruit appears as its true nature in place of the blossom. These stages are not merely differentiated; they supplant one another as being incompatible with one another. But the ceaseless activity of their own inherent nature makes them at the same time moments of an organic unity. . . .[8]

The rewriting of the history of philosophy which these programmatic remarks call for was accomplished by Hegel himself in his *Lectures on the History of Philosophy.* The history of philosophy is here in brilliant detail set forth as philosophy: an intricate dialectical development of concepts achieving closure in the system of Hegel himself.

A new concept of society, which was to have far-reaching effects upon social philosophy, social science, and human existence was implied in the cumbersome double metaphor which appears in the *Philosophy of Right:* "The State is an organism. . . ." Hegel finished the sentence by translating the language of biology into the language of idealism: "or the development of the idea into its differences." The concept of the State for Hegel comprehends more than the institutions of government; it synthesizes the opposition between the private life of the family and the public life of "civil society"; it is the embodiment of the spirit of the entire life of a people. As he says in his Introduction to the *Philosophy of History:* "The general principle which manifests itself and becomes an object of consciousness in the State . . . is the whole of that cycle of phenomena which constitutes the *culture* of a nation.[9] The State as the totality of national culture is the true Individual[10] of history. In this Individual, rather than in the particular existent human beings who are its parts, it is appropriate to locate finite mind.

> In point of fact the notion of the realization of self-conscious reason . . . finds its actual fulfillment in the life of a nation. Reason appears here as the fluent universal substance . . . which yet breaks up into many entirely independent beings. . . . They are conscious within themselves of being these individual independent beings through the fact that they surrender and sacrifice their particular individuality, and that this universal substance is their soul and essence. . . .[11]

The locus of finite mind is in the national life, in the mind of the group (*Volk*) in which the Absolute is historically manifested. The content of this group mind is the product of the social and historic processes as these are utilized by Spirit.

Spirit manifests itself in the mind of particular nations and in their role in the dialectical progress of history. That these self-fulfilling ends of Spirit are achieved, and not the desires of individual human beings, is the work of the Cunning of Reason which channels the aspirations of individuals into functions of the organic social system which they neither intend nor understand. Thus the "individual totality" of a nation in which "the constitution adopted" "makes one substance—one spirit—with its religion, art, philosophy" [12] may be understood, in the language of contemporary social science, as a social system, in which all phenomena are at once system-determined and system-determining.[13] In a similar fashion the Cunning of Reason utilizes "World Historical Individuals," charismatic leaders like Caesar, Alexander, and Napoleon to bring about the goal of progress to a new stage of history; such great men pursue personal ends which they intuit to coincide with "the requirements of the time—what was ripe for development." Although the World-Historical Individuals' actions and thoughts must be credited as "the best of their time," these unwitting agents of the World-Spirit are as removed from a comprehension of the Idea they are introducing into history as are ordinary men in their private pursuits from a knowledge of the system-functions they maintain. And so the belief in the self-determination of one's actions and the belief in independent personal reflective judgment are both illusions. Self-determination in action and independent rational judgment are properties of the Whole which is "alone reality," of Spirit and its embodiment in the State, and not of individuals who, as parts, have only the limited role of expressing aspects of the state through subserving it in specific functions.

The system-maintaining role of the ordinary man's passionate actions and the system-changing role of the leader's innovation are prototypal for Hegel's treatment of the entire range of individual thought, action, and values. All of these are totally immanent in the processes of society and history, which are the sole sources of their content. No appeal from the social and historical process to any mode of transcendence is possible: to an independent God, to natural law, or to universal rational or moral principles. The self-objectification of Spirit in particular societal organisms and in the spiritual closures of history has as its obverse side sociologism and historicism. History and society are the organic totalities which all human phenomena subserve and from which they derive their meaning.

Hegel's ethics and politics are especially instructive instances of this aspect of Hegel's thought. Just as the State is mind made objective, so is it also morality made objective:

> The state is the actuality of the ethical Idea. It is ethical mind . . . knowing and thinking itself . . . an absolute unmoved end in itself, in which freedom comes into its supreme right. On the other hand this final end has supreme right against the individual whose supreme duty it is to be a member of the state.[14]

Ethics is solely social ethics or customary morality (*Sittlichkeit*); it has its source in the life of the nation. No moral authority transcends the ethics of the society; the State itself actualizes the ethical Idea and is the Concrete Ethical Substance to which individual human beings are related only as Accidents. The Concrete Ethical Substance is a unity-in-diversity of the legal, political, economic, religious, and educational institutions of the society and the customs of group life. The moral law which is binding on all members of the group is itself a function of these institutions and activities of group life and it has as its end the welfare of the particular society itself. Hegel's view of ethics as a function of the concrete societal organism implies the relativity of ethics to specific societies, or, as W. H. Walsh points out, "the dissolution of ethics into sociology." [15] Hegel's social organicism precludes the possibility of a universal ethics to which an individual might appeal. In the *Philosophy of History* the consummation of man's historical progress in the consciousness of freedom necessarily falls with a nation-state; the consciousness that "all are free" is not universal moral consciousness but the *Geist* of the Germanic *Volk*. When Hegel insists upon the importance of the "universal" in ethics, he is not opposing universal to national-social ethics, but social to personal ethics.

The individual relates to the public morality of his own nation by interiorizing. The process of internalizing the ethical substance of culture begins within the organic unity of the family and is continued within the community. Internalization of the ethical substance makes possible the highest level of moral life attainable by the individual: the unity of "substantiality" and "subjectivity," the identity of the content of the personal will with that of the nation. With the complete internalization of the social ethics, the individual does not feel the yoke of the moral laws; he has attained the "substantial freedom" in which he wills the laws he has internalized. At the same time, this good citizen reaps the benefits of a sense of belonging, of oneness with his group, and of "the happiness of being in the substance." [16]

In organicist philosophies of society, in which the ideal is a function of the actual social process, the moral life is achieved by internalization. Alienation is the counterprocess of internalization. Alienation is the fate of all moral philosophizing which turns away from a reconciliation with the actual and attempts, through independent, personal reflection or intuition, to erect a transcendent ideal that opposes the actual. Hegel directs his attack upon the Kantian ethic of universal reason and upon the Romantic ethic of moral inwardness. Notwithstanding their divergent internal difficulties, both are linked together by Hegel as pitting reason or feelings or the self against the social order and thus as ethics of alienation. They have their source in conceit, perversion, or wickedness and, if acted upon, they result in revolutionary destruction:

> The heart-throb for the welfare of mankind passes therefore into the rage of frantic self-conceit, into the fury of consciousness to preserve itself from destruction. . . . When consciousness therefore sets up the law of its heart, it finds itself resisted by others because it conflicts with the equally individual laws of their

> heart. . . . What appears as public ordinance is thus this state of war of each against all. . . .[17]

In the *Philosophy of Right* Hegel attacks the truth-value of the ethics of private conscience (Kant): "The state cannot give recognition to conscience in its private form as subjective knowing, any more than science can grant validity to subjective opinion, dogmatism, and the appeal to a subjective opinion." [18] The point of Hegel's criticism is not directed toward disproving the validity of the principles of private conscience, but toward repudiating formal ethics as estranged from the concrete society whose activities it is the function of ethics to control. Hegel will accept neither an ethics of universal reason nor an ethics of private intuition. The rational ground of ethics is in the social system.

Politics is the obverse side of ethics in organicist theory. As the actuality of the ethical Idea, the State defines the values of the particular society and these take priority over all other values for the members of the group. The sole end of the nation-state itself as an organic totality is its own self-realization and self-maintenance. As a "substantial unity" the state is "the absolute, unmoved End-in-itself." Government does not, accordingly, rest upon logically and legally prior universal principles nor is it restricted by natural rights; the nation-state, "the Divine Idea as it exists on earth," is "absolute power on earth." Nor is it conceivable that any universal ethical principles constrain the nation-state, which "is the self-certain absolute mind which acknowledges no abstract rules of good and bad, shameful and mean, craft and deception." [19]

There remains to be considered the relationship to this "absolute power on earth" of individuals within the nation and of other nations. Since the nation-state is the actualization of Spirit, the ideal is immanent in the actual; the gap between what is and what ought to be is closed. Is there, in principle, any national political posture for the individual except that of conformity? One area for dissent remains. Although the real is the rational, Hegel distinguishes between the real and the merely existent, which may in part be only appearance. Dissent from national institutions is theoretically possible, therefore, with respect to the distinctions they draw between the essential and the unimportant, their inconsistencies in maintaining public policy, and their failure to put into practice existing law or accepted norms. Revolutionary dissent which seeks to overthrow the existing state is totally illegitimate. On the other hand, if its leadership is in the successful hands of a World Historical Individual, the Cunning of Reason will thereby have brought about a new stage in the actualization of the World-Spirit. Power legitimizes, whether of the State or of the law-breaking World Historical rebel. On such matters public opinion, with its "whole character of accidental opinion, with its ignorance and perversity, its false knowledge and incorrect judgment," is not to be trusted (nor even represented in the Legislature).

The relations among independent national powers are ungovernable by formal international law or by an external league of nations such as Kant had suggested to bring about everlasting peace. The sovereign wills of nation-states clash inevitably in warfare. Specifically, against the imperialistic dominance of the nation whose time has come as the carrier of the World-Spirit, "the spirits of other nations are absolutely without right." Moreover, war serves an essential ethical function within the group: it overcomes the drift into alienation that occurs with lasting peace: "In order not to let . . . the common spirit evaporate, government has from time to time to shake them [social subsystems] to the very centre by War." [20]

It has been said that Hegel is " 'the philosopher' behind the nineteenth century social sciences" and also "the philosopher of the various collectivistic movements of industrial society." [21] He is also, as this discussion has suggested, the philosopher behind important developments in twentieth-century social science and social philosophy and nationalistic politics.

Let us apply, then, to Hegel's potent metaphysics and social philosophy, the test of the responsibility of any metaphysics, social philosophy, or social science which was offered at the beginning of the present discussion: its ability to provide a logical ground or principle by reference to which the individual can distantiate himself from, reflect upon, judge, criticize, dissent from, defy, or rebel against the acts of other individuals or groups, including actions of his own nation, other nations, and international organizations. All of these activities are of a type which Hegel, in his own post-Revolutionary situation, feared and despised. But our interest here has been to identify the elements of his philosophy which oppose them, and thus to aid in the recognition of similar Hegelian elements in contemporary social thought.

Distantiation, criticism, dissent, and so on, insofar as they are rational actions, require, in addition to their objects, a self and a logical ground or principle. But Hegelian organicist metaphysics, in which all phenomena, including human beings and their thoughts, values, and actions, are system-determined and system-determining within the cultural organism, makes it impossible to distinguish the self from the parts of the total organism which it seeks to criticize or dissent from, or from the principles upon which the criticism or dissent are based. On this organicist metaphysics selfhood is confined to the cultural totality, to the group self which is alone capable of independent reflective judgment and of self-determination in action. Except for his psychobiological individuality, the individual member of society is wholly a social self, a carrier of the ethical and cognitive substance of the culture. The unwitting or willed dissolution of the self into the thought and values and social roles of the cultural organism maximizes group solidarity by eliminating the self as a seat of independent reflective judgment, criticism, dissent, defiance, or rebellion. The self is compensated, however, for this surrender of its rational autonomy, by the redemptive happiness of group membership. *Sola societate* replaces the *sola fide* of St. Paul as the path to salvation. The self not only *is* other-directed by the group, but *ought* to be, since no ethical authority supersedes that of the national culture. ("The ethical is subjective disposition but of objectively existing law.") Nor is intellectual transcendence of the culture possible. Philosophy, which "is its own time comprehended in thought," cannot provide the self with transcendent principles by reference to which it can make itself distant from and judge its own society. Philosophy makes possible only internal criticism. To seek to be self-directed by attempting to formulate transcendent universal moral ideals or subjective intuitive moral judgments is therefore doubly dangerous: for the self, it is symptomatic of alienation; for the society, of dysfunction. It is given only to the World Historical Individual to be the rebel; for everyone else there is the role of Eichman.

The future of metaphysics projected by the present discussion is clearly Hegelian: as Hegel himself formulated his idealistic organicism to negate the atomistic and rationalistic individualism of the Enlightenment; so now there is need for a metaphysical synthesis of these that will unite what is true within each of these positions with our present knowledge of society and of subjective phenomenology.

NOTES

1. This is true for Hegel's Absolute, immanent in history, and also for Marx's communist society, a posthistorical eschatology.
2. The politics and sociological theory of Comte in France at this time were in many respects identical with those of Hegel.
3. Cf. Herbert Marcuse, *Reason and Revoluton,* Boston, 1960, pp. 14–15.
4. *Phenomenology of Mind,* New York, 1967, pp. 81–82.
5. *Ibid.*
6. *Ibid.*, p. 83.
7. *Ibid.*, p. 75.
8. *Ibid.*, p. 68.
9. *Hegel Selections,* ed. J. Loewenberg, New York, 1929, p. 403.
10. *Ibid.*, p. 355. "But in the history of the World, the *Individuals* we have to do with are *Peoples;* Totalities that are States."
11. *Phenomenology,* p. 376.
12. *Hegel Selections,* p. 397.
13. Cf. the distinction between manifest and latent functions of society made by contemporary sociological functionalism. Cf. also T. Z. Lavine, "Karl Mannheim and Contemporary Functionalism," *Philosophy and Phenomenological Research,* 1965, XXV, 560–571.
14. *Philosophy of Right,* London, 1896, pp. 257–258.
15. *Hegelian Ethics,* New York, 1969, p. 55.
16. *Phenomenology,* p. 380.
17. *Ibid.*, pp. 397–399.
18. *Philosophy of Right,* p. 137.
19. *System der Sittlichkeit,* quoted by Ernst Cassirer, *The Myth of the State,* New Haven, 1946, p. 264.
20. *Phenomenology,* p. 474.
21. John Herman Randall, Jr., *The Career of Philosophy,* New York, 1965, II, 321.

Metaphysics and Religious Faith*

Louis Dupré

(1) THE IDEA OF GOD IS EXCLUSIVELY RELIGIOUS

For many years metaphysicians have dealt with the object of the religious act as if they had invented it. Natural theology or theodicy as a branch of philosophy was considered to be totally independent of man's religious activity. This view first appeared in Aristotle, survived in the Stoa, and disappeared in early Christian philosophy. It emerged again in late Scholasticism and reached new heights in the various systems which are loosely combined under the vague name of rationalism. Kant was at once one of its chief proponents and the main author of its decline in recent philosophy. The trend has not entirely died out, as the following quotation from Whitehead's *Science and the Modern World* eloquently proves:

> Aristotle found it necessary to complete his metaphysics by the introduction of the Prime Mover—God. This, for two reasons, is an important fact in the history of metaphysics. In the first place if we are to accord to anyone the position of the greatest metaphysician, having regard to genius of insight, to general equipment in knowledge, and to the stimulus of his metaphysical ancestry, we must choose Aristotle. Secondly, in his consideration of this metaphysical question he was entirely dispassionate; and he is the last European metaphysician of first-rate importance for whom this claim can be made. After Aristotle, ethical and religious interests began to influence metaphysical conclusions.[1]

Whitehead himself believes that the time has come to secularize once more the idea of God in philosophy.[2]

Against this thesis I posit that philosophy by itself has never reached the idea of God, that it has received it from religious faith and that the time has come to acknowledge fully this debt. In the forceful terms of Duméry:

> The philosopher *encounters* this idea; he is not the author of it. He must therefore seek to know what it signifies and what role in life can be assigned to it. But he is not to mold it as he pleases nor turn it to uses which do not answer to the fundamental aspiration of the subject. In these conditions, the God of philosophies is from the start a theft and a blunder. One pretends to believe that the idea of God is the property of philosophy, whereas it is borrowed from the religious life.[3]

The philosopher may conclude to a transcendent world ground, or if he feels unable to reach such a conclusion he may postulate this ground as a necessary condition to make the universe intelligible. But a necessary ground is not God.

Even if philosophy attains an ultimate, absolute principle of meaning and of value, it has not yet attained the Divine. For many philosophers the intelligibility of the real requires some absolutely intelligible *Logos.* Kant's theory of the constitution itself, far from having dispensed with such a requirement, implicitly presupposes it. Now, a few philosophers, such as Plato, and, more recently, certain Thomists, like Maréchal and Lonergan, would also call this ultimately intelligible the ultimately real. Others admit that the real and the intelligible are related and must at least be partially identical, but they hesitate to make the absolutely real coincide with the absolutely intelligible. With the Kantians they keep wondering: Why should the real be ultimately intelligible? That the real is not self-explanatory does not necessarily imply that *ultimately* it must be explanatory, although we would all hope it to be so. But even then many will feel the need to "postulate" a principle of intelligibility which is at the same time the ultimate ground of all reality. Whether it is postulate or conclusion, however, this principle remains purely metaphysical and, as such, clearly distinct from the idea of God.

A similar way of reasoning applies to the ultimate principle of value in metaphysics. Does it coincide with absolute being? A partial identity is evident, a total one is not. But even if we accept or assume a total identity, the principle in which it is realized still differs from the religious idea of God. A German philosopher who discusses this point at length concludes:

> That the principle of value just as the principle of meaning stands close to the religious idea of God, is undeniable. Indeed, it stands even closer, as the term "principle of value" suggests. Nevertheless we must beware of identifying them. "Principle of value" is a metaphysical, "reality of value" a religious concept. The former lacks the specifically religious moment, the moment of the sacred. Our axiological argument did not assume the values of the sacred and could not assume them, for it was based on world-realization. But that does not appear among religious values, since the sacred has neither the ability nor the need to be realized, since it is a [preexisting] *reality* of value.[4]

From the preceding it should be obvious that we do not accept "purely rational" arguments for the existence of God. But, even if such arguments could be made more successful than they are and could prove the existence of an infinite, perfect Being, they still would not reach the "object" of the religious act. Unless philosophy studies God *from within* the religious experience where his name was first heard, it will always fall into the error denounced by Scheler of identifying two differently intended objects without proving that they are identical. The absolute of philosophy solves an intellectual problem. The God of religion brings salvation. The latter originates in the religious experience (including a divine revelation), the former is a product of speculative thinking which borrows the name God from religious language where it has a different meaning. The metaphysical idea of God is never a subject, while the God of faith is. It is not merely that we speak differently *about* a person (object) than *to* a person. In the case of God we cannot talk *about* him except in a context of talking *to* him.

> God is the only one to whom we can speak only in the second person. When we speak about him, we do so only insofar as we stand in his presence. We therefore can speak of God while speaking to him, that is, while praying. When we speak in the third person, as is inevitable in human language, we speak inauthentically about him.[5]

FAITH'S NEED OF PHILOSOPHICAL REFLECTION

Nevertheless, the claim that faith is inaccessible to philosophical reflection is even more false than the one that philosophy has invented the idea of God. Albrecht Ritschl introduced this thesis into Protestant theology and it still has not been fully exorcised from it. Yet this sort of fideism is self-defeating. For if nothing in the religious experience responds to a philosophical question, it also follows that philosophy cannot find any meaning in it. Philosophy did not invent the name of God, but, unless that name gives life and depth to some dimension of which philosophy is aware, the name itself must remain as meaningless as positivist philosophy maintains it is. Moreover, since the believer makes certain statements on the nature of the real on which the philosopher also has views, the believer must compare his tenets with what reason tells him and justify them in its light. This is not a matter of apologetics. It simply means that the mind cannot simultaneously accept two views on the same subject without trying to harmonize them.

Of course, here we must face the fact that not all philosophies are fit to deal with the religious phenomenon. Any approach which rejects a priori all transcendent claims is obviously unable to regard the religious experience as religious man regards it himself. But equally unfit is a philosophy which feels so much at home with religion that it claims to do full justice to its transcendence and thereby immanentizes it. Faith claims to create a transcendent world *within* the immanent and asks the philosopher to acknowledge this transcendence while abstaining from it.

Focusing our attention now on the particular modes in which philosophers have opened their metaphysics to the transcendent dimension, we notice an almost infinite variety. The approaches range from an idea of God which is the keystone of a system (a secularization after the fashion which we denounced in the previous section) to an open and benevolent agnosticism. Few today would still claim with Descartes that all certainties collapse unless there exists a transcendent, infinitely perfect Being. But all advocates of logically stringent arguments for the existence of God share, to some extent, Descartes' position insofar as their universe must become incoherent without God. For if this universe implies the necessary existence of God, the very thought of a world without God would coniflct with the only possible conception of the present one. Some might say that the same argument applies to any philosopher who *accepts* the existence of God, insofar as the acceptance of a necessary being excludes a problematic attitude with respect to that idea: a necessary being, once admitted, cannot be "bracketed" any more. Yet this conclusion does not follow, since there is a distinction between the thought of a necessary being and the necessary thought of a necessary being. The former concept is based upon a fluid concept of reality which can alternatively include and exclude the notion of a transcendent necessary being, while the latter, which is accepted by the adherents of Anselm's ontological argument, allows only one possible logical universe of which God is a necessary component. Nevertheless, even those for whom God is such a philosophical necessity do not usually claim that philosophical discourse alone exhausts its riches. Whitehead, for instance, in the text quoted at the beginning, praises Aristotle for having stayed within the confines of metaphysics: the poverty of the Aristotelian vision of God is the sign of its authenticity. Religious faith for Whitehead is by no means a mere extension of metaphysics, but rather an attempt to infuse "that non-temporal generality which primarily belongs to conceptual thought alone" into the particularity of emotion.[6] Whether religious faith needs philosophical reflection, as this statement implies, is a question which will be treated later.

First we must discuss another position in which philosophy pretends neither to invent nor to prove the existence of God, but in which it remains open toward the transcendent. This open-ended philosophy is then confronted with a number of possible hypotheses concerning the ultimate ground of the mind and the universe. One of these necessarily imposes itself upon the philosopher's attention, because of the actual existence of a religious experience. Maurice Blondel, the main proponent of this theory, refers to it as a "necessary hypothesis," thus distinguishing it from a number of other hypotheses which the philosopher may prefer not to consider even though he does not see them as logically contradictory. Philosophy's task is to analyze the intrinsic coherence of the God-hypothesis as it is presented by religious man. In doing so metaphysics naturally develops into philosophy of religion. The transition is smooth enough, but it is all the more important that the philosopher be fully aware of it. Otherwise he will conclude, as he has done so often in the past, to some "natural" theory of God which faith or theology merely "follows up and fills out more fully." [7]

So far we have considered the problem only from philosophy's point of view. But faith itself leads normally to some sort of reflection upon its own activity. Gnosticism could become a religious deviation only because the *gnosis* is part of the religious act itself. Faith tends toward even greater clarification. The *fides quaerens intellectum* is not an invention of philosophers but of theologians, and one which in the Christian tradition has been practiced ever since the Pauline and the Johannine writings. In an advanced culture faith naturally recurs to philosophical concepts to develop its ideas. As long as his faith proposes a supersensible world, a divine Creator, and an immortal soul, the believer cannot avoid thinking about what these tenets might possibly mean. But, aside from particular beliefs, faith as the integrating factor of existence, the overall structure which assigns to all aspects of life their ultimate meaning, meets that ultimate rational interpretation of reality to which we refer as metaphysics. Windelband at one time went so far as to call religion "an intercourse with the inmost nature and foundation of all reality, a life in and with God, *a metaphysical life*." [8] Far from threatening the religious activity, philosophical reflection brings it to a heightened awareness of itself. Philosophical reflection helps the movement of faith along in its restless desire to go beyond its present state and to approach closer to vision.

Yet, as we realized even in the first section, this affinity to reflection is fraught with danger both to metaphysics and faith. The believing metaphysician may be tempted to take the religious integration for ultimate metaphysical answers. As Heidegger pointed out, God is not the final answer to the question: Why is there something rather than nothing? [9] On the contrary, he is part of the problem, for metaphysics must question his Being as much as that of all finite beings. On the other hand, all too eager a desire for philosophical insight may tempt religious man to substitute independent speculation for the living experience. Thus he may end up pretending to understand what in another respect he declares to be beyond understanding.

But these dangers must be braved since religious man has no choice but to take the risk which is inherent to the nature of his experience. Whitehead forcefully expressed the need of reflection when he declared that faith to maintain its religious status must remain aware of its metaphysical implications, more so than science.

> Science can leave its metaphysics implicit and retire behind our belief in the pragmatic value of its general descriptions. If religion does that, it admits that its dogmas are merely pleasing ideas for the purpose of stimulating its emotions. Science (at least as a temporary methodological device) can rest upon a naive faith; religion is the longing for justification. When religion ceases to seek for penetration, for clarity, it is sinking back into its lower forms.[10]

The degeneration to which Whitehead refers consists in a flight into the purely emotional and the wildly phantastic, denounced by all students of the religious experience. Tylor presented his evolutionary theory as a gradual rationalization which subdues the unruly forces of religious inspiration. Rudolf Otto, from an entirely different viewpoint, considered the interpretation of the rational elements into the nonrational ones an axiomatic process whose inner necessity is felt to be self-evident.[11] The category of the sacred does not reach its fullest meaning until the non-rational numinous fact is "schematized" by rational elements.[12] Otto Karrer mentions the constant threat of a "Verwilderung" of the elements of imagination in religion.[13] We find the need for rationalization mentioned in Plato, in Locke, and in Hegel. Of course, the need for reflection in the religious act is not the need for philosophy, but one leads to the other.

THE AUTONOMY OF PHILOSOPHY AND RELIGIOUS FAITH

The philosophical reflection upon the religious act, which is usually called philosophy of religion, is to be distinguished from the general metaphysics which we discussed at the beginning of this paper. Although the latter must refrain from talking of God in the strict, religious sense, the former must embrace the full content of the religious experience. But the desire for an intrinsically unified philosophical system may lead the philosopher to make this reflection part of general metaphysics. Something of that nature seems to have occurred in Hegel's philosophy. For Hegel philosophy of religion says the same thing as the general philosophy which he calls *Logic*. "Philosophy has its own content, its need and interest common with religion; its object is the eternal truth, that is, nothing but God and his explication. Philosophy explicates itself only when it explicates religion, and while it explicates itself, it explicates religion." [14] But, although its general object is the same as that of philosophy *as such,* philosophy of religion does not stay with pure thought: it descends to the religious representation in order to study thought in its external manifestation. At the same time, philosophy of religion does not consider the finite forms which the Spirit gives itself in nature and in the finite spirit and which general philosophy must also study. Instead it concentrates directly on the Idea as it appears in its infinite form, as absolute Spirit.[15] It is obvious that the unity between philosophy of religion and metaphysics here becomes uncomfortably close.

Related to this "religionization" of metaphysics is the position held by some Catholic theologians in recent years. Here philosophy is simply made subordinate to the theological reflection which occurs *in* the religious experience itself. Thus philosophical reflection is made dependent upon extraphilosophical norms and the autonomy of philosophical thought is jeopardized altogether. The nonbeliever is said to live an inauthentic existence and thereby to be at a definite disadvantage in philosophizing. The rejection of faith is thought to compromise the quality of his philosophical reflection. This position is a clear instance of an illegitimate intrusion of religion into the domain of metaphysics. We might even say: into the domain of philosophy, for, when a thinker so widely extends the boundaries of theology, there is no proper domain for philosophy of religion left.[16]

A somewhat similar view, although more restrained, is implied in Etienne Gilson's notion of Christian philosophy.[17] Gilson, whose position is based upon Thomas' *Summa Theologiae,* considers Christian philosophy an integral part of Christian theology. This position obviously rings the death bell for an autonomous philosophy of the Christian experience. If this is Christian philosophy, there is no Christian *philosophy*.[18] If philosophy is an *autonomous* reflection upon living experience, it must be entitled to reflect upon the religious experience, in this case the

Christian experience, without having to sacrifice its independence. Of course, all here depends on the meaning of "autonomy." If it means that philosophy must create or at least entirely reconstitute the religious concepts, then it will either have to admit that it is unable to do so, or it will in its own way reinvent these concepts, but then religious man will no longer recognize them as his own. But, if "autonomy" means a critical interpretation of a *received* experience, then there can be a philosophy of religion acceptable to religious man.

It is not always clear which one of the two positions an author adopts. In the case of Hegel this is a matter of dispute to the present day. Hegel accepts the unique authority of the Christian revelation. Yet he also argues that faith does not fully come into its own until it has philosophically *thought* the representational content of this revelation. This view may appear similar to the one proposed in the beginning of the preceding section. But for Hegel philosophy is not merely a reflection upon faith: it is *faith itself* reaching its own truth. This does not mean, as has been argued so often in the past, that philosophy is a substitute for religion. How could it be a substitute for what it presupposes? But it does mean that religion cannot be fully true in its own right until it has become philosophy. Many a religious man will balk at this conclusion, because it places an exclusive emphasis upon the cognitive, the gnostic elements of the religious act. Certainly, a desire for clarification is essential to the act of faith, but it is not the whole act, nor can it ever change the act into a different one, an act of knowledge. Religious faith spontaneously tends toward philosophical reflection, but it never gives up its own identity in order to become an act of philosophical reflection. Once the philosopher identifies these two acts, he basically changes the nature of the religious experience. It then becomes *primarily* an intellectual insight—which it was not before—and it pretends to understand its object *exhaustively* —which faith never does. To remain religious the gnostic drive of faith must be kept within the boundaries of faith. A religious act can never be transformed into one of reflection and still preserve its original religious character. Hegel seems to set no limits to the gnostic drive. For him the act is its intellectual content. This appears even in the order of development of the *Philosophy of Religion*. How else could he claim that the Greek (indeed, the

Roman) religion marked a higher stage of development than the Jewish? Or that the Greek mysteries constituted a more "primitive" religious expression than the Greek mythology? [19] If "primitive" means "more crudely religious" and not merely "more ancient" this statement is patently false.

The exhaustive character of the (philosophical) religious insight is the other trait which makes Hegel's position suspect to the believer. The God of faith remains hidden, at the end of the clarification process as much as in the beginning. It is essential to faith *not* to understand. Hegel's philosophical religion has no such restrictions. Philosophical knowledge for him is knowledge of the absolute and in the religious act it pursues its drive until there remains nothing of the original darkness. But is this still true *religious* insight? One sympathetic commentator wonders: "Does speculative thought grasp the mystery as well as it thinks? Does the perfect knowledge, the spiritual gnosis, of the Trinitarian mystery not impose another negation, an abnegation, a passion of which the patient Idea does not seem to be overly aware? Perhaps it is not a mere figure of representation that a surplus of knowledge remains promised from the Spirit to the Spirit. But does the relentless idealist thought ever know a surplus?" [20]

Hegel's case shows how difficult it is to keep the relations between philosophy and religion such that both preserve their full integrity. We are inclined to think that the impact of religion, via the philosophy of religion, upon general metaphysics is more modest. It consists mainly in the awareness of a new dimension in the Being which the metaphysician studies. This means not that all reality is to be interpreted with reference to theology, but that philosophy must adopt a consciously expectant attitude with regard to the foundation of human existence. Philosophy then becomes what Rahner calls "the ontology of a *potentia oboedientialis* for revelation." [21] This would also be the true religious philosophy. The methodological problems of the idea of Christian philosophy are caused by its unwillingness to reveal its true sources or by its willingness to abandon the autonomy of philosophy. Once it has abandoned these spurious attitudes, there is no reason why the idea would not become meaningful again.

NOTES

1. *Science and the Modern World,* New York, 1959, p. 156.
2. *Process and Reality,* New York, 1960, p. 315.
3. *Le problème de Dieu,* Paris, 1957, p. 15.
4. Johannes Hessen, *Religionsphilosophie,* 1955, II, 299.
5. Karl Heim, *Glauben und Denken,* Berlin. 1931, p. 316, quoted in Hessen, *Religionsphilosophie,* p. 181.
6. *Process and Reality,* p. 23.
7. Karl Rahner, *Hearers of the Word,* New York, 1969, p. 13.
8. "Das Heilige," in *Präludien,* 1903, p. 357.
9. *An Introduction to Metaphysics,* trans. Ralph Manheim, New York, 1961, pp. 6–7.
10. *Religion in the Making,* New York, 1961, p. 83.
11. *The Idea of the Holy,* New York, 1958, p. 136.
12. *Ibid.,* p. 45.
13. *Das Religiöse in der Menschheit und das Christentum,* Freiburg, 1934, p. 134. See also, Johannes Hessen, *Religionsphilosophie,* II, 36.
14. *Vorlesungen über die Philosophie der Religion,* I, 29.
15. *Vorlesungen,* I, 31–33. See also Albert Chapelle, *Hegel et la religion,* Paris, 1963, I, 212–213; André Léonard, *La foi chez Hegel,* Louvain: pro manuscripto, 1968, pp. 216–217, Claude Bruaire, *Logique et religion chrétienne dans la philosophie de Hegel,* Paris, 1964, pp. 43–44.
16. We find this position well articulated in Henk van Luyk, S. J., *Philosophie du fait chrétien. L'analyse critique du christianisme de Henry Duméry,* Paris, 1964, pp. 190–280.
17. See, for instance, "What Is Christian Philosophy?," in *A Gilson Reader,* ed. Anton Pegis, Garden City, N.Y., 1957; also *Elements of Christian Philosophy,* New York, 1960.
18. For a critique see, George P. Klubertanz, "Metaphysics and Theistic Convictions," in *Teaching Thomism Today,* ed. George McLean, Washington, D.C., 1963, pp. 271–306, and Germain Grisez, "Etienne Gilson: Elements of Christian Philosophy," in *Thomist,* 1960, 448–476.
19. *Vorlesungen,* III, 138.
20. A. Chapelle, *Hegel et la religion,* Paris, 1967, II, 79.
21. *Hearers of the Word,* p. 25.

Metaphysics and Religion*

George Bosworth Burch

Two basic concerns of religion are orthodoxy and liberalism. We want to be orthodox, that is, hold right opinion, and we want to be liberal, that is, enjoy freedom. But the two are incompatible. Man cannot both stick to the straight path and gather the daisies in the field. The orthodox man has logic on his side, and his armor is the law of noncontradiction. With two contradictory doctrines, it may be difficult to determine which is true, but once he has determined it he can reject the other. His formula is *this not that.* The liberal man, on the other hand, is illogical. Not that he rejects reason, but he has his own brand of logic, based not on the law of noncontradiction but on the law of Hegelian dialectic. If a thesis is true, its antithesis is also true, and they can be resolved in a synthesis on a higher level of thought. The business of thought is not to determine which of two antitheses is true but to find the synthesis which includes both. The formula of the liberal man is *this and that.* We are both right even if we disagree. There are many paths leading to the same mountain top. Truth is one, but men call it by different names. You go your way and I will go mine, and we shall meet as our paths converge into one. Liberalism has a powerful attraction for the magnanimous man, who condemns orthodoxy as narrow-minded. At a fork in the road near Wellesley there used to be a sign which read, "Boston either way." That is liberalism.

* This paper is a summary of an unpublished book *Alternative Goals in Religion: Love, Freedom, Truth.*

Both orthodoxy and liberalism have difficulties. Orthodoxy *is* narrow-minded. It is unabashed provincialism to assert that our way is the only way. We know that there are other churches, other faiths, and other philosophies besides our own. It is hard for an educated person to be orthodox. He knows too much. But if he knows too much to be orthodox, he thinks too much to be liberal. If he accepts a premise, he also accepts its consequences. The liberal meets the difficulty by abstracting the common part of opposing views, considering this their essence, and ignoring their differences as superficial. But this presumed synthesis on a higher level is all too often on a lower level. It is possible to be both a Christian and a Buddhist simultaneously, but one has to sacrifice two things, the essence of Christianity and the essence of Buddhism. The issue between orthodoxy and liberalism cannot be solved logically. It is a metalogical question: what sort of logic are we to recognize? If we accept the logic of truth and falsity, our problem is to find the truth, and having found it to defend it as orthodox. If we accept the logic of liberalism, our problem is to synthesize opposed ideas as best we can. Neither is fully satisfactory. The logic of orthodoxy fails to recognize the equal claim of the alternative, while the logic of liberalism is either illogical in uniting incompatible ideas or inadequate in ignoring much of their content.

If we ask the metalogical question whether there is a third sort of logic besides these two, one such logic immediately suggests itself. Besides negation and conjunction there is also disjunction. Besides *not* and *and* there is also *or.* I mean *or* in the exclusive sense: *this or that but not both.* "Boston either way" is liberalism. If the sign read, "Left Boston, right dead end," that would be orthodoxy. But who says we must go to Boston? Suppose the sign read, "Left Boston, right New York"? Who is to say that Boston is better than New York? With this sign we have a choice, but it is necessary to make a commitment. *This or that* is the formula of commitment. When the menu offers steak, chicken, or lobster, we do not insist that only one is edible, neither do we order a little of each, but we make a choice and having made it are committed to it. Life is like that. We freely choose a wife, a vocation, a religion. In retrospect the choice seems the only possible one, for our commitments make us what we are, but at the time of choice there was a real choice. We can judge how well we have abided by our commitments, but we cannot judge the commitments themselves. The logic of disjunction is the logic of faith, which requires indemonstrable and therefore arbitrary choice. If not the logic we think by, it is usually the logic we live by. It is a dynamic logic. The ordinary logic of *not* is static, merely making explicit theorems already implicit in the premises. The Hegelian dialectic of *and* is only apparently dynamic, finding a more comprehensive formula for antithetical ideas. But the free choice of *or* involves progress, as one possibility is actualized and thus generates new possibilities and so a continuing progress which ends only with the attainment of the Absolute. But this Absolute, unlike the inevitable Absolute of Hegelian dialectic, has alternatives. A religious man can take, toward other religions, the attitude of orthodoxy or liberalism or commitment. Psychologically, orthodoxy reflects pride in the exclusive superiority of one's own way. Liberalism reflects excessive humility prepared to eliminate from one's own way anything incompatible with others. Commitment reflects a true humility which, while maintaining its own way without compromise or qualification, still recognizes the equal validity of other ways not as errors to be tolerated but as alternatives also freely chosen.

With this metalogical preamble, let us turn to metaphysics, which is the speculative search for the Absolute, and religion, which is the practical escape from our nonabsolute or sinful situation. Metaphysics, if it is to be existential and not mere analysis of concepts, must start from experience. Experience always includes consciousness and its content, subject and object. There are three ways in which they can be related. The content may determine the consciousness: this is *knowing*. The consciousness may determine the content: this is *willing*. Consciousness and content may mutually determine each other: this is *feeling*. In ordinary experience these three functions are confused. Our knowledge of truth is perverted by wishful thinking arising from the will or emotional prejudices arising from the feeling. Our freedom of will is restricted by what we know and what we feel. Our aesthetic enjoyment is corrupted by overemphasis on the object enjoyed or on the enjoying consciousness. The scientist who seeks truth must purge his knowledge of subjective prejudices, and the philosopher who seeks absolute Truth must purge his knowledge of all subjectivity. This involves sacrifice.

Objectivity can be obtained only by abandoning subjectivity. Truth can be obtained only by giving up freedom. If one is going to accept facts as a scientist does, one cannot impose his own fancies on the world as a poet does. The search for truth is an austere discipline. But who says I must search for truth? I may prefer to glory in the freedom of my will, in the Godlike activity of freely creating. In that case I will follow the opposite procedure, purging my will of the objective influences which keep it from being pure subjectivity, which is absolute Freedom. But who says I must seek either objectivity or subjectivity? I may prefer to combine object and consciousness in an emotional appreciation of aesthetic value. I can do this by a third procedure, purging my feeling of separateness. Union of subject and object is love, and feeling freed from all separateness is absolute Love. In ordinary experience we have some truth, some freedom, and some love, but they result from incompatible functions of the mind, and the more we have of one the less we have of the others.

To attain absolute objectivity, that is, absolute Truth, is the goal of Vedanta. Moksha is pure truth purged of all subjectivism, that is, all error. To attain absolute subjectivity, that is, absolute Freedom, is the goal of Buddhism. Nirvana is pure freedom purged of all realism, that is, all constraint. To attain absolute togetherness, with God and each other, that is, absolute Love, is the goal of Christianity. Beatitude is pure love purged of all separation, that is, all sin. In each case the goal is the Absolute. But the three forms of the Absolute are not identical. They are opposite extremes. The paths do not converge. They diverge. They are not three paths leading to the same mountain peak. They are three paths leading to different mountain peaks. What they have in common is not their goal but their starting point, the valley of ignorance, suffering, and sin in which we find ourselves. Their goals are different, opposed, incomparable—alternative Absolutes.

Religion, if it is practical and not mere worship, is escapism, an attempt to change our condition, to escape from the state in which we are. There are different religions because different teachers have emphasized different imperfections in our actual condition, envisaged different better possibilities, and taught different techniques for attaining these goals; but the fact of original sin, that man is by nature bad, is the common presupposition of all. It is difficult to appreciate other religions. Our first impulse is to deny their existence, since religion is Christianity, and so the heathen, not being Christian, obviously have no religion. When further knowledge makes this position untenable, we say that the heathen do indeed have their own religions, but that these are false religions. Still further appreciation of heathen religions leads to the position that they are good and true so far as they go, but that ours goes further and is in fact the very truth others are groping for. Still deeper insight leads us to say that all the great religions, including our own, are of equal value, coordinate and equally valid ways leading to the same goal of eternal beatitude in union with God (*our* goal, of course), and in saying this we pride ourselves on our scholarship, tolerance, and liberalism. This broad-minded view recognizes that there are many ways, but it keeps the old dogmatic and provincial prejudice that there is only one goal. We must face the fact that divergent roads do not lead to the same destination. What the various religions have in common is not their goal but their starting point, the common state of sin, suffering, and ignorance.

Christianity, Buddhism, and Vedanta emphasize the wickedness, the suffering, and the ignorance of this life, respectively. Christianity is less concerned about suffering, which it sometimes considers as having a sort of value in itself, or about ignorance, since knowledge is not required for sanctity, which is best sought in the attitude of a little child. Buddhism is less concerned about wickedness, which is compensated through the law of karma, or about ignorance, Buddha refusing to discuss metaphysical problems on the ground that such knowledge is useless. Vedanta is less concerned about wickedness, since salvation is by knowledge alone, or about suffering, which it considers illusory. Our actual experience is a mixture of the three. Insofar as the subject is separated from the object of his experience, he opposes his interests to those of others, hence the selfishness, wickedness, and hatred which constitute sin. Insofar as the subject is thwarted by objective facts he cannot control, suffering results. Insofar as the object appears distorted by subjective conditions of awareness, we are ignorant of the objective reality.

The trouble with this life is its poverty. This is a poor life. Our love is reduced almost to zero by our selfishness, our happiness is reduced almost to zero by unlimited desires inevitably frustrated, and our knowledge of reality is reduced almost to zero by our subjective forms of intuition and categories of understanding. The life to which we aspire is a rich life. Attaining the religious goal does not mean giving up the good things of life. It means getting greater goods. Our love of God is greater when we are no longer separated from him, and our love of neighbor is richer when we love all men in God. Our happiness is richer when our freedom is no longer restricted. Our knowledge of truth is richer when we know reality in the richness of its concrete being instead of in some abstract form of our own imposition. Each of these consummations is possible, so we are taught. Nevertheless, it does not follow that they are possible together. We must beware the fallacy of composition: because three girls are willing to marry you, it does not follow that you can marry all three. Absolute Love, Freedom, and Truth may be incompatible. In that case we may have to give up something after all.

The prejudice that the Absolute is one is a consequence of that unity-mongering which has always been the bane of philosophy. That these three absolutes are really one Absolute is not even plausible, since going in opposite directions is an unlikely way to arrive at the same destination. But if in practice the way determines the goal, so in theory the goal defines the way. The metaphysical absolutes of Love, Freedom, and Truth define the religious ways of Christianity, Buddhism, and Vedanta, respectively. Let me speak first of Christianity. All Christian sects accept theism, rejecting the alternatives of atheism and pantheism. Atheism and pantheism are not incompatible with religion, but they are incompatible with a religion of absolute Love. If there is no God, there is no absolute object of love. If there is nothing except God, there is nobody to love God. Atheism may be the theology of freedom and pantheism the theology of truth, but theism is the theology of love.

By love I mean *eros,* not *agape* or charity. Christians have never gone in for *agape* very seriously, in spite of their professed commitment to it. Except for some saints like Francis, Christian charity finds its widest expression in a pacifism which teaches love for all men, whereas some other religions teach compassion for all sentient beings or even all living beings. If *agape* is the essence of religion, Christianity is not one of the more advanced religions. Faith, hope, and charity are the ways of the Christian life. But love is its goal. *Agape* presupposes inequality, but *eros* produces equality, and even the love of God generates an ineffable quasi-equality in which the metaphysical difference between creature and Creator is somehow lost in the existential union of lover and Beloved.

If love is union, lack of love is separation. This is sin, and its expression is malevolent behavior. Petty sin is separation from anybody; high sin is separation from God. This is our natural state; that is the doctrine of original sin. Love, consequently, has to be acquired; that is the doctrine of grace. Love is emotion or feeling. Charity may be performed as duty, without any feeling, as when we contribute money without really wanting to, but love is never reluctant. Love is appreciation of beauty, and the meaning of love is found in the meaning of beauty. According to one theory of aesthetics the beauty of a symphony is in the hearer's consciousness, since objectively it is a mere scratching of sheep's intestines by horses' hairs. According to another theory its beauty is its objective form of rhythm, melody, and harmony, independently of being heard. Neither theory is adequate. Neither a beauty in the mind nor a beauty which need not be experienced is the beauty which is *felt*. Feeling is union of subject and object. In knowing or willing subject and object are contrasted, with one subordinated to the other, but in feeling the attempt to contrast them results only in destroying the feeling.

This is even more obvious when appreciation of the beauty of a person is exalted to love. Love is sympathy, feeling with, neither objective nor subjective. To be lovely is not to be loved, and to be in a loving mood is not to love. The lovely object needs a lover, not as a foil for her beauty, but to actualize what is otherwise a mere potency. The loving subject needs a beloved, not as a stage for his conscious mood but to transcend it by transcending himself. Metaphysically, feeling is union of subject and object, that is, of consciousness and content. It means sacrificing both truth and freedom. On the one hand, just as there is no place for feeling in science, so there is no place for science in feeling. To know a girl as she is is a project for an anthropologist, not a lover, and to know God as he is is a project for a theologian, not a mystic. Truth is to apprehend something as it is objectively, love to apprehend something as merged with yourself. Knowing frees the object from its subjective conditions. Feeling binds the object to its subjective conditions. On the other hand, to feel is also to sacrifice freedom. To be free is to act voluntarily, imposing your own will, but you cannot impose your love. In feeling or love you must submit, not to the object, as in knowing, but to the togetherness. Aesthetic enjoyment and love are restricted by knowing, which lets the object dominate consciousness, and willing, which lets consciousness dominate object. We purify our feeling by giving up either of these forms of separation and attain pure feeling when all separation is gone.

Mystical love differs from other love not in its nature, for it too is union of consciousness and content, nor in its intensity, for a trivial or carnal love may be intense, but in its object. The mystic loves God, the absolute Being, and so is united with him. Theologians have a word for the union of God and man. The word is *Christ*. For Christians Christ is not only teacher and savior but salvation itself. Christ *is* the union of God and man, which is salvation from sin, which is the separation of God and man. Christians become members of Christ in baptism, and are nourished by Christ in communion. Whether interpreted symbolically or literally, the sacraments are already the love of God. What remains is to perfect this love, to attain eternal and absolute love of the absolute Being.

Such absolute Love is the highest good, justifying lesser goods as means to it, itself needing no justification. It cannot be justified, but it can be analyzed. In ordinary experience consciousness and content are apprehended as distinct. Feeling is the uniting of the two, and absolute feeling or love is perfect union of consciousness and content with all separateness eliminated. As separateness is reduced, the subjective forms and categories which define finite phenomena are eliminated, so that love tends inevitably to become love of the infinite object, God. Absolute Love of absolute Being is the goal toward which the process of purging the feeling faculty proceeds. It is the ideal of the Christian way, and Christians believe by faith that it is attainable. It is the Absolute beyond which there is nothing more. But it does not follow that absolute Love is the only absolute. This brings us to a consideration of other religions.

The life of Buddha was that of a Hindu guru, and his doctrine was only to call attention to matters of common knowledge and ordinary experience. He said that life is suffering, that the cause of suffering is desire, that elimination of suffering comes with elimination of desire, and that this is accomplished by following the path of right living and thinking based on moderation and temperance. Buddhism, like every religion, is a form of escapism. What it wants to escape from is the suffering of this life. "Some have perverted notions, others have right notions, but all suffer the same pain," says the Lotus Sutra. We may need revelation to know that we are in a state of sin or ignorance, but we know suffering by immediate experience. Buddhism needs no revealed scripture, but only attention to the obvious. The Buddhist virtues are simply those of ordinary and universal morality—noninjury, chastity, honesty, and temperance. Buddhist monks, like Christian monks, also take vows of celibacy and poverty, but they do not take a vow of obedience, and the vows they do take are not irrevocable. Renunciation of freedom is the very heart of Christian monasticism, but a Buddhist monk never gives up his freedom. Truth as such is not important. Buddha teaches whatever doctrines may be effective for the various persons he is concerned with saving. There is no revealed dogma. Metaphysical problems are ignored partly because they are insoluble, since they are based on the false presupposition of substantial being, but also because, even if they were soluble, the solutions would have no practical value. Buddhism is not a theoretical system of knowledge seeking truth but a practical way of life seeking freedom.

Buddhist philosophy, consequently, is analytical rather than speculative. Buddhism does not believe in God or soul. Scientific study enables us to find order and causal laws within the world, but experience does not show us any eternal reality underlying phenomena. Neither experience nor reason proves the existence of God or the soul or, for that matter, any substance at all. These are metaphysical fictions which we would not even think of except through the influence of allegedly revealed scripture. Reality, including the individual self, is not substance but process, like a flame or a wave of the sea, which seems to be a thing because it maintains a more or less constant form, but really is nothing but a process, the matter constantly changing, the form constantly renewed by causal necessity. The flame will go out if the temperature is lowered, the wave will die down if the wind stops, and the individual person will no longer suffer when the force of desire ceases. But in none of these cases is anything destroyed, because neither flame nor wave nor person is a thing. Does the person then cease to be? Yes, if by being you mean to continue the suffering characteristic of life; no, if by being you mean to be a substantial self, because he never was in that sense. The person who attains nirvana simply ceases to be disturbed.

A common technique of Zen Buddhism is to meditate on some insoluble problem, not to sharpen the intellect but to discredit it. The meditation is terminated when it is rejected as absurd. Then the self is freed from thought. The purpose of Zen discipline is to realize the Formless Self, the self freed from all those forms which make it limited, definite, or individual. The purpose of the Zen arts is to express the Formless Self. These arts have a universal appeal. We can appreciate a Japanese flower arrangement without considering the theory involved. Our concern here, however, is with the theory. Experience is a relation between consciousness and content. In willing, consciousness determines content. If what we know is truth and what we feel is love, what we will is freedom. Suffering, desire, knowledge, and feeling accompany ordinary willing, but are incompatible with absolute willing. Insofar as we will, we are indifferent to all claims of objects. Such freedom is the Buddhist ideal of serenity undisturbed by objects, especially supposed substances, which demand either to be known or to be felt. Free of the objective world which he desires neither to know nor to feel, the Buddhist has an unassailable refuge of pure consciousness.

The Absolute is always ineffable, but absolute Freedom is especially so. Truth is at least known, even if it cannot be formulated in words. Love is felt, which is something like being known. But Freedom is only willed. It cannot be made a content of consciousness, because that is just what it is not. Absolute Freedom or nirvana is consciousness without content, subject without object, willing without willing anything, so that *will* becomes an intransitive verb. We do not differ from each other by our consciousness; that is the fallacy of the substantial self. We differ from each other by the content of our consciousness, and where there is no content there is no difference and so no individuality. Nirvana can be called annihilation, since everything which can be conceived or pointed to is lacking. But that which cannot be conceived or pointed to, the will, still is; and because it is will it is active, acting on things in creative art and on men in compassionate charity, but not acted on. This is absolute Freedom, awakening the mind without fixing it anywhere.

If nirvana or absolute Freedom, the goal of Buddhism, is pure activity, moksha or absolute Truth, the goal of Vedanta, is pure passivity. We know when our consciousness mirrors whatever objectively is. Philosophy is rational analysis of experience. It distinguishes between awareness of reality, which is truth, and awareness of illusion, which is error. Rational philosophy alone, however, only makes and demonstrates this distinction, as Kant did. It does not actually free us from the phenomena which it proves to be unreal, or enable us to see the reality which it posits as the ground of phenomena. This is accomplished gradually, as we purge the knowing function of the willing and feeling functions by which the consciousness either determines or is joined to its objects.

We attain truth by sublation of illusion, and we attain absolute Truth by sublation of all illusion, even the illusion of individuality. The meaning of sublation is best seen in the common experience of waking up from a dream. On waking we have an immediate, intuitive, and certain awareness that the dream experience from which we have awakened was unreal. We realize that the waking experience, on the other hand, is real—real, that is, relative to the dream, though it may itself be later sublated and so prove unreal. Waking is a passive process: it means cessation of the activity by which we created the dream experience from our own substance, and opening our eyes to perceive what is there around us. But knowledge of reality is possible only by sublation of error. If we never woke, there would be no reason to call our dreams illusory, and if we never dreamed there would be no reason to call our waking experience real. Truth is meaningful only by contrast with error, not hypothetical error but error actually experienced. Just as freedom presupposes bondage and love presupposes separateness, so truth presupposes error, apart from which it is meaningless.

Reality or truth is that which is not sublated, and absolute Truth is that which cannot ever be sublated. All objects of experience can be sublated. The only thing which cannot ever be sublated is the Self which has the experience. To realize one's identity with Brahman the absolute Reality is not to become Brahman, any more than waking from a dream is to get into bed, but is to attain by pure knowing the absolute Truth which is the goal of Vedanta.

The search for truth is an austere discipline; it is only for those who are willing to sacrifice both freedom and love. Its goal is only for those who go all the way. Realization of the Self as absolute Being, Consciousness, and Bliss is its consummation.

The conclusion is that the world is one but there are many paths leading from it—three paths, to be precise. A religion is a way of escape from the world, and consequently there are three types of religion. The world—that is, ordinary experience—is a mixture of knowing, willing, and feeling. It is characterized by ignorance because knowing is not pure, suffering because willing is not pure, and sin because feeling is not pure, each being modified by the others. Escape from the world is accomplished by a psychological abstraction which takes one function and gives up the others. One can keep all three, remaining in the world and renouncing religion. But if any one function is partially purified, one is leaving the world, and if it is perfectly purified, it is completely freed from the others, and these three perfections are the alternative forms of the Absolute, which are the alternative goals of religion. To stay in the world requires doing nothing, as we are already there. To follow any way requires commitment to it. To follow more than one and so seek incompatible goals leads to religious frustration. Christianity, Buddhism, and nondualist Vedanta are examples of the three types. They cannot be integrated, because they fix the mind at different places—Christianity on God, Vedanta on the Self, and Buddhism nowhere. They cannot judge one another, because they have no positive ideal in common. But they are alike in aspiration, although not in the object of aspiration, and they can agree in opposing irreligion. Their attitude toward each other should be neither dogmatism nor tolerance nor liberalism but coexistence.

Coexistence, which avoids both the destructiveness of dogmatism and the poverty of liberalism, is important in many fields. In international politics disaster is imminent as the nations strive to impose their own political systems on each other, instead of coexisting in mutual respect on a planet big enough for alternative ways of life, and it would be also unfortunate if social progress should be undone by the various governments liberally becoming alike through reducing their activities to the bare essentials of a laissez-faire system. Our concern here, however, is with coexistence in religion. Today there is no isolation. Religions can no longer ignore each other. But they do not have to fight each other because of their differences or abolish their differences to avoid fighting. It would be a catastrophic disaster to civilization for the great religions to destroy each other either by dogmatically attacking each other or by liberally merging into some watered-down world religion. Christianity must distinguish between its friends and its enemies. Its enemies are secularism and humanism. But its friends are Buddhism and Vedanta and Islam. In the world today they must live together as alternative religions or else they may perish together, because there are powerful forces opposing religion as such. Nevertheless, any religion, with its commitment to the Absolute, should be strong enough to stand against the outer forces of secularism. The great dangers are the inner forces of the logic of *not* and the logic of *and,* dogmatic orthodoxy and shallow liberalism, both attitudes fraught with disaster, the former threatening mutual destruction, the latter leading to the withering away of religions as everything incompatible with the others is eliminated, either leaving secularism triumphant. Religions are incompatible. Liberalism reduces them to a bare minimum in which the essence of each is rejected and so essentially they cease to exist. But religions which do not exist cannot coexist. Gandhi, a great liberal, asked: "What does it matter that we take different roads so long as we reach the same goal? wherein is the cause for quarreling?" I ask: What does it matter that we reach different goals? wherein is the cause for quarreling?

A sound theory of religion is possible only by clear thinking, which analyzes experience, indicates the Absolute, and exorcises the demon of monism. What is important, however, is not the theory of religion, based on alternative forms of the Absolute, but the practice of religion, based on commitment and coexistence. This is only a dream. It is a dream which has been fulfilled in other aspects of life, aspects in which our civilization has attained some degree of success. It is fulfilled in academic life by departmentalization of the university, in social organization by division of labor, in domestic relations by monogamy. But it has not been fulfilled in the two most important aspects of life, politics, which maintains peace, and religion, which seeks ultimate values, aspects in which our civilization is conspicuously unsuccessful,

unsuccessful just because either dogmatic violence or liberal non-commitment, not coexistence of alternatives, has been the rule.

We all have a dream, a dream revived after each world war, not of nations fighting each other and not of a world state with a homogeneous culture but of many diverse nations each sovereign and demanding its own citizens' loyalty but coexisting in a League of Nations or United Nations. I also have a dream of religions neither opposing each other nor abandoning their commitment to the Absolute, each to its own form of the Absolute, coexisting in their coordinate but radically different aspirations. Then will be fulfilled the word of the Prophet Micah: "For all people will walk every one in the name of *his* god, and we will walk in the name of the Lord *our* God for ever and ever."

The Future of Metaphysics

Richard McKeon

I

The facts alleged about the confusions and dilemmas of past metaphysics reflect problems encountered in present philosophical oppositions. The recurrent interest to predict the future of metaphysics is usually expressed as a prognosis, not only of progressive therapy of present ills but also of progressive success of a present method of diagnosis and cure. The future of metaphysics is determined by the controversies of philosophers as well as by the ontology of things or the epistemology of thoughts; and its course is often marked more clearly by suggestive paradoxes than by indubitable certainties.

Kant found the problem of the *Prolegomena to Any Future Metaphysics* in the fact that there had been no *actual* metaphysics in the past or the present. Therefore his first task was to demonstrate that metaphysics is *possible*. Twenty years after he had shown incontrovertibly that there had been no actual metaphysics before the critical philosophy, he completed, in the year of his death 1804, a treatise on the real progress (*die wirklichen Fortschritte*) of metaphysics in Germany since the time of Leibniz and Wolff. When Feuerbach wrote his *Principles of the Philosophy of the Future* in 1843, as "the continuation and further justification" of his *Theses on the Reform of Philosophy,* he laid down as a first principle (rather than a thesis): "The task of the modern era was the realization and humanization of God—the transformation and dissolution of theology into anthropology." The truth and reality assumed by the old metaphysics or ontotheology had to be traced back to psychological or anthropological determinations.

The BBC broadcasts which were published under the title *The Revolution in Philosophy* in 1956 were followed by later broadcasts, published under the title *The Nature of Metaphysics,* in 1957. In the first, A. J. Ayer set forth the achievement of the Vienna Circle in metaphysics (p. 74): "Metaphysics, which they construed as covering such allegedly philosophical enterprises as the attempt to describe Reality as a whole, or to find the purpose of the Universe, or to reach beyond the everyday world to some supra-sensible spiritual order, was condemned by them not as being unduly speculative, or even as being false, but as being literally non-sensical." In the second, Gilbert Ryle gives two reasons for preferring Kant's form of anti-metaphysics to the Logical Positivist form (pp. 128–129), first, because the Positivistic attack seems merely to define metaphysics out of existence, while Kant gives a serious diagnosis of the actual character of metaphysical assertions, and, second, because the Positivistic attack makes it almost incredible that so much industry and intelligence should have been devoted to propounding nonsignificant doctrines, while Kant undertakes to explain why metaphysical theorizing should be so very strong in men of high intelligence. Metaphysical questions are still unanswerable, but they are also recognized to be unavoidable.

The paradoxes of a future metaphysics have a form, a pattern, and a continuity. It is clear from the history of the discussion of its future that metaphysics has always been necessary as well as contingent, and possible as well as impossible. Consideration of its future at any time depended on determination of senses in which all the modalities apply to the enterprise of metaphysics, as they do indeed to any contemplated future action. The facts about past metaphysics are ambiguous and contradictory, indisputable and incredible. Examination of the future of metaphysics and of the history of the progress of metaphysics since Leibniz and Wolff, or since Descartes, Kant, Fichte, and Hegel, or since Hume and Kant, permits the differentiation of two varieties or perspectives of ambiguity: (1) "metaphysics" has always had a plurality of meanings and methods, and (2) metaphysics has developed by using a plurality of facts and categories determined by a new "method" borrowed from science, practice, and art in order to emulate the progress, revolution, or renaissance they have achieved. The semantics of "metaphysics" and "method" must be made clear before the facts proper to metaphysical inquiry can be discovered, examined, or stated. The methods determine the necessity of a metaphysics, the impossibility of a metaphysics which is undertaken by use of other methods, the contingency of any particular statement of metaphysics, and the possibility of metaphysical progress.

The term "metaphysics" was invented to apply to the theoretical science which Aristotle called "wisdom," "theology," and "first philosophy." It was a science of *first* principles or of being *qua* being, that is, it provided an analysis and grounding of the principles of the other sciences—theoretical, practical, and poetic or productive sciences—and a demonstration of their parts and methods. Aristotle examines the history of philosophy to discover that such an inquiry had been impossible prior to his analysis of causes; he ties the future of such inquiry to the progress of the sciences and their development of methods; he relates the unity of a first philosophy and of its subject matter to the being and operation of a first cause. A first philosophy, or inquiry concerning being, is essential if philosophy itself is to consist of many particular sciences with different subject matters, methods, and principles. It is meaningless if philosophy itself is unified, or consists of sciences unified in one science, for then philosophy would not depend on a separate science of first principles of *being* but on principles which express *beliefs* about the nature of being. Aristotle refutes three such philosophies: those based on beliefs about separated forms or model ideas which provide transcendental conditions for intelligibility and existence; those based on beliefs about ultimate forms or indivisible atoms which provide underlying physical conditions for knowledge, perception, and pleasure; and those based on beliefs about language and action which show that all statements are true or false, that being is nonbeing, that whatever is is in motion or that motion is impossible, and that determination of the good and the true is conventional or arbitrary. Paradoxically, the history of metaphysics since this beginning has been a history of controversial oppositions among fundamental beliefs about the nature of reality—oppositions of idealism, materialism, and skepticism—in which an independent science of first principles was seldom if ever propounded. Even during the Middle Ages, the possibilities of metaphysics were expressed in beliefs about the transcendental God of revealed theology, in which the principles of philosophy and science were derived from divine wisdom; or in beliefs about nature and human nature, which provided two ways to the principles of science and action, one by induction from experience, the other by deduction from the word of God; or in skeptical beliefs about the art of discourse, which laid the foundations of law, civil and canon, and of the scholastic method and casuistry in arguments *sic et non.*

The term "science" took on a different meaning in the seventeenth century which set the course of the progress of metaphysics from Hobbes and Locke or from Leibniz and Wolff. Philosophers undertook the task of applying the methods of the new sciences to human understanding and action. The term "ontology" was invented in the seventeenth century. In the course of the eighteenth century, ontology became *metaphysica generalis,* and the parts of metaphysics, *metaphysica specialis,* were found to be "cosmology," "theology," and "psychology."

It was against this conception of theoretical metaphysics that Kant revolted at the end of the eighteenth century. Once more, he found three strands in the tradition against which he revolted: he was moved by Hume's "academic skepticism" to abandon his dogmatism and to use the skeptical method to develop a critical, rather than a skeptical, philosophy; he adapted Locke's empirical analysis of understanding and knowledge, and transformed it to the analysis of possible experience; and he showed the contradictions involved in the application of the concepts of the understanding to the ideas of God, the self, and the world in theoretical transcendental ontology. Kant's question concerning the possibility of metaphysics was based on the recognition of the absence of metaphysics in any of these approaches, and it had to do with the possibility of a metaphysics based, like mathematics and physics, on synthetic principles *a priori.*

During the nineteenth century, philosophers differentiated two kinds of science, a science of nature or of universal laws, and a science of spirit or of particulars and values. Metaphysics was conceived in terms of both kinds of science. It might be critical or idealistic, or it might be empirical or materialistic, and the way to ontology or being had to be prepared by a propaedeutic examination of ways of thinking or modes of thought, by epistemology or methodology.

During the twentieth century, "history" or the "science of culture" undertook the task of resolving the separation and opposition of the particulars and values of spiritual science and the laws and facts of natural science. *Kulturwissenschaft* related and interpreted *Geisteswissenschaft* and *Naturwissenschaft* according to the characteristics they had developed or acquired in the course of history and in the structures of cultures. In so doing it took over many of the functions which had once been exercised by metaphysics or epistemology in establishing principles and determining methods. The history of the progress of metaphysics since Locke and Leibniz has entered into a third phase—(1) ontology or being, (2) ideology or knowing, (3) culture or communication. The future of metaphysics must be found in our times in what we do and in what we say. From the semantics and topics of communication we may be able to clarify the methodology of thinking and knowing and proceed to the metaphysics of what is and what takes place.

II

I have inverted Kant's order by giving the history of the progress of metaphysics before treating the future of metaphysics. I have questioned Kant's facts by placing them in a context of circumstances in which they cease to be facts which universally and uniquely condition metaphysical inquiry, provide the marks by which to judge when metaphysics is present or absent in philosophy (or in theoretical, practical, and aesthetic thought in general), and determine the questions which must be answered critically before metaphysics can take its determined form in a metaphysics of necessity and a metaphysics of freedom. I retain his paradoxes, however, but in somewhat altered form. He traced the history of metaphysics after having shown that no metaphysics had ever actually existed. The statement of his enterprise runs through all the modalities to focus on the need to demonstrate the possibility of metaphysics: there is no *actual* metaphysics, and a speculative metaphysics is *impossible;* yet metaphysics is *necessary* if truth is to be distinguished from illusion, and it is *contingent* on the completion of a critique of pure reason; the *possibility* of extending metaphysical judgments, which use the categories of understanding, beyond the bounds of sense experience can then be shown analytically. I have traced the history of metaphysics through many stages of ontology (which Kant rejected as a possible science), methodology (which Kant employed to prepare for metaphysics), and culture (which provides no grounds for the possibility of an *a priori* of metaphysics designed to exhibit the whole body of philosophical knowledge in systematic connection). I shall try therefore to show that metaphysics is *actual* today, *contingent* not on necessary forms of thought but on circumstantial developments of culture, in which it is both *impossible* as an apodeictic science of connections and *necessary* to provide the ordering principles of *possible* interacting communications and interrelated communities.

The paradoxes of the history of metaphysics and of culture—of thinking, making, doing, and saying—are the result of semantic changes in all the words used in making statements about what is known, about the nature and use of what is made, about the criteria and consequences of what is done, and about the meanings and applications of what is said, as well as about the interrelations and priorities among them. Despite these semantic ambiguities, or even because of them, it is possible to make unambiguous statements about substantive inquiries and objective situations which might be undertaken in metaphysics and which would contribute to revealing objective situations and to effecting changes in them.

The semantic paradoxes can be removed easily from the statement of purpose which I have just made. I am interested in metaphysics as a first philosophy or science of first principles. I do not think it is properly an ontology devoted to establishing certain first principles on the analogy of mathematical principles or the principles of natural philosophy; nor is it in need of a methodological propaedeutic devoted to the study of universal laws or particular values; nor does it depend on the establishment of a unified syntactic, semantic, and pragmatic, or on the construction of a universal grammar or of a general characteristical lexicon or of a moral technologized rhetoric. On the other hand, I am more interested in understanding the meanings, applications, and objectives of these programs for metaphysics than in refuting them as meaningless, impossible, or useless. They make use of ideas and methods that have always been part of the metaphysical enterprise broadly considered, and the long history of controversial opposition among them has apparently not lessened the attractiveness or reduced the effectiveness of any one of them. The metaphysics of the future should make use of them as supplementary aspects rather than as incompatible opposites. I am convinced that the orientation of our times—in theory, practice, and art—is to the study of concrete facts of existence and experience, and I see no reason why the ontological study of principles and the epistemological study of methods should not find their propaedeutic in the study of concrete facts and values. Philosophy still continues to seek a model in science, but "science" has ceased to be knowledge of universal necessary laws; it has ceased to be divided between two methods, one for the universal laws of nature, the other for the particular facts and values studied in the social sciences and the humanities; it has found no one logic of discovery or of proof, no grammar of assent or of negation, no rhetoric of falsification or of action. It takes the form of a great variety of operations and formulations, and we have invented a word to relate universal laws to concrete operations, "technology," the "science of art," and in the process of exploring that science the distinction between science and technology, pure theory and concrete operation has become the subject of a controversial metaphysical dispute.

Once these semantic changes have been noted, the semantic continuity which connects our task today with the task of Kant in the eighteenth century becomes apparent. Kant, while seeking the possibility of a science of metaphysics and finding such a science lacking, did grant the actuality and even the indispensability of a metaphysics of concrete particularity which was short of being an apodeictic *a priori* science and therefore of no interest to him in his search for a science of metaphysics. After solemnly and legally suspending all metaphysicians from their occupations until they have answered the question, How are synthetic cognitions *a priori* possible? Kant continues in the *Prolegomena* (pp. 29–30, J. P. Mahaffy and J. H. Bernard translation): "If they on the other hand desire to carry on their business not as a *science*, but as an *art* of persuasion wholesome and suited to the general common sense of man, they cannot in justice be prevented. They will then speak the modest language of a rational faith, they will grant that they are not allowed even to *conjecture,* far less to *know,* anything which lies beyond the bounds of all possible experience, but only to *assume* something (not for speculative use, which they must abandon, but for practical only) that is possible and even indispensable for the guidance of the understanding and of the will in life." Common sense and rhetoric are not alien to the spirit of contemporary philosophy. They too have been transformed and have been put to other uses than those which they had in the pejorative senses which Kant gave them. Transformed into methods of examining and changing concrete facts of existence, "common sense" and "rhetoric" have taken over many of the functions once exercised by "reason" or "sense" or by "dialectic" or "criticism." They may lead therefore not only to a variety of metaphysics of belief or "rational faith" about the nature of things, the laws of thought, and the uses of language, and to "assumptions" which make life, alleged facts, credited thoughts, and linguistic usages possible, but also to metaphysics of "scientific inquiry" concerning the principles of being, thought, action, and expression, and to "principles" which make possible the grounding of principles of knowledge, action, and production.

The *inevitable* practice of metaphysics today may be differentiated and classified under the four headings used to describe the position of Kant concerning one *possible* metaphysics in contrast to three *impossible* metaphysics among the four *necessary* forms of metaphysics, the history of three of which he traced as background to the prolegomena which prepared for the future of the fourth. When one has passed beyond ontology and methodology to a philosophy of culture, all four forms of metaphysics are recognized to be actual, contingently, and are rejected as impossible, necessarily. In the long history of his encounters with culture, man has reacted skeptically to its manifestations of deception, idealistically to traces of a rational plan and of purposiveness found in experience, and materialistically in his search for underlying grounds for its operation in nature and human nature. Throughout that history he has also rejected beliefs that the structure of culture is symbolic, ideal, or material and has sought, in the place of beliefs, a science of principles for the processes of knowing, thinking, doing, and communicating which constitute culture. (1) In the skeptical metaphysics, which still continues and still goes back with reverence to Hume, the conventional structure of language and the intentional structure of action are examined as facts and as the language of action and the action of language. (2) In the transcendental metaphysics, which still continues and which has transformed the metaphysics of Kant and the transvaluation of Nietzsche, the modeling influence of a universal language, of a transcendental "We," and of a transcendental ontology are detected in the facts of existence and experience in a lived world. (3) In the empirical metaphysics of human character and natural processes, which still continues and which still builds on the differentiation of natural law and historical sequence, the facts of natural events and human actions are traced back and adjusted to the structure of nature and of human nature. (4) In the circumstantial metaphysics, which still continues and which still recalls and makes use of Bacon's conception of knowledge as power and Mill's search for the criteria of knowledge and action in their consequences, the interplay of man and his natural, biological, and cultural environment are investigated as data and facts.

Three of these actual forms of metaphysics are statements of "beliefs" about the nature of reality and investigations of what follows from these beliefs in statements of what happens, of what can be said to be known, of what should be planned and carried out in action, and of what can be said significantly and relevantly. The skeptical metaphysics is an elaboration of the belief that nothing is except existence and experience. The transcendental metaphysics is a development of the belief that what is experienced and what exists here and now takes on intelligibility and being by reference to something which transcends experience. The empirical metaphysics works on the belief that what happens and what is done owes its meaning and relevance to a structure which underlies experience and existence. The fourth of the actual forms of metaphysics is a science of first principles constructed to relate man to the circumstances and problems he encounters in his environment and to the principles which render intelligible and resolvable the problems presented by his natural, his biological, and his cultural environment and the problems presented by their interrelations. A metaphysics of culture will run through all the modalities to focus on the necessity of metaphysics. There is no *actual* metaphysics which binds men together in community and communication, and an *a priori* ideology of culture, accepted freely or imposed by constraint, is *impossible;* yet metaphysics is *possible* if the contentious oppositions of beliefs of action groups, pressure groups, and propaganda groups can be transformed into ongoing action in which the *contingent* pursuit of particular interests contributes to common interests, and the clarification of the *necessity* of metaphysics contributes to motivation and action to realize the *possibility* of that transformation.

III

The metaphysics of the future will continue the pluralism of approaches and perspectives in which "that which is" will be rendered apparent by examination and interpretation of the "facts" of concrete experience and the "data" of existence. But the pluralism of approaches need not terminate in a series of antithetical metaphysics from which to choose one true belief singled out in the host of demonstrably false suppositions, presumptions, and prejudices. When communication is recognized to provide the bases and the criteria, in what is said and what is done, for what is said to be thought, for what is done as thought, and for what is said or made to be, when communication and culture are the sources of ideology and methodology and also of ontology and metaphysics, no appeal can be made to antecedent or independent criteria of meaning and truth or of reality and objectivity. The criteria of meaning and of being are provided by communication and action, since they determine what is known and what the knowledge is about. A metaphysics based on communication should take full advantage of the pluralism of orientations, and it should constitute a single metaphysics by relating the variety of approaches to the ongoing inquiry opened up by continuing communication; it should not block off the developing richness of inquiry concerning facts and values, structures and consequences, by building an exclusive single metaphysics on one chosen approach.

Communication has begun to assume primacy in the interpretation and use of facts and data, but much inquiry is still guided and dominated by appeal to criteria provided by distinctions of authoritative methodology and by concepts of antecedent reality which delimit and restrict communication and predetermine both the ways of inquiry and the bounds and properties of what is and of what must be. Philosophers still go to what they present as the findings of physics for knowledge of a reality on which to ground the principles and model the methods of philosophic speculations, but physicists have long been aware of the dependence of their laws and principles on communication. Niels Bohr thus explains "experiment" by "communication."

> Notwithstanding the power of quantum mechanics as a means of ordering an immense amount of evidence regarding atomic phenomena, its departure from accustomed demands of causal explanation has naturally given rise to the question whether we are here concerned with an exhaustive description of experience. The answer to this question evidently calls for a closer examination of the conditions for the unambiguous use of the concepts of classical physics in the analysis of atomic phenomena. The decisive point is to recognize that the description of the experimental arrangement and the recording of observations must be given in plain language, suitably refined by the usual physical terminology. This is a simple logical demand, since by the word "experiment" we can only mean a procedure regarding which we are able to communicate to others what we have done and what we have learned. ["Causality and Complimentarity" (1958), *Essays 1958–1962 on Atomic Physics and Human Knowledge,* 1966, p. 3.]

In his lecture on "The Solvay Meetings and the Development of Quantum Physics" in 1962, Bohr recounts the sequence of meetings which led through numerous stages to the development by reformulation, and by inquiry suggested by reformulation, of the theories and investigations of quantum physics (*ibid.,* pp. 79–100). "Theory" and "experiment" were both "communications."

The common problems and the continuing functions of a metaphysics of communication and culture have a continuity, under transformation, with the problems and functions of metaphysics of being and ontology and of metaphysics of knowing and ideology. The statement of those problems and functions depends on recognition of two kinds of pluralism. One is the pluralism of selections which has distinguished the orientations to metaphysics in the history of the development of metaphysics; the other is the pluralism of interpretations which has separated the hypotheses formed within each orientation from which the controversies of philosophy and the oppositions of interpretations of facts have arisen. The continuing functions which have marked the presence and operation of metaphysics have been two: an architectonic function of organizing science, action, production, and language, and of relating their principles, and an originative function of grounding principles in the exercise and in the products of each of these related functions. A metaphysics of ontology makes theoretic sciences architectonic; seeks the principles of being in things; and adapts the principles of language to the properties and functions of things. A metaphysics prepared for or assumed by a critical or experimental examination of forms of thought or associations of ideas makes practical reason or action architectonic, as Kant and Mill do; seeks principles of knowledge in thought or perception; and adapts the principles of language to the categories of thought or the impulsions of emotion. A metaphysics prepared for by an experiential or existential examination of communication and culture, seeks to discover, to use, and to test principles of production and discourse in communication; makes production—art or technology—architectonic by producing a community of culture; and adapts the principles of language and the principles of action to each other.

The first kind of pluralism, which marks off characteristic approaches to metaphysical problems as stages of historical development, has in the past presented a choice between (1) using and improving current philosophic idioms and modes of operation to restate metaphysical assumptions, and (2) abandoning current idioms and modes to revive old methods or inaugurate new ones. In an age in which the metaphysical idiom is cultural, it is a choice between (1) working on metaphysical problems in one of the current anti-metaphysical philosophical idioms, while disputing concerning whether or not they are metaphysical; and (2) abandoning those idioms to return to the idiom of a refurbished perennial philosophy or to instaurate a new stage in the historical evolution by formulating the ontology implicit in philosophies of existence and experience. The second kind of pluralism, which is encountered in the different approaches made within a current idiom, has in the past presented a choice between (1) participating in the controversies among the varieties of philosophic interpretations of the facts of experience and the data of existence to formulate beliefs about reality or to establish principles for understanding and motivation; and (2) abandoning philosophic controversies for scientific examination of the facts and systems of communication, information, history, and language. In an age in which the metaphysical idiom is cultural, it is a choice between (1) working on metaphysical problems in one of the schools of philosophy that find bases for beliefs about what is the case in language, in transcendental hermeneutics, or in descriptions or lawlike statements, and find principles in the circumstances of inquiry, action, and expression; and (2) abandoning those schools in the recognition that philosophy and metaphysics are now being done not in the schools or departments of philosophy, but elsewhere in universities and communities in which architectonic principles of culture are coming into being and originative principles of action and communication are coming into operation.

An age in which the metaphysical idiom is cultural also presents the opportunity to depart from the traditional patterns of intellectual evolution and intellectual debate. It is possible to preserve the pluralism of stages of development by forming new structures of communication and culture which continue rather than supplant the processes and functions characteristic of what had been considered preparatory stages. A metaphysics of communication and culture may be used as a propaedeutic to a metaphysics of knowing and methodology and to a metaphysics of being and ontology, and ontology and epistemology may in turn be used as propaedeutics to a metaphysics of communication and culture, once it becomes involved in controversies among the variant modes of carrying out such a metaphysics. In a metaphysics of communication and culture, propaedeutic approaches can be merged with metaphysical interpretations by universalizing the architectonic functions of cultures and by differentiating the productive processes of communication. The new structures of communication and culture can be used to preserve rather than reduce the variety of approaches which are the basis of controversial oppositions by merging beliefs about objectivity, intelligibility, and expressibility and by relating the grounds of beliefs to the principles of communication and culture.

It is possible that both pluralisms may be preserved and utilized in developing a single diversified and progressive metaphysics of the future. Controversy among approaches and schools will not be lessened, nor will consensus or mutual understanding among ideologies be advanced, but the different approaches and inquiries will be oriented to common problems presented by experience and even by common sense under the influence of a more and more clearly conceived common concern with the concrete facts of culture and communication. The increased importance of communication in resolving common problems and in testing and using proposed resolutions has contributed to the abandonment of theoretical *a priori* and empirical *a posteriori* sciences of physics and metaphysics, and the erosion of dogmatism has broadened and strengthened tolerance of those lesser arts and methods, the use of which Kant was willing to grant to nonscientific, nonmetaphysical men who would not pause to determine whether synthetic conceptions *a priori* are possible—the arts of persuasion, of presentation, of tracing consequences, and of ordering. The reorientation to concrete facts of experience and to common data of existence has changed the meaning and the direction of the methods used to relate "principles" to what is in "fact" and to what is "thought" to be; and in the process "facts" are made and presented and "principles" are sought and posited. Culture and communication have assumed the architectonic and originative functions of ontology and methodology, for communities are formed by communication, and they in turn provide the context and possibility of communication. The pluralism of the stages of the history of metaphysics is preserved and grounded in a metaphysics of communication and culture. The pluralism of the four actual forms of metaphysics serves as a prolegomenon for a future metaphysics in which the architectonic functions of culture are universalized and the productive processes of communications are differentiated. The transformations of each of these forms, which are already in process, inverting methods and changing facts, suggest possible forms of a single metaphysics which makes use of a plurality of methods and a plurality of hypotheses concerning systems of communication and culture—systems of things, thoughts, actions, and expressions, and systems presenting connections and consequences among them and revealing aspects and grounds of their processes.

(1) The skeptical metaphysics, which approaches the forms and processes of thought and the truths and probabilities of occurrences by examining language and action, has always had an affinity with the methods of rhetoric and sophistic. Gorgias treated speech, arguments, and persuasion as "deception" in poetry, science, rhetoric, and philosophy; Isocrates inverted Plato's divided line and sought philosophy in opinion not knowledge; the Middle Academy developed the Platonic philosophy by skeptical and probabilistic methods; Cicero used the academic method to distinguish the special cases of demonstrative, judicial, and de-

liberative rhetoric from the general questions of philosophy; Hume acknowledged that he followed the academic mode of philosophizing. The emphasis in the skeptical tradition is appropriately (since *"skepsis"* means "perception," "observation," "examination") on invention and discovery. "Deception" is a creative activity which turns from commonly or authoritatively accepted data to open up unaccustomed apperceptions. When metaphysics is conceived to be a science, as it is in the metaphysics of ontology and of methodology, "demonstration" is an apodeictic proof which exhibits true conclusions as necessary consequences from necessary principles, and even in rhetoric "demonstrative" persuasion is an epideictic exhibition of virtues for praise and of vices for blame. In a metaphysics of communication and culture, "demonstration" is the exhibition, preferably in active manifestations, of injustices and evils, which incite actions, and of estimable actions and manners, which are misesteemed and misrepresented; scientific "demonstration" is the communicable construction of experiments and probabilistic examination of their consequences. The new demonstrations are continuations of the methods of inventing and discovering new data from which to construct new facts and new principles to guide inquiry and action.

The direction of the method of demonstration has been inverted from the derivation of conclusions which state facts or laws governing facts to the invention or discovery of facts which open the way to new principles. The data of demonstration do not cease to be "given" when it is recognized that they are "invented," and the "deception" of an invention does not become a "falsehood," but is recognized to be an approximation to the newly established and accepted deception and the new data which it gives. Culture and communication depend on creativity, and metaphysics has been, and must be, inventive, heuristic, and constructive. We have become interested once more in creativity and in the simple elements of science, art, action, and language, but we continue to treat them as fixed elements in the manner of ontology or methodology. The tradition of the metaphysics based on language and action has treated them as variables or "topics"—"places" within which the simples that constitute data may be found by interpreting variables in constants—rather than as simple, fixed entities or simple, fixed ideas. The metaphysics of communication and culture may enter into creative demonstration if present controversies concerning "categories" are turned into inquiries concerning "topics" to be used for expression, invention, and discovery.

(2) The empirical metaphysics, which seeks bases in nature and human nature underlying phenomena and appearances, has always had an affinity with the constructions of grammar and the judgments of interpretation. The emphasis in the empirical and critical traditions is appropriately (since *"empeiria"* means "experience," "practice," "craft," and *"krisis"* means "distinction," "decision," "judgment," "interpretation," "criticism") on facts and distinctions, on statements of facts, and on interpretations of facts and of statements. Propositions are distinguished from other statements: unlike commands, prayers, and persuasions, statements of feeling and desire, propositions are statements which may be true or false. A true proposition states a fact. Experience, criticism, and hermeneutics are therefore closely related, although each is variously interpreted and developed. Aristotle's *On Interpretation* (*Peri Hermeneias*) treats propositions, after distinguishing them from other sentences; Demetrius' *On Interpretation* differentiates four styles—elevated, elegant, plain, and forcible—relative to composition, subject matter, and diction, and in contrast to their misuses. When metaphysics, conceived as a science, moves from ontology to epistemological methodology, "propositions" become "judgments." "Judicial metaphysics" is a grammar in which the elements or letters ("*stoicheion*" was applied to letters and to parts of speech in grammar, to elements of matter in physics, and to elements of proof in science, as in the title of Euclid's treatise) are combined and synthesized in composite bodies, and the modalities of sensation, feeling, and thought result from the movements and impacts of bodies. The "judicial rhetoric" of an age of communication and culture moves "judgment" out of the law court, and universalizes the "processes" by which legal issues are adjudicated to apply to all processes and to interpret all issues by trying alternative hypotheses in adversary opposition. Hypotheses are refuted by being falsified, and a proposition is shown to be true by resisting falsification.

The direction of the method of judgment has been inverted: judgment was the verification of true judgments to determine what is the case and the grounding of appearances and phenomena in an underlying reality and certain knowledge; it has become the falsification of proposed judgments to test what is supposed to be the case, and the grounding of statements of principles and objectivity in warranted judgments and established facts. The facts of judgment do not cease to be hard, solid, and irresistible when it is recalled that they are *facta,* made, and the making of facts is still distinguishable from the making of fictions. The distinction between fact and fiction is established by interpretation, and interpretation may show that what had been accepted as facts are fictions and that acknowledged fictions may function as facts and may come to be recognized as facts in fact. Culture and communication depend on information and the interpretation of information, and metaphysics has been, and must continue to be, informative, presentational, judicial, and critical. We have become interested once more in judgment and information, even to the extent of forming systems and sciences of information, but we continue to treat the facts of informations as fixed entities or fixed judgments in the manner of ontology or methodology. The tradition of metaphysics based on language and action has employed hermeneutics to consider the interpretations and the styles of statements and of actions when they are taken to present facts and feelings. There is considerable interest today in developing a new hermeneutics applicable both to texts and to experiences The metaphysics of communication and culture may enter into judicial interpretation if present controversies concerning hypotheses and their transformation into information systems are turned into inquiries concerning interpretations and concerning how they may be used for presentation, judgment, and criticism.

The topics of the metaphysics of invention may be joined to the interpretations of the metaphysics of judgment to relate the judgment and proof of what is already known to the discovery and expression of what is not yet known in order to clarify the choice between continuing the interpretation of new facts within an established structure of metaphysical hypotheses and inventing a new structure of hypotheses to bring to attention new data which provide the grounds and suggest the consequences of new facts.

(3) The transcendental metaphysics, which seeks being and intelligibility in a reality and intelligence which transcends becoming and opinion, has always had an affinity with the assimilations

of dialectic and the construction of systems based on hierarchies of values. The emphasis in transcendental or systematic traditions is appropriately (since *"systema"* means "a whole," "a constitution," "a flock," "a company," "a musical scale") on organic wholes, on syntheses and systems in which wholes and parts mutually influence each other. Fundamental principles or first principles are found in systems, in the dominant determination either of the whole by the properties and functions of the parts or of the parts in the constitution of the whole. As we have moved from ontology and methodology we have ceased to seek a fundamental system of things or of thoughts on which to base order, but we have gained confidence in the discovery and institution of a system of communication and a system of communities by which to order what we say and do, and even what we think and what we know about the order of things. We hope to transform partial discussions with their divisions, oppositions, and polarizations by providing an originative principle of discussion in what we like to call "dialogue," and to transform partial economic, social, and political communities by reorienting them in the inclusive cultural community of mankind. The ordering of the new architectonic principle of culture will be an open-ended use and advancement of freedom and universality, and the operation of the new originative principle of communication depends on the use and advancement of activity rather than passivity and of diversity rather than repetition.

The direction of the method of systematization and ordering has been inverted: systems of things and thoughts were classificatory wholes used to order and relate parts; systems of culture and communication are generative constructions used to open up meanings and values and to remove limitations to action and insight. Culture and communication depend on ordering principles and systems, and metaphysics has been, and must continue to be, systematic ordering of parts in wholes holoscopically and systematic constructing of wholes from parts meroscopically. We have become interested once more in systems, but we continue to treat them as organizations of fixed items of information and of ascertained positions with respect to alleged facts and the issues they raise. Not all positions are principles, and the tradition of metaphysics based on language and action must build structures within which principles may be detected and used in the advancement of freedom, activity, diversity, and universality.

(4) The demonstrative metaphysics of expression, the judicial metaphysics of presentation, and the speculative metaphysics of systematization are metaphysical formulations of beliefs about the fundamental nature of reality. They are transformations of traditional beliefs that the ordering of science, action, art, and reflection is found by examining the structure of language, of things, or of ideas. Those beliefs are stated in the course of discovering and presenting the results of scientific inquiry, policy formation, moral judgment, and artistic creation and criticism. They do not require a separate inquiry, nor do they constitute the subject matter of a separate science. The circumstantial metaphysics, which distinguishes the invention of forms in art from the discovery of causes in science, and which differentiates sciences according to subject matters, methods, and principles, has always had an affinity with the inferences and consequences of logic. It is a metaphysics of the principles of other sciences, and since they are first principles and not demonstrable or testable by the methods employed in the science of which they are principles, they form the subject matter of a separate science of metaphysics in which they are treated by a metaphysical method distinct from the method of other sciences. In a metaphysics of culture and communication, that method is a universalization of the method of "deliberative rhetoric" taken out of the legislative assembly and applied to all problematic situations and *aporiai*. We deliberate and make decisions not only about practical actions to be taken with respect to things within our power, which was the original scope and function of deliberation and choice, but also about anything we know, or think, or conjecture, or make, or formulate. The presuppositions and objectives of deliberation are principles.

The direction of the method of deliberation has been inverted: deliberation made decisions concerning available means to be employed in particular circumstances to achieve desired ends. The circumstances and the ends were not subjects of deliberation. In an age of technology new means which have never been applied to circumstances or problems and for which purposes have not been devised or projected have become available, and deliberation may be applied to the choice of circumstances and to decisions concerning purposes and ends. The sequences of action and statements are not modeled to observed consequences of things or conceived consequences of thoughts but are built from ratios, relations, proportions, rhythms, and analogies. A variety of methods may be used on the same set of relations to bring into focus and existence different aspects and possibilities of the situation, and aspects and consequences may move from field to field, from art to art, like a theme traced through different circumstances and processes. Human knowledge and human experiences are arranged in a vast number of such themes, and the variations of arts and methods used to develop them may constitute a dynamic substitute for rigid methodologies, separated fields, and static subject matters. The metaphysics of communication and culture may enter into dynamic deliberation in the study of principles in a science of first principles.

The topics of the metaphysics of invention and the interpretations of a metaphysics of judgment may be joined to the principles of a metaphysics of organization and the themes of a metaphysics of deliberation to relate the functions of expression, presentation, systematization, and arrangement in the ongoing processes of communication and culture.

The future of metaphysics is one of cultural communication. Metaphysics is inevitable in such communication, and it inevitably takes many forms. The search for principles of cultural communication is under way in science, practice, and art. That search is confused by the fact that it seems, as a consequence of semantic changes, to be contrary to what the search for principles has been; and it often passes unnoticed, or even seems to involve the rejection of metaphysics, because it is the opposite to what it is expected to be. Philosophers can contribute to the success of that search, and it seems inevitable that they should. Even if they do not, however, progress is inevitable in the ongoing quest as long as men seek to know, to act, and to make. Any meeting or conference is a contribution to metaphysics as an art of communication and culture. The results to be sought in such applied metaphysical conferences should not be, as is frequently the case, conversion of others to one's own metaphysical faith, or establishment of a single formulation of metaphysics and achievement of consensus on it, but new insights provided and new problems encountered, which had not been seen clearly or stated explicitly before, but which will open up, when the memory of semantic oppositions, defeats, and victories fades away, a field of data and problems within which to start the work of metaphysical discovery, judgment, ordering, and inquiry.